2/1/78

Karen

TRENDS IN BRITISH POLITI

Also by Chris Cook and John Ramsden
By-Elections in British Politics

TRENDS IN BRITISH POLITICS SINCE 1945

edited by

CHRIS COOK
and
JOHN RAMSDEN

First published 1978 by
THE MACMILLAN PRESS LTD
London and Basingstoke
Associated companies in Delhi Dublin Hong Kong
Johannesburg Lagos Melbourne New York Singapore Tokyo

ISBN 0 333 19777 1 (hardcover)
ISBN 0 333 19779 8 (paperback)

Printed in Hong Kong

British Library Cataloguing in Publication Data

Trends in British politics since 1945
  1. Great Britain – Politics and government – 1945 –
I. Cook, Chris II. Ramsden, John, b. 1947
320.9'41'085   JN231

ISBN 0–333–19777–1

Contents

Notes on the Contributors

CHRIS COOK was educated at St Catharine's College, Cambridge, and Oriel College, Oxford; Research Student of Nuffield College, Oxford, 1968–70. After five years as a Senior Research Officer at the London School of Economics, he is now with the Royal Commission on Historical Manuscripts. His previous publications include the five-volume *Sources in British Political History, 1900–1951* and *A Short History of the Liberal Party, 1900–1976*. He is a Fellow of the Royal Historical Society.

STANLEY HENIG was educated at Corpus Christi College, Oxford; Research Student of Nuffield College, Oxford, 1962. Subsequently Lecturer in Politics at the University of Lancaster. Labour MP for Lancaster, 1966–70. He has written widely on European affairs and is Assistant Editor of the *Journal of Common Market Studies*.

IAIN McLEAN was educated at Christ Church, Oxford; Student and Research Fellow, Nuffield College, Oxford, 1967–71. Lecturer in Politics at the University of Newcastle-upon-Tyne since 1971. His previous publications include a biography of Keir Hardie.

GILLIAN PEELE was educated at Durham University and St Anne's College, Oxford; Student of Nuffield College 1971–3; member of Gray's Inn; Lecturer in Politics, St Catherine's College, Oxford, since 1972. Research Fellow, St Antony's College, Oxford, since 1973. Currently Fellow and Tutor in Politics, Lady Margaret Hall, Oxford. Co-editor of *The Politics of Reappraisal, 1918–1939*.

ALAN BUTT PHILIP is a Research Fellow at the Centre for European Industrial Studies, Bath University. After taking first class honours at St John's College, Oxford, he was a Research Student of Nuffield College. His previous publications include *The Welsh Question*. He is joint author of *Power to the People*, a report of the Liberal Party's Machinery of Government policy panel.

JOHN RAMSDEN was educated at Corpus Christi College, Oxford; Student of Nuffield College, 1969–72; Lecturer in Modern History, Queen Mary College, University of London, since 1972. Co-author of *The Conservatives* (edited by Lord Butler).

PETER SINCLAIR was educated at Corpus Christi College, Oxford; Student of Nuffield College, Oxford, 1967. Appointed Fellow and Tutor in Economics, Brasenose College, Oxford, 1970.

DAVID STEEL was educated at Jesus College, Oxford. From 1969 to 1972 he was a Research Student of Nuffield College, Oxford, before moving to the University of Exeter as Lecturer in Politics.

ROBERT TAYLOR was educated at Wadham College, Oxford. From 1965 to 1968 he was a Research Student of Nuffield College, Oxford. He was subsequently Lecturer in Modern History at the University of Lancaster before moving to the staff of *The Economist*. His previous published works include a biography of Lord Salisbury. He is currently Industrial Correspondent of the *Observer*.

Introduction

John Ramsden

Categorisation and periodic reassessment are the stuff of history. Historians delight in discovering or rediscovering the elements of continuity within a given period, only for a subsequent generation to stress instead the elements of change within it, so opening the way for a further rediscovery of the period's essential unity later. In so far as political scientists and commentators are drawing their evidence from the recent past, they are subject to the same tendencies. If history may be defined as 'past politics', then political scientists may be described as present historians.

There is a distinct tendency among those who have recently written about the British past to disparage the search for turning-points or closely-defined periods. Rather, it is fashionable to stress the complementary facets of tradition and change as the two sides of the same coin. So 1485, 1603 and 1714 have all lost their magic as historic moments of change: not only is 1485 abandoned as the start of 'the Early Modern Period' of British history, but it is implicitly assumed that the advent of the Tudors did not make any sea-change in the directions of British history anyway. Nearer to the present, the watershed of the Industrial Revolution is no longer stressed in quite the same way as it once was, the origins of the political parties have been shown to be far more complex than was once thought, and the point at which Britain 'entered the modern world' of the twentieth century can be variously dated at 1897, 1901, 1906, 1909, 1914, 1916 or 1918. And yet in this general collapse of the signposts of historical direction, the most recent has survived unscathed with hardly a challenge. Writings on Britain since 1945 have assumed in one way or another that it was a 'post-war' situation that they were describing; the Second World War was allowed as a watershed when most others had been abandoned, and it was assumed not only that the war had marked (if not created) a shift in British politics, but also that the period since 1945 was characterised by the essential unity of a period when the longer-term trends of 1939–45 were still working themselves out.

Several understandable reasons for this can be cited. Universities have not as a rule taught much post-war British history in their undergraduate syllabuses, and professional historians have rarely ventured into the post-war field in their own writings on Britain. It is indeed methodologically more difficult to consider Britain since the last war than in any other age; Government papers are now becoming available for the late-1940s, but only just so, and there are few collections of the private papers of post-war politicians that are yet available to historians. Post-War British history is still predominantly history written from the outside, whereas the history of every other generation can be viewed differently by looking at the opinions of participants from the inside. It can also be seen that the post-war years did actually seem to possess an objective unity that justified their consideration as one unified period, a unity that is only to be broken down by a longer perspective. Finally, it may also be difficult for the generation that lived through the Second World War to accept that it was not such a decisive change in Britain's destiny as it seemed to be at the time, or that we have now entered a new phase of development in which the influences are not much related to the events of 1939–45. For all of these reasons, it has perhaps been inevitable that Britain since 1945 has been seen as a post-war society, without much concentration on differentiation within that period.

In every sense though, this is changing and will go on changing. The passage of time casts a lengthening perspective on the Second World War and more recent events demand an ever closer scrutiny. The developing techniques of instant historians in the press – 'Insight' in the *Sunday Times* and many imitators – have done much to fill the gap left by academic historians. Sir Norman Chester's *The Nationalisation of British History 1945–51*, published in 1975, is the first to apply the techniques of the *Official History of the Second World War* to a new peacetime history, the first authoritative work of scholarship on the post-war years to be based on free access to Government records. Other volumes are planned and in any case the slow forward march of the thirty-year rule will gradually open up the files that have so far remained closed. The academic historian can now be expected to venture more often into post-war British history, and one consequence of this will most certainly be a reassessment of how lasting was the impact of changes initiated during the war years. This process has indeed begun with the opening up of papers for the war itself. Paul Addison's *The Road to 1945* has demonstrated the extent to which the apparently new directions of 1939–45 were actually based on trends of policy-making that were firmly established in the 1930s. He has also emphasised the break in continuity *since* 1945; his conclusion on 'Attlee's Consensus' after 1945 is that 'we were all Keynesians then'; even a few years ago, he would have been forced to conclude that 'we are all Keynesians now'.

It may not therefore be premature to re-examine the current trends in British politics in order to see how far they still stem from wartime roots. The conclusion of most of the contributors to this volume is rather to stress that in most areas Britain is now reacting to influences that are much more recent than the 1940s. What has emerged is that we should consider post-war politics as a period of three distinct phases rather than one and that only the first of these can be appropriately called 'post-war'.

Between the end of the war and the late-1950s, almost every area of British politics was still dominated by the political and economic legacy of the war years, and equally by the political legacy of the inter-war years. The overriding concern was the prevention of a slump like that of the 1930s, with its attendant stagnation and mass unemployment; the techniques of Keynesian economic management seemed to provide politicians with powers of whose existence they had scarcely even dreamt before; some, like Harold Macmillan – Keynes's publisher – had discovered the secret in the 1930s, but most had to wait for the demonstration of the success of demand management in the 1940s. In the social field, Beveridge occupied much the same role that Keynes occupied in the economy, a symbol more of the practicability of a better system than of its desirability. The language of British politics was still that of the 1930s and 1940s, and it was spoken for the most part by politicians whose own careers had spanned the war. Nationalisation remained the central area between the parties, but it was an area that they chose for a ritual dance rather than for a real battle, as David Steel shows; this was much as it had been ever since the Labour Party committed itself to a real policy of nationalisation in 1918. In the field of foreign affairs, Britain clung to great-power status with the victory of 1945 well to the front of the national mind; in the field of defence planning, Britain's strategy in the 1950s was heavily influenced by the desire to prevent war from breaking out as it had done in 1939. Heavy spending on defence would deter possible Russian aggression and a firm commitment to NATO would prevent a repetition of the diplomatic errors of appeasement. Meanwhile, the British economy seemed to have recovered from the strains of war and appeared to be performing very well; so long as British people compared Britain's economic performance to Britain in the past rather than to other countries in the present, then the achievements would seem considerable. Such was the Butskellite consensus that shaped British politics in the 1950s, compounded equally of the policy consequences of total war and the political achievements of Ramsay MacDonald and Stanley Baldwin. Neither Conservative nor Labour parties suggested much in the way of radical reforms, and in so far as they did so the roots of their radicalism were distant rather than contemporary. In short, little happened in the decade after 1945 to disturb the policies that had emerged during the wartime National Government or the political life that had been resumed on the defeat of Germany.

However, the decade after the retirements of Churchill and Attlee in 1955 marked a new mood altogether. The twin shocks that produced this change were the Suez failure of 1956 and the economic recessions of 1956–7 and 1961–2. Together these two shocks produced a great loss of national confidence that had profound effects on the political parties, as I have sought to show in my own essay in this volume; but individually and collectively they also affected every other area of British politics. Suez certainly shattered the illusion that Britain could continue to play an imperial role on the world stage; at the same time as exposing the weakness of the Commonwealth as a prop of British world power, it also illuminated the unreality of the 'special relationship' with the United States. Of the three areas of British international involvement that her statesmen had identified, only the European one remained as an inviting opportunity. Europe, in the shape first of EFTA and then of the EEC, was made more attractive by Britain's relative economic decline; invidious comparisons were made with other European countries, so that Britain's affluence looked unattractive when set alongside the West German 'economic miracle'. Hence, by the end of the 1950s, the orientation of Britain's international position was being changed, and in a direction which few had foreseen in 1945; by 1967, the leaders of all three major parties regarded British entry to the EEC as a central policy objective. By then too the last vestiges of a world role had been given up with the withdrawal of British armed forces from east of Suez, a decision dictated – appropriately enough – by economic rather than strategic necessities. Henceforth, British politics began to be Europeanised, with significant results for the parties and for the constitution, as Stanley Henig and Gillian Peele describe.

At home, the loss of confidence was marked by a new wave of reformism, a reformism that assumed British failure and looked abroad for models to be emulated. Every institution has been subjected to critical analysis and almost all of them have been reconstructed at least once. It was all strikingly reminiscent of the National Efficiency Movement that flourished briefly between the Boer War and 1914; in the 1960s as in the Edwardian period the drive for institutional reform was impelled by a sense of relative national failure and was concentrated on means rather than ends. Through the 1960s, politicians of all parties continued to assume that the end-products of policy should be rapid (or at least faster) economic growth and the maintenance of world influence. Hence, they followed each other from Butskellism into a new Heath-Wilson political consensus that Paul Foot aptly called 'the collapse into technology'. The trend began with Harold Macmillan's attempt to modernise and revitalise his government in 1962; one feature of this was the promotion of younger men, following the growth of a new world fashion for youth at the helm since John Kennedy's election to the US Presidency in 1960, but another feature was the adoption of more technocratic and managerial methods in government, characterised by the appointment of Ministers for Science and for Technical Co-operation. Harold Wilson managed to make this particular issue his own during 1964, promising that a Labour Government would harness the 'white heat of the technological revolution' to the promotion of greater prosperity, and his Government followed Macmillan's lead with the creation of a Ministry of Technology. With Edward Heath as their leader from 1965, the Conservative Party jumped wholeheartedly on to the same bandwagon of technocratic reformism; reviews of *Putting Britain Right Ahead*, the official Conservative statement of policy of September 1965, concentrated on the similarity of language and style with Harold Wilson's speeches of the past two years. Within a few years, Liberals were campaigning with a poster that showed Harold Wilson and Edward Heath together and the slogan 'which twin is the Tory?'. In the 1950s, Liberals had argued that they alone could moderate the dangerous antagonisms of the other parties; in the 1960s they had to argue that the other parties were the same and that they alone could offer a real alternative. So the first response of the parties to Britain's loss of real confidence in herself and in her institutions was actually to increase the consensus between the major parties in a more-technocratic-than-thou auction. Of course, the major parties reached different parts of the consensus at different stages: the Conservatives were quicker to grasp the international aspects and the apparent necessity of Britain joining the EEC, while Labour was quicker to attack domestic sacred cows and responded more quickly to the re-discovery of poverty as a political issue.

In one area, though, the development was continuous, that is the increasing readiness of governments of both parties to seek advice from outside Whitehall, to involve powerful interest groups in the formulation of its policies. This is perhaps best understood as the attempt by governments that have been decreasingly confident of their ability to find acceptable answers to the political questions of the day and so have been increasingly ready to share their responsibility. More critically, it can be regarded as a steady drift towards a more corporate system of statecraft. The first major developments in this form were the creation of the National Economic Development Council and the National Incomes Commission by the Macmillan Government, although there were certainly precedents for these – for example in the Economic Advisory Council of the 1930s. The Wilson Government made further advances with the creation of 'Little Neddies' to assist the NEDC in their own regions or industries; it also initiated a newly corporatist trend with tripartite negotiations between Government, trade unions and industrialists. With Government support, the Federation of British Industries merged with other industrial organisations to form a single organisation for the whole of British industry, the Confederation of British Industry. In 1965, the CBI and the TUC joined with Government to sign a Declaration of Intent regarding their hopes for better industrial relations. Similar negotiations surrounded the incomes policy decisions of both the Wilson and Heath Governments and bodies like the Prices and Incomes Board of 1966 included members from all three groups. This increased involvement of both sides of industry was not greatly welcomed by either side; Robert Taylor shows how unwillingly the trade unions have been drawn into a form of partnership with government and much the same may be said of industry. Within this broad trend there

have been party variations – Conservatives moved towards a quadripar-
tite form of bargaining by introducing the Retail Consortium (another
body created like the CBI to make collective representation to government
more convenient), while Labour has more recently prefered bilateral
negotiations with the trade unions – but the trend has been continuous. So
far indeed has the corporatist approach become a reflex for government
that it has sometimes needed to play off one corporatist method against
another to achieve its purposes. So the Schools Council represents all
interested parties in the educational field in an appropriately corporatist
manner; when the Callaghan Government wished to change its approach
to education in the schools in 1976 and wished to impose its new approach
on the Schools Council, it initiated a series of national and regional
conferences through the TUC and the CBI.

Linking political trends in the very recent past is of necessity a
speculative affair, but it does seem that a third phase of post-war history
has now begun, occasioned by the failure of both Labour and Conservative
parties to achieve their common purposes through technocratic reformism.
This latest phase has been characterised by deepening economic
problems – the energy crisis, higher levels of unemployment and inflation,
and continuing trade deficits – and by a more bitter and more overtly
ideological mood in the parties. Britain has indeed come a long way from
the stable political environment of the 1950s, when almost the entire
electorate could be divided between two parties which kept their
disagreements within narrow bounds and did not seek to make irreversible
changes in the balance of society. Continued economic decline provides a
major part of the explanation for this development; not only can the parties
not succeed if they promise substantial increases in the size of the national
cake, they cannot even plausibly offer the prospect of continuous increases
in the first place; hence the struggle to divide the cake has become more
bitter and more contentious. Linked with this, partly as cause and partly as
result, has been the increasing militancy of the trade unions, no longer
content like their predecessors in the 1930s to accept that a slump must
bring cuts in their members' standards of living. Relations with the trade
unions have thus become the central problem for any Conservative
Government – as they were in the 1920s but they had not been in the
intervening years. Paradoxically, economic decline, while cementing the
ties between the Labour Party and the trade unions, has actually
weakened those on the other side between Conservatives and industry.
Hence, when the Labour Government was threatened by defeat in a vote
of no confidence in March 1977, the stock market fell sharply and sterling
lost ground on the money market.

The left wing of the Labour movement led the way in the adoption of a
more ideological stance, a change that has contributed signally to the
increasing bitterness of politics. Marxists now play a more significant role
in the trade unions as well as in the local and national Labour parties. A

recent survey for the magazine New Society showed how far this trend had progressed when Labour MPs were asked which books and people had most influenced them; it can be seen that now at least the Labour Party owes more to Marx than to Methodism. The failure of the Heath Government has produced a similar reaction on the Conservative side, so that there is now an identifiable radical right-wing current in the mainstream of British politics. There is also, for the first time since 1945, a serious threat to the established parties from outside the mainstream, a phenomenon that must be closely related to economic factors. In Scotland and Wales the very survival of the major parties seems to be threatened and there seems to be very little chance that politics in either country will return to what it was even ten years ago. Outside the mainstream, on the right there is a threat to the major parties from the National Front, a party that feeds on economic troubles and the national lack of confidence in the traditional manner of fringe parties from the right – traditional in European terms, that is, rather than British.

Finally, the changing balance between the parties and the increasing conflicts that have occurred between parties and between government and unions have challenged many of the basic precepts of the constitution that still seemed unshakeable only a decade ago. The House of Lords is threatened with abolition, Collective Responsibility and the rule of law seem to be threatened; conversely, there is more talk of the possibility of a Bill of Rights, of the referendum, or of electoral reform. This last point may indeed remind a historian – or a citizen with a very long memory – that it is not all as novel as it may seem to us in this generation. In the 1920s, when the British party system was struggling to respond to the emergence of the Labour Party and at the same time to deal with the damage done to the economy by the First World War, many of the same debates took place. Labour was seen, quite wrongly, as a revolutionary force that would upset all of the conventions of the constitution; in defence the partisans of the right argued out the need for some means of containing Labour through electoral reform, the referendum or a reform of the House of Lords; trade unions and Conservatives found it difficult to coexist. And with the passage of time, the passions of the 1920s faded into a long period of political calm and stability. It would be premature to predict any such outcome for Britain in the 1980s, but the advent of North Sea oil does at least suggest a pause from the economic pressures that have beset government for the past twenty years. In the long run, de Tocqueville may again be proved right in his assertion that 'history is a picture gallery where there are many copies, but few originals'.

1 The Developing Constitution

Gillian Peele

The task of analysing the constitutional developments of contemporary Britain is not an easy one. Even in countries where there is a basic constitutional text, a settled procedure for resolving constitutional disputes and a specialised vocabulary for constitutional debate, there is sometimes a lack of consensus about where the boundaries of the constitutional realm should be drawn and an element of imprecision in the content of the constitutional rules themselves. Britain, however, can identify no single document which might serve as the primary reference point in the search for the rules and principles which constrain and structure the distribution of authority in the state and which prescribe the relationships between the several parts of government and the individual citizen.[1] Moreover this country has no equivalent of the United States Supreme Court or the West German Federal Constitutional Court to deal with clashes between institutions in a principled manner, above the fray of party politics; and, as has become painfully obvious in the devolution debate, as a people we have very little familiarity with the language of constitutional argument.[2] Any student of the British constitution therefore must recognise the inchoate nature of the subject and is likely to fall back upon a definition of the constitution such as Herman Finer's characterisation of it as a country's 'system of fundamental political institutions'.[3] To that extent, a description of the British constitution has to rely heavily on the behaviour of the politicians themselves as a source for new constitutional norms and as a way of testing whether older norms still govern behaviour: the pronouncements of the judiciary and the words of the statute book alone are not enough. Unfortunately the actions of politicians are frequently difficult to interpret and the area of disagreement about an alleged precedent is correspondingly great. Inevitably perhaps the consequence of such ambiguity has been to convince many commentators that the 'dark saying' of de Tocqueville's about the British constitution was indeed correct and that Britain really had no constitutional rules which could be distinguished from the rules of the common law on the one hand or mere political practice on the other.[4] Or, as Ian Gilmour has recently put it, 'if everything is part of the constitution, then in a sense nothing is'.[5]

These traditional impediments to the study of the British constitution are particularly acute in the latter half of the 1970s when the pace of social, economic and political change has so quickened as to make Burkean metaphors of gradual evolutionary change appear wholly inappropriate. Indeed, whatever approach one adopts to constitutional analysis, the British constitution as an integrated system of fundamental institutions resting upon certain crucial, if rarely formulated, political ideas may have reached the end of its natural lifespan; the creativity which enabled it to adapt over four centuries of conflict has disappeared. What sort of constitutional framework will replace the present somewhat derelict structure is rather hard to predict at the moment but it would be difficult to deny that we are witnessing a period of constitutional transition. The qualitative change which has come over the British constitution can be seen both in the operation of British political institutions and in the tone of recent political commentary. Until a short while ago for example the features which writers on the British polity emphasised were stability and predictability. As recently as 1969 Ian Gilmour was able to describe the British constitution as one which was 'excellent for the securing of consent, so excellent indeed that it almost eliminates dissent' – although he personally rather regretted the mood of torpor and inertia which that 'consent' represented.[6] Other twentieth-century authors applauded Britain's constitutional development and traced the way in which the good fortune of the English had given them an ordered system of cabinet government, a mass electorate, a highly professional and incorruptible bureaucracy and judiciary and, above all, a party system capable of accommodating the conflicting interests of an industrial society. Substantive policies like the institutional structure also seemed to give cause for congratulation since they appeared to suit the attitudes of a relatively prosperous and homogeneous population; in the welfare state and the mixed economy there was a practical compromise which accorded well with the political environment.[7]

Today there is almost no remnant outside Parliament of that constitutional complacency which used to permeate comparisons of our political institutions with those of other countries. Not only have major changes in the machinery of government been set in motion by such constitutional events as our entry into the European Community, but further changes seem likely as a result of the Labour Government of 1974's initial commitment to devolution and subsequent difficulties in securing the passage of appropriate legislation. And to the problem of assemblies for Scotland and for Wales must be added the continuing trauma of Ulster where the suspension of Stormont brought the question of the status of Northern Ireland back into Westminster politics. The comfort of the insular centralised state has thus been shattered in the past decade and a question-mark now hangs over many of the most familiar relationships and practices of the British parliamentary system. Moreover, in the eyes of many observers the consensus of values so vital in a political order dependent upon unwritten and therefore informal constitutional conventions appears to have disintegrated. The complex web of shared habits, ideas and beliefs which enabled the British system of democracy to work without formal statements of powers, rights and obligations no longer binds either the political elite or the electorate at large. The body politic has, in a sense which has still not been universally grasped, lost its personality.

One indication of the change which has come across the face of Britain is that constitutional questions are once again on our political agenda, although as yet there is little evidence that many political leaders have much idea about how to cope with them. It is perhaps worth stressing how important such a development is in a political culture which unlike the American has only rarely been marked by wide-ranging and basic questioning of the premises of the political order. The seventeenth century obviously experienced constitutional conflict of a very basic kind—and one which left its intellectual stamp on our institutions—while the period immediately prior to the First World War was also a time of political and constitutional ferment.[8] Apart from these two exceptional periods of British history, however, constitutional argument has usually centred upon the extension of the franchise, so that in the nineteenth century the literature of constitutional theory is richest when, as in the period immediately prior to 1832 or the 1860s, some major electoral reform is envisaged. The period covered by Sir Harold Wilson's first two administrations and that of Mr Heath—the years between 1964 and 1974—witnessed a large amount of limited administrative reorganisation preceded by Royal Commissions or committees of inquiry. Many of these changes—in the organisation of the higher civil service, of local government, and of the health service for example—had some potential constitutional significance but they were primarily seen as attempts to secure greater efficiency, often in accordance with tenets of management theory, within the framework of the existing set of values and assumptions about the institution's role. In short these exercises in reform were limited readjustments of the institutional machinery in the time-honoured tradition of British constitutional growth. Even such evident absurdities as attempting to strengthen local government without confronting the problem of finance did not cause British administrators to question this approach at the time;[9] and a Royal Commission established to investigate the constitution itself contrived to avoid thinking deeply about the basic constitutional structure of the United Kingdom, as its hasty rejection of federalism revealed.[10]

By contrast with that decade of limited institutional tinkering the period since the fall of the Heath government in 1974 has been one in which deep dissatisfaction with our 'fundamental institutions' has been voiced and the possibility of further *ad hoc* reforms seems unlikely. The ease with which the constitution secured consent, according to Ian Gilmour, would hardly be acknowledged by a critic of the British political scene in the years between 1974 and 1977. Indeed the keynote of this most recent period of political history has been dissent even when, as in the relationship between the Labour Government and the trade union movement, the theme was public harmony. Since 1974 we have seen a gathering mood of discontent in relation to the two institutions which are perhaps the most fundamental parts of our political system – the first-past-the-post single-member-constituency method of electing representatives and the political parties. There has also been evidence of an increase in demands for a written constitution together with an incorporation into British law of some kind of bill of rights or statement of individual liberties.[11] Support for a formulation of the proper relationship between the individual and the state, implying as it does a limitation on political sovereignty and some kind of judicial review, constitutes perhaps the most eloquent evidence that there has been an erosion of confidence in the traditional constitution with its unspoken and informal norms, its series of compromise settlements and its spirit of incrementalism. And, of course, there has been considerable evidence in Scotland in particular of dissatisfaction with the unitary and centralised nature of the state, although it is doubtful whether some politicians have appreciated the strength of this criticism even now.

The origins of a more probing questioning of the nature and form of our political processes can perhaps be found in the confused party situation which followed the February 1974 general election and which was not greatly ameliorated by the second general election in that year. The general election of October did, it is true, produce a tiny overall majority for Labour but that majority was soon eroded by defections and by-election defeats. It thus became necessary for the Government to learn to live in a climate in which the normal verities of political life in Britain no longer held good. It was a lesson which was only partially learnt, however, since the size of the Government's majority initially did nothing to impede its presentation to Parliament of radical legislative measures; nor did it inhibit the party from claiming a mandate for them. In addition, it did not significantly reduce the conviction with which Labour MPs resisted the claims of the House of Lords to amend legislation coming from the Commons. (Indeed shortly after one display of strength by the upper house, the Labour Party published proposals for the abolition of the second chamber.[12]) To many observers, the situation in the Commons was a desirable one since it in theory provided some check on the Government's legislation; in practice, at least until it became clear that the nationalists had nothing to gain from keeping the Government in office (because the devolution bill had foundered in committee) the separated forces of the opposition were unlikely to unite and could do little to restrain the

Government once it was determined on a measure. The passage of legislation became a matter of chance and the major result was that the political process took on an even more unprincipled and incomprehensible appearance to the ordinary voter than before. Government could feel secure of neither electoral support nor parliamentary loyalty, to say nothing of the strains within the Labour party as a whole.

The growing division between the Labour Government and the Labour Party as a whole had its roots in the leftwards shift of opinion in the unions and constituency parties towards the end of the 1966 – 70 administration of Sir Harold Wilson. This movement of opinion, which became most marked during Labour's period of opposition between 1970 and 1974, was constitutionally important because it revealed the extent to which the orthodox practices and conventions of British political life required an atmosphere of muted ideological controversy. The move towards the left by Labour, which was paralleled by a rejection of centrist policies in the Conservative Party, heightened partisan tension and destroyed the common orientation towards the exercise of political power which had survived from 1945 until the early 1960s. The traditional constitution, as some were wont to call it, represented a *modus vivendi* between competing parties and interests but it had also been the embodiment of a tacit agreement to limit the extent to which the power of the state would be directed towards the ends of a temporary majority. In other words the informal compromise of those years entailed a guarantee to minority interests and that guarantee was extremely difficult to maintain as political conflict became more severe. Political tensions were also heightened by the realisation that Britain's economic resources were unlikely to expand. The language of priorities is proverbially the religion of socialism and that language was spoken more frequently as Britain's economic performance declined. In these circumstances it was hardly surprising if there was speculation about methods of curbing the ability of the state to put its policies into practice; since 1964 Labour governments seemed in electoral terms more successful than Conservative ones, and the measures they were promoting had become more directly redistributive in purpose. What *is* perhaps surprising is that there should have been such a long period, between the advent of Labour into the British political system and today's debate, when the threat to certain group interests and possible constitutional safeguards against that threat were ignored. After all, the Founding Fathers of the American constitution had accurately identified a threat to individual interests, especially property, in undiluted majoritarian government at the end of the eighteenth century and had developed the concepts of judicial review and constitutionalism to cope with it.

The analysis of specific constitutional trends and developments has to be placed against this background of diverging opinions about what constraints there should be on the exercise of power in Britain. And it must also be borne in mind that changes in one ostensibly discrete area of the political system may in fact have repercussions on the polity as a whole, even if these effects are not immediately apparent. The constitution is a delicate and integrated mechanism even if politicians are skilled at concealing the extent to which specific proposals are likely to alter the constitutional balance.

The first major area in which the British constitution has changed is our role in relation to the European Community. The decision to apply for membership was itself a recognition of the transformation of Britain's status in the international system and represented a significant reappraisal of the links both with the Commonwealth and with the United States.[13] Much of the political debate prior to our accession to the European Community was focused upon the question of whether entry into a supranational grouping of this kind would erode parliamentary sovereignty. For according to Dicey, and to a large number of commentators on our constitutional arrangements, parliamentary sovereignty is the principle which, from a legal point of view, dominates our political institutions. Dicey's own definition of parliamentary sovereignty was a clear and simple one; it meant that under the English constitution Parliament has the right 'to make or unmake any law whatever' and that 'no person or body is recognised by the law of England as having a right to override or set aside the legislation of Parliament.'[14] From this principle, according to Dicey, flows the advantage of constitutional flexibility but also the difficulty of ensuring that today's solemn legislative commitment will not be undone by tomorrow's legislative majority. And certainly most implicit and explicit challenges to this pre-eminently Austinian doctrine have failed in the nineteenth and twentieth centuries, from an attempt to provide rules for the assessment of compensation in all future compulsory purchase cases to an attempt to challenge the validity of a Race Relations Act because it curtailed freedom of speech.[15]

Yet the point to be remembered in discussions of parliamentary sovereignty in the legal sense is that it is no more and no less than a rule of statutory interpretation applied by the judiciary, albeit perhaps the most important one in the legal system as a whole.[16] In other words it is a doctrine which finds its continuing sanction in the behaviour and conduct of the judges; and the judges, as was evidenced by the House of Lords' action in restricting the doctrine of precedent in 1966, can amend their own guiding norms and practices.[17] Few English judges would strike down a major part of a parliamentary statute with the confidence with which the American Supreme Court has dealt with Congressional legislation from the Judiciary Act of 1789 to the recent Campaign Finance Act of 1974;[18] but British judges can and do interpret statutes in a way which does not necessarily conform with the actual intentions of those who drafted the legislation. Sometimes this is the result of the application of technical presumptions of statutory interpretation – for example it is generally assumed that Parliament, in the absence of explicit evidence to the contrary, does not intend to exclude the requirement of *mens rea* from a statutory crime and that it does not intend to interfere with vested rights;[19] sometimes it is the result of judicial activism or, as its supporters call it, 'creativity' even when faced with a statute, such as the Foreign Compensation Act of 1950, which purports to exclude review by the courts.[20]

The European Communities Act of 1972 – which incorporates the Community treaties into the British legal system – defines the rules of statutory interpretation which the judges are to apply when there appears to be a conflict between a piece of parliamentary legislation and an item of European legislation. Section 3 (1) of the European Communities Act explicitly provides that any dispute as to the interpretation, effect or validity of the Treaties, or of secondary legislation made under them, is to be treated by the British judges as a question of law. If such a case reaches the House of Lords there must be – under Article 177 of the Treaty of Rome – a reference to the European Court for a definitive ruling on the subject; but even in the lower courts, the principles which must govern the case are those of European law, and there may at any stage of the litigation be a request for a ruling from the European Court on the meaning and interpretation of the Treaties.[21] In fact what the European Communities Act has done is to change the *grundnorm* of our legal system and amend the rules to which the judges will look in their attempt to settle legal disputes. Judges now have to refer to principles of law which are, in short, superior to parliamentary legislation. Thus, while Britain as a matter of political fact chooses to remain a member of the European Community, Dicey's first principle of the British constitution has to be set aside. Doubts had been cast on the theory of parliamentary sovereignty prior to our entry into Europe; those doubts have surely now become a certainty.[22]

The period between the passage of the European Communities Act is too brief to allow for many definitive statements by the judiciary on how they intend to cope with this fundamental change in the British constitution. Nevertheless there are some signs of judicial awareness of the impact of Community membership upon our traditional constitutional concepts and practices. Lord Denning, who along with the late Lord Reid and Lord Scarman, will probably be remembered as one of the remarkable contributors to the development of the common law in a changing political environment, emphasised the impact of Community membership in a case prior to our accession to the Treaties. That case – *Blackburn* v. *Attorney-General* – was an attempt to prevent the Government from signing the Treaty of Rome because, it was claimed, membership of the Community was incompatible with the fundamental principle of parliamentary sovereignty.[23] Lord Denning agreed with some of Mr Blackburn's contentions about the impact which entry into Europe would have:

It does appear that if this country should go into the Common Market and sign the Treaty of Rome, it means that we will have taken a step that is irreversible. The sovereignty of these islands will thenceforth be limited.[24]

Lord Denning's remarks in that case were admittedly *obiter dicta*; but they do underline the extent to which, as he put it, although we have all 'been brought up to believe that, in legal theory, one Parliament cannot bind another', legal theory was now out of harmony with constitutional and political reality.[25] Parliamentary sovereignty might join the series of 'inapt words' or maxims 'of which the truth is ceasing or has ceased' which Bagehot saw as the inheritance of every generation.[26]

Lord Denning supplemented his remarks in *Blackburn* v. *Attorney-General* when, in 1974, he was called upon to decide whether it was necessary to refer a point of law to the European Court from the Court of Appeal. Although he decided in that case that it was not necessary to refer the problem – which related to the legality of Bulmer's description of their beverages as *champagne* cider and *champagne* perry even though they were not produced in the Champagne district of France – Lord Denning took the opportunity to draw the now famous and graphic picture of the effect of the Treaties on English law. English law, he said, could no longer be comprehended in isolation from European law:

> . . . when we come to matters with a European element, the Treaty is like an incoming tide. It flows into the estuaries and up the rivers. It cannot be held back. Parliament has decided that the Treaty is henceforward to be part of our law. It is equal in force to any statute.[27]

No longer must English courts in cases of conflict examine the words 'in meticulous detail' or confine themselves to the 'English text' in attempting to interpret such matters: they must 'divine the spirit of the Treaty and gain inspiration from it.'[28] And in 1974 there was in fact a reference to the European Court from the Chancery Division when it was suggested that Article 48 of the Treaty of Rome might preclude the Home Secretary from regulating the entry into Britain of EEC nationals on grounds of public interest or national security.[29]

The detail of these cases is perhaps secondary to the general point that, for good or ill, the British legal system is no longer autonomous. The ringing definition of parliamentary sovereignty to be found in the legal treatise of Dicey or the constitutional history of Maitland needs to be revised in the light of a change which has diverted the course of British constitutional development from a path followed since the late seventeenth century.[30] Dicey, of course, had analysed the British constitution in terms of principles other than parliamentary sovereignty and one such principle to which he accorded special authority was that of the rule of law. Now this concept is at least as difficult as that of parliamentary sovereignty but at its most general it obviously connotes a set of ideas and values which together demand that power is exercised in a 'climate of legality and of legal order'; and it also suggests that the ultimate justification of any claim to authority is rooted in the electoral process, and the notion of democratic representation.[31] More specifically it has been taken to mean that governmental power should not be exercised in an arbitrary manner but rather should be suffused with certain principles of 'fairness', whether these are defined in narrow procedural terms or in broader substantive ones.[32] And the rule of law has also been invoked to defend the proposition that the law, whether in statutory form or not, should apply with equal force to individuals, groups and public authorities. One of the most interesting constitutional developments of the past twenty years, however, has been the way in which the threat to this principle from government has generated new approaches and institutions to limit and control executive action, while the main challenger to Parliament and the rule of law has been the variety of groups within society which have had recourse to direct action to achieve their ends. Indeed these challenges have become so frequent a part of British political life that they have almost ceased to excite condemnation outside the ranks of a few highly individualistic and right-wing organisations. What is not clear, though, is whether there is a need to revise the individualistic conceptions of legal theory to accord with what might be understood as the realities of power in a post-industrial society, or whether we need a more activist and vigilant constitutionalism to cope with these new accretions of power.

Although there were challenges to the rule of law by a variety of 'protest' groups throughout this period (including one by a wing of the Liberal Party in relation to the presence of juggernauts in Britain) the main challenge to the principle has undoubtedly been seen in the activities and claims of the trade union movement. The most obvious example of a trade union challenge to the rule of law was when the movement clashed with the Conservative Government over the implementation of Industrial Relations Act of 1971. The legitimacy of this piece of legislation was denied by the trade unions and it often seemed that the unions denied also the general right of Parliament to pass legislation to regulate industrial relations.[33] And certainly some trade unionists have claimed that criminal acts performed in the course of an industrial dispute should equally be immune from the processes of law.[34] On the other hand some constitutional theorists, such as Sir Ivor Jennings, have argued that governments have a constitutional duty to consult affected interests before legislating on a topic which is central to their well-being and in fact there was unusually little interchange between the Department of Employment and the TUC over the content of the bill in its pre-legislative stages.[35] Moreover, for many trade union leaders and even some Labour MPs, both Parliament and the legal system embodied values which were alien to socialism almost by definition, so that an argument for the rule of law necessarily entailed an argument against the 'real interests' of the working class. The confidence with which the trade union movement in Britain exercised its powers – which was exhibited as much in the defeat of Labour's legislative proposals of 1969 as in the defeat of the Industrial Relations Act of 1971 – in part reflects the development within the Labour Party of a more Marxist, class-based ideology. But it also reflects the growing role of organised labour in the polity as a whole, a role Parliament itself has fostered by the legitimisation of policies of wage restraint and the attempt to incorporate the unions into the long-term planning of the economy. It may be that after a period in which both Labour and Conservative Governments sought to regulate this growing power by legislation, both parties will return to a policy of encouraging 'responsible unionism' in a new guise through such expedients as industrial democracy or, more speculatively, the revival of the idea of an Industrial Chamber in new dress as a substitute for the House of Lords as presently constituted. Either way the problem of how to integrate the corporate strength of the union movement into a political system welded to principles of representative democracy of a highly individualistic kind is likely to remain in the mainstream of British political discussion.[36]

The discovery that Parliamentary legislation would not automatically be obeyed by those whom it was designed to regulate was not simply a feature of the years in which Mr Heath's government clashed with the unions. In Northern Ireland too, Parliament found that its ability to legislate was severely constrained. It was originally hoped that the reintroduction of direct rule would increase respect for the law in Ulster by removing a sectional Parliament at Stormont which lacked legitimacy in the eyes of the minority Roman Catholic portion of the population. Unfortunately it seemed that Westminster's legislation lacked legitimacy for both the majority and the minority groups of the electorate. Thus the complex constitutional solution of 1973 – the so-called power-sharing arrangements – could command no real support in the Province when it was actually put into operation. That constitutional settlement was destroyed as a result of a fourteen-day general strike by the Protestant Ulster Workers' Council and no political solution to the Ulster problem has been agreed since that date. Parliamentary legislation and political methods generally seemed impotent in a situation where large sections of the population had abandoned the values of constitutionalism and preferred extra-parliamentary means of imposing their preferences on their fellow citizens.[37]

By the beginning of 1977 therefore the processes of parliamentary democracy in Britain had been forced to bend to some extent to the pressures of external constraint, partly as a result of a voluntary commitment to a supranational organisation, and partly as a result of a decline among some sections of the population of respect for the rule of law as traditionally understood. But even apart from these changes, the last decade and a half has seen sustained, if occasionally confused, questioning of Parliament's role in the British body politic. The major themes of the debate about Parliament have undoubtedly been the adequacy of the House of Commons as a legislative body and the efficiency of Parliamentary techniques of administrative scrutiny.[38] In the period immediately following the general election of February 1974 criticism of the performance of the law-making and accountability functions was complemented by growth in the movement for electoral reform which, it could be argued, constituted a major criticism of the capacity of the House of Commons to fulfil its representative function. Together these doubts about the relevance of the House of Commons' activities to the nation's affairs reveal a serious loss of confidence in the fundamental elements of the British style of representative democracy.[39]

Criticism of the House of Commons' part in the legislative process was in many ways a product of the increasing amount of legislation which Parliament had to examine and the consequent frustration felt by backbenchers whose time was taken up in activity which, as far as they were concerned, was largely ritual. (The extent of the normal impact of backbench opinion on the government's legislative proposals can be assessed from the calculation that over three legislative sessions – 1967 – 8, 1968 – 9, and 1970 – 71 – only 39 amendments were successfully moved by members of the opposition or the Government backbenches; and of these 39 amendments only nine were of substantial importance.[40]) Richard Crossman's period as Leader of the House of Commons witnessed a series of procedural experiments and the development of the Select Committee system, but it seemed in 1971 that many of the familiar problems of parliamentary reform were still unsolved.[41] Thus the Select Committee on Procedure in that year in a special report on the process of legislation commented:

> . . . there has been an increasing volume of criticism of the legislative work done by Parliament to the effect that many statutes are difficult to interpret, to comprehend and to apply in practice. Your Committee have received evidence of the increasingly active and informed part in proceedings played by Members who have entered the House in recent years. Often, however, they have been frustrated in being excluded from debates by the large number of members wishing to speak, and in being required to attend committees on Bills whose proceedings appeared to offer little opportunity of securing changes in the majority of Bills before them.[42]

MPs, it appeared, had become more professional but there was little scope for them to exercise their professionalism. Indeed one of the assumptions on which the limited reforms of the mid-1960s had been made was that the legislative process – and hence most of Parliament's time – was the

Government's by right. MPs won such favours as they could in terms of additional debating time and novel specialist committees only if prepared to subscribe to what one authority has called a 'package deal' in which the executive's business was expedited in return for these concessions to the backbenches.[43] Such incidents as the refusal to allow a Select Committee to travel abroad or to allow a key minister to give evidence before a Select Committee were simply indications of the constitutional reality: it was the executive which controlled the legislature and not vice versa, although the confused party situation within the House of Commons after 1974 has tempted one or two MPs to use their new-found bargaining power and to rebel against the party whips.[44] Yet even in the context of a Parliament in which a Government can lose a second reading debate for the first time since the Second World War and in which significant amendments to a bill can be achieved by backbench rebellion, the norms of party discipline and solidarity remain overwhelmingly strong, and the room for backbench initiative correspondingly weak.[45]

Dissatisfaction with the manner in which the House of Commons passed its legislation was not only a symptom of a desire by ordinary MPs to participate more fully in the decision-making process. It was also a product of the House of Commons' failure to achieve a consistently high standard of legislative output in technical terms. The pressure under which parliamentary draftsmen had to work, the piecemeal nature of amendments, and the highly complicated nature of many legislative proposals meant that obscure and even internally contradictory bills reached the statute book. The Second Report from the Select Committee on Procedure, (1971) as a Law Commission Report had done before it, examined ways of improving the form and drafting of bills in order to achieve a greater degree of clarity in the law but, although the committee recommended that draftsmen be made available to MPs who wished to introduce private members' legislation, the task of making more concrete improvements in the legislative process was avoided by suggesting that a specialised committee be established to review the form, drafting and amendment of legislation, and the practice in its preparation.[46] That committee—the Renton Committee on the Preparation of Legislation—commenced its report by underlining how difficult it was in practice to improve the quality of legislation without radical changes in parliamentary attitudes:

> . . . little can be done to improve the quality of legislation unless those concerned in the process are willing to modify some of their most cherished habits. We have particularly in mind the tendency of all governments to rush too much weighty legislation through Parliament in too short a time with or without the connivance of Parliament, and the inclination of Members of Parliament to press for too much detail in Bills. Parliamentarians really cannot have it both ways. If they really want legislation to be simple and clear they must accept bills shorn of

unnecessary detail and elaboration. We cannot emphasise too strongly that Government and Parliament have a clear responsibility for the condition of the statute book.[47]

Despite a thorough examination of the problem, the actual proposals of the Renton Committee were modest. Perhaps its most significant suggestion was that a procedure for incorporating improvements of a purely drafting and non-policy nature should be devised so that formal amendments of this kind could be made in between a bill's passage through all its parliamentary stages and its receipt of the Royal Assent. (The fact that such an amendment was technical would have to be certified by both the Speaker of the House of Commons and the Lord Chancellor.) The problem with such a proposal is that it would sometimes be difficult to draw the line between amendments which really were politically neutral and ones which were simply designed to tighten up legislation not acceptable to the Opposition. Indeed it may be that Opposition members of the House of Commons have an interest in technically deficient legislation reaching the statute book since this allows scope for political attack on the substance of the legislation (witness for example the way in which drafting deficiencies in the Sex Discrimination Act and the Scotland and Wales Bill have been exploited) and permits judicial rather than legislative tidying up of the measure.

The techniques of parliamentary scrutiny of the administration were also reappraised when the 1966 general election brought into the House of Commons a large number of able, full-time politicians anxious not to become mere lobby fodder, and sceptical of the relevance of traditional constitutional theories to the realities of administrative practice in a highly developed welfare state. There was thus a search for new machinery to substitute for outworn or discredited informal practices. One casualty of this renewed questioning of the way in which parliament operates was the doctrine of ministerial responsibility which traditionally lay at the heart of the process of control and accountability in Britain. The classic doctrine was that a minister was responsible for every act and omission of his department whether he had made a personal contribution to the error or not. Parliament therefore had the right to question the Minister on the subject if it was felt that some policy error or some act of maladministration had occurred. In the last resort the doctrine assumed that a Minister who failed to give Parliament a satisfactory explanation for a departmental error would have to resign. This doctrine was used to justify a number of constitutional practices – such as the sanctity of civil service anonymity and the initial refusal of ministers to allow civil servants to appear before Select Committees.[48] Its importance in British political mythology also explains to some extent the slow development of legal techniques for controlling the administration in the twentieth century: the primary redress for an aggrieved citizen was political.

The inadequacies of this theory to secure a measure of accountability had been underlined in the immediate post-war period.[49] Parliament was powerless to demand the resignation of a member of the executive because, unless the individual minister happened to be one whom the Prime Minister was anxious to dispose of anyway, party solidarity would usually ensure that an attack on the conduct of a department could be overcome. Even where the minister was willing to admit that an error had been made and even when *he* might perhaps have thought it necessary to offer his resignation, the Government would generally prefer to deny the charge if it reflected adversely on the administration as a whole. Sir Thomas Dugdale's resignation over the Crichel Down affair in 1954 should be interpreted therefore not as a sign of the health of the convention but as an indication of the insignificance of the error in policy terms or of the weakness of the minister concerned. In such a situation resignation was not a punitive measure imposed by Parliament but the cheapest and quickest way of closing the matter politically.

Scepticism about Parliament's willingness to impose sanctions on the minister was reinforced by scepticism about the ability of any politician to control and supervise the inner workings of his department. The trend towards larger government departments made the theory of ministerial responsibility more evidently fictitious and indeed the problem of deciding which minister was answerable to the House of Commons for the affairs of a 'super-department' was one factor in the gradual liquidation of these vast Whitehall empires. (By 1977 only the Foreign and Commonwealth Office and the Ministry of Defence remained of the 'super-departments' and they had been created for reasons other than those of administrative theory.[50]) The erosion of belief in the doctrine of ministerial responsibility perhaps made MPs more receptive to the suggestion that other techniques for controlling the executive could be relevant to Britain. Growing awareness of their collective impotence *vis-à-vis* the executive may thus have prevented MPs in the late 1960s from immediately rejecting the proposal for an Ombudsman as a threat to one of their most cherished functions; and it may also have made them more sympathetic to the judicial elaboration of individual rights against the Government.

The establishment of the Parliamentary Commissioner for Administration in 1967 represented a public admission that Parliament's traditional methods of securing the redress of individuals' grievances needed to be supplemented. But it also hastened the demise of many of the conventions which had previously constrained the investigatory process in the United Kingdom. For one important corollary of the theory of ministerial responsibility had been the rule that civil servants themselves were immune from criticism and that any attempt to distinguish the acts or policies of a minister from those of his advisers would be resisted. Select Committees initially encountered difficulty when they tried to question civil servants directly but that resistance was to some extent overcome and the practice of senior civil servants testifying before such committees is now fairly common.[51] The Parliamentary Commission whose office is associated with a Select Committee which may examine his reports and any aspect of his work, placed another nail in the coffin of bureaucratic anonymity. Some of the implications of the Parliamentary Commissioner's operations became clear in the first sensitive case which arose, the so-called Sachsenhausen affair. In that case the Foreign Secretary, George Brown, attempted to protect his civil servants after criticism in a report by the Parliamentary Commissioner on the way in which compensation under an Anglo-German scheme to recompense concentration camp victims had been administered.[52] Moreover the Foreign Secretary argued very strongly that once the Parliamentary Commissioner had investigated a case it was not appropriate for the Select Committee to try to follow up his reports, by themselves questioning officials, even where satisfaction had not been obtained from the department in question. In other words the screen which covered the actions of civil servants and advisers could only be lifted to a limited extent by the Parliamentary Commissioner and it could be replaced at any time in the investigatory process by a minister who chose to make the issue one of political confidence.[53] In his diaries, which were themselves to erode the conventions of civil service anonymity still further, Richard Crossman has claimed that the Foreign Secretary's assertion that he was personally responsible for the decision to deny compensation to certain individuals was 'a lot of nonsense' and that George Brown was misguided in his attempts to stymie an investigation.[54]

Regardless of the merits of the Sachsenhausen case itself, the incident reveals both that some members of the government had not thought about how the Parliamentary Commissioner's powers would affect the traditional theory of ministerial responsibility or the orthodox relationship between politicians and civil servants and that, once lifted, the screen of anonymity might be difficult to reimpose. Certainly experience since the Sachsenhausen debates – most notably in relation to the Court Line affair—suggests that public knowledge of the differences in outlook between a minister and his advisers is being extended.[55] This development was probably compounded by increasing sophistication on the part of the media about the official contribution to policy-making, particularly with respect to financial decisions, so that over the period between 1967 and 1977 the image of the civil service as a politically neutral tool of the Cabinet became increasingly hard to maintain. And as a response to increased understanding – though some would say exaggeration – of the influence of senior officials, the 1960s saw a growth in the practice of importing temporary policy advisers into government to counteract the permanent civil service's alleged monopoly of information. Such a trend could be discerned in both the Wilson and the Heath Governments although each Prime Minister employed different sorts of advisers. Some civil servants seemed to welcome the greater flexibility and publicity which these changes brought to them and some movement has been made towards easing the restrictions which are put on members of the civil service engaging in political activity.[56] However, if a decade after the introduction of the Parliamentary Commissioner for Administration it seems that 'the constitutional chain of linked conventions' has been torn asunder and can never be quite the same again, it would be wrong perhaps to see Britain as moving towards a politicised civil service.[57] The Parliamentary Commissioner and the Select Committee have promoted the *identifiability* of civil servants and have exposed them to more open criticism. Yet judges and diplomats have long been in this position and no one has suggested that their offices should be 'political' in the sense that each administration would appoint only their own men to these posts.

The central position which the nebulous concept of ministerial responsibility occupied for so long in the British system of government has meant that the judiciary has been relatively slow to develop its own techniques for controlling administrative activity. But as the number of occasions on which the individual citizen has to deal with public authorities have multiplied, so the likelihood of judicial intervention has increased. It is not surprising therefore that the past few years have seen the courts struggling to reconcile conflicting private and public claims and openly acknowledging the need to articulate more general principles of administrative justice irrespective of the opportunities for political control of the government through Parliament. Concern with both judicial and parliamentary methods of protecting the citizen had been promoted by the Franks Report of 1958 which drew attention to the importance of the principles of openness, fairness, and impartiality in the realm of administrative adjudication;[58] but from 1964 onwards it was difficult to ignore the degree of progress made in the refinement of legal principles and standards applicable in the administrative arena. The task of constructing a system of administrative law, of laying the ghosts of the prerogative courts as well as of Dicey, often required judicial ingenuity. Here, however, as Lord Diplock put it in an introduction to a comparative survey of English and American methods of regulating executive power, 'there were . . . effective weapons rusting in the judicial armoury' which the courts could clean and sharpen.[59] The ways in which those weapons have been used have varied but recent controversial decisions such as the Laker Skytrain case, the Tameside decision and the judgment of the Court of Appeal in the Post Office boycott case have underlined the general role which the courts are assuming in the process of administration.[60]

Some specific features of this new pattern of judicial activity deserve to be mentioned, although it must be remembered that this area of the law is extremely fluid and that courts are not always entirely consistent.[61] First the doctrine of natural justice has been developed by the judiciary so that it can now cover *administrative* decisions as well as decisions deemed to be *judicial* or *quasi-judicial* in character. The transcedence of the distinction between administrative and judicial decisions – which was crystallised in the Donoughmore Report of 1932 – was achieved in the 1964 case of *Ridge* v. *Baldwin*.[62] In that case a Watch Committee's decision to dismiss a Chief Constable was held to be a nullity because no opportunity was afforded to him to make representations to the committee. Thus the Watch Committee had failed to observe one of the fundamental principles of natural justice which insists that 'no party ought to be condemned unheard.'[63] Lord Reid noted in his judgment that the concept of natural justice might often seem so vague in modern times as to be meaningless; but such a suggestion, he thought, suffered from 'the perennial fallacy' that because something cannot be cut and dried or nicely measured it does not exist. On the contrary, according to Lord Reid, the rules of natural justice were inherent in all judicial thinking even if they might have to be applied to a host of new situations. And Lord Morris of Borth-y-Gest echoed Lord Reid's opinion of the importance of the principles of natural justice by describing them as 'something basic to our system' and stating that the importance of affirming them far transcended the significance of any particular case.[64]

The idea of natural justice – or 'fair play in action' – has been elaborated since 1964 and applied to the range of public authorities which determine the rights of individuals in the modern welfare state. Thus the duty to allow the affected party to make his case heard has been imposed on tax tribunals, on immigration officers, on the Monopolies Commission and on the Race Relations Board.[65] And the courts have also begun to elaborate its implications by insisting that a party has a right to be represented by counsel and to know the reasons for an authority's decision.[66]

A new determination to subordinate the exercise of public power to juristic principles can be seen in the manner in which the House of Lords in 1968 treated the questions of executive or Crown privilege and ministerial discretion. In *Conway* v. *Rimmer* the House of Lords held that a refusal by the Home Secretary to produce certain documents in the course of litigation could be reviewed by the court.[67] This decision, which one authority has called 'the most startling piece of judicial activism . . . since the war', was justified by the House of Lords on the grounds that although the executive might think that the public had an interest in preventing the circulation of potentially damaging material, the public also had an interest in seeing that justice was done. The court might therefore in appropriate circumstances question the reasonableness of a claim to Crown privilege and substitute its own judgement of the public interest for that of the Minister.[68] In *Padfield* v. *Minister of Agriculture, Fisheries and Food* the House of Lords considered the constraints which operated when a minister exercised discretionary powers.[69] The case involved a refusal by the minister to establish an investigatory committee to review prices under a statutory milk marketing scheme, giving as his reason the fact that he might be embarrassed by its recommendations. Although the House of

Lords acknowledged that the decision as to whether or not to establish such a committee was discretionary it declared that a discretionary power was not an unfettered one. Discretionary powers had still to be exercised in accordance with legal standards and they were exercised unreasonably if irrelevant considerations were allowed to enter the decision-making process. The question of political or other embarrassment was not a relevant consideration for the purpose of reaching a decision and was unlawful since its intrusion tended to frustrate the purpose for which discretion had been given to the minister by the statute.[70] Moreover, Lords Reid, Hodson, Upjohn and Pearce went further in their judgments and said that where there was even *prima facie* evidence of irregularity the courts could infer from the Minister's refusal to give any reason for a discretionary decision that he had acted unlawfully.[71] These constraints on ministerial discretion were to become the subject of intense debate in 1977 when the Court of Appeal, or at least Lord Denning, made remarks which suggested that they had indeed inferred unlawfulness from the Attorney-General's refusal to furnish reasons for his decision with regard to an application for an injunction against the Post Office union.[72]

In retrospect the Post Office boycott case may prove an interesting touchstone of popular attitudes towards judicial activism: broadly speaking collectivists favoured the time-honoured methods of controlling the exercise of discretionary power via Parliament and argued that courts were both socially unrepresentative and unaccountable, while individualists looked with favour upon imposing relatively strict legal standards upon government and its officers.[73] Clearly the use which has been made of the legal process in recent years in Britain has tended to be anti-socialist in character, but as American experience has revealed this need not necessarily be so. Even here the division is perhaps not so clear-cut since a socialist who disapproved of legal intervention in education, for example, might well approve of the civil libertarian element in *Conway* v. *Rimmer*.

Judicial activism in the field of government secrecy and civil liberties was also apparent in 1975 when the Court of Appeal elaborated the circumstances in which it would intervene to restrain the publication of Cabinet discussions and documents. The case arose out of the decision of the executors of Richard Crossman to publish extracts from his diaries even though they had not received the customary permission of the Cabinet Secretary. It was alleged by the Cabinet Secretary, presumably on behalf of the Prime Minister, that the restrictions which normally prevented former Cabinet ministers from revealing the details of Cabinet affairs were firm conventions which flowed from the 'two complementary principles of the collective responsibility of the government as a whole and the personal responsibility of individual ministers'.[74] The matter was not one which depended upon the draconian restrictions of the Official Secrets Act or indeed, as Lord Widgery pointed out, upon the binding nature of the Privy Councillors' oath. Rather, it was a claim based on the inherent needs of government and the mutual trust which is demanded between ministers themselves and between ministers and their advisers. Secrecy, according to this view of British government, was 'an essential feature' of the doctrine of collective responsibility and that in turn was at the centre of the British political system. What the Attorney-General was saying also, of course, was that where the convention was breached the courts had the power to intervene and enforce the rule, a claim which if accepted would open up an extremely wide area for potential judicial intervention in future. Lord Widgery's judgment seemed indeed to confirm some of the Attorney-General's allegations and to suggest that parts of the convention of collective responsibility and Cabinet secrecy were binding in law as well as morally. According to Lord Widgery it was the case that Cabinet proceedings were to be regarded as confidential and hence subject to legal protection similar to that which protected marital and financial confidences from being blazoned abroad. However, what precisely constituted impropriety in this area was a question for the court to determine in the light of the particular circumstances of each individual case: mere breach of the convention was not in itself a matter for judicial intervention. Thus the courts have neatly substituted their assessment of what is in the public interest for the assessment offered by the Cabinet itself. In a way this is logical, for just as Lord Reid noted in *Conway* v. *Rimmer* the need to balance different conceptions of the public interest against each other and to take into the equation the public interest in the fair administration of justice, so Lord Widgery noted a public interest in 'a right to free publication'.[75] Therefore there was a time limit after which the duty of the court to restrain publication of political confidences would lapse and that limit was not necessarily the limit of thirty years imposed upon scholars since there was no reason to believe that such revelations as the Crossman diaries contained would necessarily threaten the doctrine of collective responsibility. Thus even though the court acknowledged much of the Attorney-General's case, it made itself the determinant of what should be published and when; and, as is well known, in the case of the Crossman memoirs it permitted the publication of material which was of a kind which hitherto had definitely been confidential. Moreover the court asserted along the way that, while there was ground for protecting Cabinet confidences, there was no basis in law for treating either civil service advice or the discussions about civil servants as inherently deserving protection from publicity.

The Crossman affair thus represents two significant trends in the British way of conducting constitutional debates: the tendency for the informal consensus of values about proper conduct to become ineffective and the tendency for more formal statements, often of a legal character, to be substituted for implicit understandings and ambiguous relationships. (In the case of ministerial memoirs the legal formulation offered by Lord Widgery was supplemented by a code produced by a committee established under Lord Radcliffe, although as with the attempt to 'improve' the Official Secrets Act it is open to doubt whether a new streamlined statement of the rights of the executive is preferable from a libertarian point of view to the old and discredited set of laws and conventions.[76]) If the doctrine of collective responsibility found some legal sanction as a result of the Crossman diaries affair, it was also the case in the 1970s that the doctrine had been to some extent modified in the light of other developments, most notably the divisions within the Labour Party on the question of Europe and on the accommodation with the Liberal Party in March 1977.[77]

The classic doctrine of collective responsibility had been as much honoured in the breach as the observance since the Second World War, but changing norms and practices in this respect became most apparent under the Labour Governments of 1964–70 and in the period following 1974. Although there were many ways of interpreting the doctrine, it was generally thought to mean that once a majority had decided on a policy inside the Cabinet that policy was to be regarded as the policy of the Cabinet as a whole. An individual who opposed a given course of action might resign, but if he chose to stay on then he was under an obligation not to oppose the collective Cabinet decision. (Obviously the individual opponent was under no obligation to support enthusiastically a policy he disliked and there had developed a practice of asking for dissent to be recorded in the Cabinet minutes.[78]) Over the period from 1945, however, the critics of a majority position in the Cabinet have increasingly been identifiable, sometimes by unattributable leaks to journalists and sometimes by their participation, as far as Labour is concerned, in party activities which indicate disagreement with the tenor of Government policy. While there was broad harmony between the Labour Party and the Labour Cabinet this opportunity for the public to seize on Cabinet divisions did not perhaps matter unduly and indeed one former Cabinet minister has suggested that without such flexibility the convention could not have survived at all.[79] But in a period where strains developed in the relationship between a Labour government and the extra-parliamentary party, as was increasingly the case after 1969, one has to question whether or not so many exceptions to the convention have been allowed as to remove most of its meaning.

Sir Harold Wilson has commented in his own writings on the problems created by dual membership of the Cabinet and the National Executive of the Labour Party. It seems that there have had to be constant reminders that Cabinet Ministers should not become too closely identified with NEC policies and in 1969, a time of tension in Labour circles because of the Cabinet's industrial relations proposals, a formal statement of the doctrine of collective responsibility was actually read to the Cabinet. Similarly in 1974, when there was disagreement between the NEC and the Cabinet over some aspects of foreign policy, the Prime Minister felt it necessary to write to three Cabinet ministers who had expressed disagreement with the government's policy on these matters.[80] Finally in 1976 Sir Harold Wilson had to introduce a rule that no minister who was chairman of an NEC sub-committee could undertake press briefings on its behalf if it meant announcing policies which in any way differed from those of the Government.[81] (It is perhaps worth noting that Labour Cabinets seem much more given to embodying their codes of behaviour as formal rules than Conservative ones; another example would appear to be the rule that matters discussed in committee could not be brought to full Cabinet without the consent of either the committee chairman or the Prime Minister – a rule which it appears Mr Heath had no need to employ.[82])

Yet even against the background of divisions over industrial or foreign policy, the public display of Cabinet disunity produced by the referendum campaign of 1975 was spectacular. The device of a referendum on the European issue had been introduced to extricate the Labour leadership from a difficult position created by party divisions while in opposition. The justification for the decision was that the issue was so important that normal practices of political life did not apply and hence anti-European Ministers were allowed to campaign publicly against the policy of the Cabinet as a whole in the expectation that once the votes had been counted all would return to normal. Such an expectation was not fulfilled, however, since the European question had produced – or rather reinforced – patterns of political behaviour among Cabinet Ministers which proved difficult to break. Thus Mr Tony Benn had no reservations about campaigning for the leadership on an economic platform markedly distinct from that of the government of which he was a member in 1976 and the press had little difficulty in establishing which ministers in the Cabinet had resisted the parliamentary compact with the Liberals in 1977.[83]

The Labour Prime Minister's decision to enter into an arrangement with the Liberal leader Mr Steel in March 1977 was made in order to survive a non-confidence motion. Although there had been tacit agreements between Labour and the Liberal Party in the past, this compact was constitutionally novel in that it took the form of a published agreement to allow the Liberals to veto Cabinet legislative proposals prior to their introduction into the House of Commons. To many observers the bargain represented a belated recognition of the facts of both parties real political situation. From Labour's point of view it suggested that the Government – or most of its members – had come to terms with the fact that it had neither a parliamentary majority nor popular support for radical policies. And as far as the Liberals were concerned it implied a willingness to enter into a diluted form of coalition. Such a course of action was to some extent the logical result of the party's advocacy of electoral reform and criticism of the two major parties' gladiatorial combat. (As Mr Heath was swift to point out, however, the Liberals had settled in March 1977 for a less advantageous pact than that offered by the Conservatives in

February 1974 when it seems that both a seat in the Cabinet and some examination of the electoral system were dangled before the Liberal leadership.) Yet the manner in which the agreement had come about – as a hasty response to potential parliamentary and electoral defeat – seemed to provide a very poor basis for developing a new mode of constitutional government which could transcend the perceived sterility of the existing structure of party competition, or adversary politics as it has come to be called.[84] For the agreement reflected – as the devolution debate had done before in that parliamentary session (indeed it was the failure of the system to be able to cope with the devolution issue which transformed the nationalist parties in the House of Commons to opponents rather than supporters of the Labour government) how wedded British politicians are to the short-term bargain, the *ad hoc* solution and incrementalist approach in preference to anything which might promote more fundamental, and possibly more effective, change.

The question of devolution is dealt with in detail elsewhere in this collection[85] but the manner in which both major parties treated the issue, ignoring or concealing its constitutional implications and in the Conservative Party's case denying the reality of a grievance which was not of an economic character, illuminates the dilemma which the British political system confronts. For although the emergence of the Scottish National Party as an electoral threat to the two major parties was effective in placing the topic of regional autonomy on the country's political agenda after nearly fifty years, the habits of thought, the conceptual apparatus and the political imagination of the political elite were not such as to enable the problem to be solved. A major constitutional question, offering an opportunity for constructive reappraisal of the balance between centre and region and a chance to develop political thought, was treated in the same rather pragmatic and limited fashion as the reforms of local government, the civil service and the health service had been.[86] Devolution – and the Government only realised this when its bill became enmeshed in committee in the House of Commons – *could* be treated as a minor readjustment to the constitution but to do so and to fail to draw out the implications of the change would be both dishonest and ultimately self-defeating. The defeat was paradoxically more a defeat for the Conservatives than for the Labour Party, whose short-term interests might have corresponded with a measure of devolution but whose long-term values certainly did not. For the Conservatives on the other hand it was perhaps a mark of their inability to overcome the habits of mind and behaviour into which they had fallen, that they could not see how devolution might serve their long-term goals, both in breaking down the over-centralised state which they purported to deplore, and in promoting some new form of constitutional settlement based upon more formal guarantees of rights and powers. However, it is difficult to see how such a long-term goal can be achieved if it is dependent upon political actors whose primary concern is the immediate and the short term.

The experience of devolution underlines the fundamental nature of the British constitutional problem. For although there may be mounting pressure from many parts of the political system for constitutional change, ultimately the achievement of constitutional reform is dependent upon the two institutions who have most to gain from the preservation of the *status quo*—the major political parties. The constitution is in a very real sense what the Labour and Conservative parties say it is and however great the impetus for formalisation produced by membership of a legally defined community such as the EEC., at the centre the parties' grip on political life is still almost total. It matters little that the electorate's loyalty to these two parties has declined or that in financial and membership terms these parties are less than healthy. In the absence of some political or constitutional trauma, the pace of change and the nature of the changes introduced will reflect not the interests of the electorate at large but the constraints of the two-party system. Whether the filtering of constitutional demands through Smith Square can actually produce the sort of institutional adjustment which is likely to be required – much less the rebuilding of the consensus on which those institutions will depend – remains to be seen. One would not be unduly pessimistic to suggest that if any way of arresting the spiral of constitutional decline is to be found it would be best not to place exclusive hope in the established political leadership as the mechanism to provide it. The system's ability to respond to change (which was so amply demonstrated by the realignments of the mid-nineteenth and early twentieth centuries) has to a great extent been eroded by the introduction of the referendum and the greater degree of public division within the Cabinet; badly divided parties need not split so long as, on balance, what holds them together is greater than what threatens to tear them apart. Thus the tension between the emergent forces of constitutional innovation and the imperviousness of the existing party structure to change is likely to increase rather than diminish.

NOTES

1. There are many excellent surveys of constitutions and constitutionalism. Perhaps the best introductions are Geoffrey Marshall, *Constitutional Theory* (Oxford, 1971) and Leslie Wolf-Phillips, *Comparative Constitutions* (London, 1972).

2. The point about understanding the language of constitutional argument has been expanded in an illuminating and original work by N. Johnson, *In Search of the Constitution* (Oxford, 1977).

3. Herman Finer, *The Theory and Practice of Modern Government* (London, 1962) p. 116, quoted in L. Wolf-Phillips, op. cit., p. 9.

4. See A. V. Dicey, *Introduction to the Study of the Law of the Constitution* (10th ed., London, 1959) chap. 1 for Dicey's view as to the nature of constitutional law and the difficulties of studying that subject.

5. Ian Gilmour, *The Body Politic* (2nd ed., London, 1971) p. 3.

6. Ian Gilmour, op. cit., p. 61

7. For an excellent study of the emergence of the welfare consensus see Paul Addison, *The Road to 1945* (London, 1976).

8. For an essay drawing attention to the significance of the Stuart period in explaining the underdeveloped state of public law in England see J. D. B. Mitchell, 'The causes and effects of the absence of a system of public law in the United Kingdom', in W. J. Stankiewicz (ed.), *British Government in an Era of Reform* (London, 1976). On the seventeenth-century constitution generally a useful source book is J. P. Kenyon, *The Stuart Constitution* (Cambridge, 1966). On the period prior to the First World War see R. Jenkins, *Mr. Balfour's Poodle* (London, 1954) and the first issue of *Political Quarterly*, February 1914.

9. The Report of the Committee of Inquiry into Local Government Finance (Cmnd 6453) commented on the way that the separation of their financial review from structural issues imposed 'significant limitations' on some aspects of their work. For a useful volume of articles on the Layfield Report see *Public Administration* (Spring 1977).

10. *Royal Commission on the Constitution* (London: HMSO, 1973). The Majority Report (Cmnd 5460), commenting on federalism's applicability to the United Kingdom, said that such a legalistic system would 'appear strange and artificial' and would be foreign to the British system which was 'based upon the complete sovereignty of Parliament and upon the complete dissociation of the judiciary from matters of political policy'. Ironically the Labour Government's proposals for a Scottish assembly finally contained a highly significant role for the judiciary and seemed more artificial and strange than any system since dyarchy was introduced in the Raj in 1919. Lord Kilbrandon also suggested in a television interview that perhaps the federalist alternative had been inadequately considered. The Minority Report (Cmnd 5460–1) was a much more convincing document but it hardly provided the starting-point for a new constitutional departure, since its basic assumption was the need to maintain a strong central control of policy.

11. On the bill of rights debate see Lord Hailsham, 'An Elective Dictatorship' (Dimbleby Lecture, 1976); F. Stacey, *A New Bill of Rights for Britain* (London, 1973) and N. Johnson, op. cit.

12. The Home Policy Committee of the National Executive Committee (a sub-committee chaired by Mr Benn) endorsed in January 1977 a report of a study group under Mr Heffer's chairmanship. The House of Lords had previously rejected the Aircraft and Shipbuilding Bill.

13. On the development of British foreign policy in the post-war period see U. Kitzinger, *The Challenge of the Common Market* (Oxford, 1961) and his account of how Britain joined the EEC, *Diplomacy and Persuasion* (London, 1973). For longer-term views see M. Beloff, *The United States and the Unity of Europe* (London, 1963) and *Imperial Sunset*, vol. 1 (London, 1969).

14. A. V. Dicey, *Introduction to the Study of the Law of the Constitution*, 10th ed. p. 40.

15. *R.* v. *Jordan* (1967) C. L. R. 483; 9 J. P. Supp. 48.

16. On statutory interpretation generally see Rupert Cross, *Statutory Interpretation* (London, 1976).

17. The change in the extent to which the House of Lords was bound by precedent was achieved by a Judicial Practice Statement read by the Lord Chancellor on 26 July 1966.

18. The best introduction to the Supreme Court is probably R. McCloskey, *The Modern Supreme Court* (Harvard, 1972). A magisterial history of the Supreme Court is in the process of being written under the editorial direction of Paul Freund but as yet only a small number of volumes have appeared.

19. See Lord Reid's judgment in *Warner* v. *Metropolitan Police Commissioner* (1969) 2. AC.

20. *Anisminic* v. *Foreign Compensation Commission* (1969) 2 AC 147; but see also *R.* v. *Secretary of State for the Environment, ex parte Ostler* (1976), 3WLR 288.

21. The treaties are collected in a useful book, Sweet & Maxwell's *European Community Treaties* (London, 1975).

22. There is an enormous literature on parliamentary sovereignty but a useful introduction can be found in G. Marshall, op. cit., pp. 35–72.

23. *Blackburn* v. *Attorney General* (1971) 1 WLR.

24. Ibid.

25. Ibid.

26. Walter Bagehot, *The English Constitution* in N. St John Stevas (ed.), *The Collected Works of Walter Bagehot*, vol. v. (London, 1974) p. 203.

27. *H. P. Bulmer Ltd* v. *J. Bollinger* (1974) AC.

28. Ibid.

29. See *Van Duyn* v. *Home Office* (1975) ch. 358, 2WLR. 760.

30. See F. W. Maitland, *The Constitutional History of England* (London, 1909).

31. This phrase is taken from E.C.S. Wade's summary of the conclusions of the University of Chicago's colloquium of 1957 entitled 'The Rule of Law as understood in the West'. Professor Wade's remarks may be found in his introduction to the 10th edition of A. V. Dicey op. cit., pp. xcvi – cli. See also J. Raz, 'The Rule of Law', in *Law Quarterly Review*, Vol. 93 (1977).

32. For an interesting discussion of the idea of discretionary justice and the rule of law, see K. C. Davis, *Discretionary Justice* (London, 1969).

33. There is as yet no authoritative study of the development of industrial relations policy after 1969. But reference should be made to Peter Jenkins, *The Battle of Downing Street* (London, 1970), D. E. Butler and M. Pinto-Duschinsky, *The British General Election* of 1970 (London, 1971), D. E. Butler and D. Kavanagh, *The British General Election of February 1974* (London, 1974). Also Brian Weekes et al., *Industrial Relations and the Limits of Law* (Oxford, 1975).

34. The cause of the so-called Shrewsbury martyrs was an interesting touchstone of trade union and Labour Party attitudes towards the limits of picketing. See *R v. Jones and others* (1974) I.C.R. 310.

35. Sir Ivon Jennings, *The Law and the Constitution* (5th edition, London, 1959) pp. 102 – 3: 'It is now recognised that in framing social legislation the appropriate department must consult the appropriate outside interests' . . . and 'it is clear that soon the appropriate interests will claim a "right" to be consulted'.

36. The Bullock Committee on Industrial Democracy's Report (London, 1977: Cmnd 6706) can perhaps best be viewed as an attempt to educate the public and to 'annex' the union establishment to the political establishment. There is an interesting discussion of the Committee's proposals in *Socialist Commentary* (March 1977).

37. The Northern Irish situation is too complex to investigate here but the elements of the situation may be ascertained from two books by Richard Rose: *Northern Ireland: A Time for Choice* (London, 1976) and *Governing without Consensus* (London, 1974).

38. There is an enormous literature on parliamentary reform but the best introductions are probably B. Crick, *The Reform of Parliament* (London, 1966), A. H. Hanson and B. Crick, *The Commons in Transition* (London, 1970) and the study by J. G. Griffith, *Parliamentary Scrutiny of Government Bills* (London, 1974).

39. On the case for electoral reform see S. E. Finer, *Adversary Politics and Electoral Reform* (London, 1975).

40. See J. G. Griffith, op. cit. pp. 195–207.

41. Richard Crossman's period as Leader of the House of Commons is covered in R. H. S. Crossman, *The Diaries of a Cabinet Minister*, vol. 11 (London, 1976). The survey of parliamentary processes can be found in the *Second Report from the Select Committee on Procedure 1970–71* (July 1971). See also S. Walkland and M. Ryle, *The Commons in the 70's* (London, 1977).

42. *Second Report from the Select Committee on Procedure*, para. 5.

43. Nevil Johnson, 'Select Committees as Tools of Parliamentary Reform', in A. H. Hanson and B. Crick, op. cit., pp. 224–48.

44. See for example the refusal by Brian Walden and John Mackintosh to support the Government's bill to nationalise the ship-repairing industry in November 1976; and the massive rebellions of MPs over the devolution bill in February 1977.

45. This was the Reduction of Redundancy Rebates Bill which was defeated by 130 votes

to 129 on 7th February 1977.

46. *Second Report from the Select Committee on Procedure 1970 – 71*, para. 68.

47. *Report of the Committee on the Preparation of Legislation* (London HMSO, 1975: Cmnd 6053)

48. The Vehicle and General affair of March 1971 (when an insurance company crashed leaving a million policy holders uninsured) prompted a good deal of discussion of the convention of ministerial responsibility, since it was followed by a Tribunal which attempted to apportion responsibility for the collapse between officials and ministers. For an account of the issues see R. J. S. Baker, 'The V & G Affair and Ministerial Responsibility', in *Political Quarterly*, vol 43 no. 3 (1972); and in the same issue Lewis A. Gunn, 'Politicians and Officials: Who is Answerable?' For the Report itself see *Report of the Tribunal appointed to inquire into certain issues in relation to the circumstances leading up to the cessation of trading by the Vehicle and General Insurance Company Ltd* 80 HC. 133 (HMSO 1972).

49. A useful introduction to the topic of Britain's techniques of accountability is Sir K. C. Wheare, *Maladministration and its Remedies* (London, 1973).

50. For the development of the 'super-department' see Sir. R. Clarke, *New Trends in Government* (HMSO, 1971) and the Conservative Government's White Paper, *The Reorganization of Central Government*; for descriptions and analysis see Peter Self, *Administrative Theories and Politics* (London, 1969) and J. Garrett, *The Management of Government* (London, 1972).

51. Though there is still difficulty in establishing the right of these committees to send for Ministers, as the experience of the Trade and Industry Sub-Committee of the Select Committee on Expenditure revealed. (It wanted to question Harold Lever in connection with the Chrysler Affair but Sir Harold Wilson ruled that the only ministers who could appear before the committee were those with direct departmental responsibility for the issue under investigation.) See Sir Harold Wilson, *The Governance of Britain* (London, 1975) pp. 152–155. See also J. M. Lee, 'Select Committees and the Constitution', *Political Quarterly* vol 42 (1971).

52. R. Gregory and P. Hutchesson, *The Parliamentary Ombudsman* (London, 1975), have a full account of this episode. Also *First Report from the Select Committee on the Parliamentary Commissioner for Administration, 1967 – 68* (Sachsenhausen).

53. R. Gregory & P. Hutchesson, op. cit.

54. R. H. S. Crossman, op. cit., p. 662.

55. On recent developments in the Civil Service generally see Eleventh Report of the Expenditure Committee with Minutes of Evidence taken in sessions 1975 – 76 & 1976 – 77. (H. C. 535 – 1) 1977.

56. The Armitage Committee is currently examining the restrictions on civil servants' political activities.

57. The phrase is Lewis A. Gunn's. The government itself during 1977 seemed anxious to promote wider participation in decision-making by the device of 'greener' papers. Yet a bill to allow the P.C.A. to see Cabinet papers was not given a 2nd reading.

58. See Franks Committee Report, and the interesting discussion by W. Robson in M. Ginsberg (ed.), *Law and Opinion in England in the Twentieth Century* (London, 1959).

59. B. Schwartz and H. W. R. Wade, *Legal Control of Government*.

60. *Secretary of State for Education and Science* v. *The Tameside Metropolitan Borough Council* (1976) 3WLR; *Laker Airways Ltd.* v. *Dept. of Trade* (1977) 2WLR 234; *Gouriet* v. *Union of Post Office Workers* (1977) 2WLR 310. But see also 1977 3WLR, p. 300.

61. The classic work in this area is S. de Smith, *Judicial Review of Administrative Action* (London, 1973).

62. *Report of the Committee on Minister's Powers* (1932: Cmd 4060); *Ridge* v *Baldwin* (1963) 2 WLR p. 935.

63. See Donoughmore Committee's Report at pp. 75 – 80 for a discussion of the doctrine.

64. *Ridge* v *Baldwin* (1963) 2WLR, p. 983.

65. See *Wiseman* v. *Borneman* (1970); *re H. K.* (1967); *re Hoffman la Roche* (1973) *Selvarajan* v.

Race Relations Board (1975); see also the stimulating article by Michael Beloff, 'The Silkin Squeeze', in *New Society*, 10 Feb. 1977.

66. The case of *Breen* v. *Amalgamated Engineering Union* (1971) 2 QB saw Lord Denning commenting that Britain could by then be said to have a 'developed system' of administrative law – thanks to judicial action between 1964 and 1971.

67. *Conway* v. *Rimmer* (1968) AC. 910.

68. See the comment by S. de Smith in *Constitutional and Administrative Law* (3rd ed. London, 1977) p. 610.

69. *Padfield* v. *Minister of Agriculture, Fisheries and Food* (1968) 2WLR.

70. Ibid. p. 941.

71. Ibid. pp. 945–69.

72. *Gouriet* v. *Union of Post Office Workers* (1977). The House of Lords reversed the Court of Appeal's decision.

73. See W. A. Robson, op. cit.

74. *Attorney-General* v. *Times Newspapers Ltd.* (1975)2 QB. On the attempt to prevent publication generally see Hugo Young, *The Crossman Affair* (London, 1976).

75. *Attorney-General* v. *Times Newspapers* (1975)2 QB.

76. *Report of the Committee of Privy Councillors on Ministerial Memoirs* (London: HMSO, 1976, Cmnd. 6386). Also K. Middlemas in *Political Quarterly*, vol. 47 (1976).

77. On the Cabinet generally see John Mackintosh, *The British Cabinet*, 3rd ed. (London, 1977).

78. See J. Mackintosh, op. cit., and K. Middlemas, op. cit.

79. Patrick Gordon Walker, *The Cabinet* (London, 1972). See also J. Mackintosh, op. cit. p. 533 and for general discussion of the events of 1974–5 A. Silkin's article in *Political Quarterly*, vol. 48 no. 1. (1977).

80. Sir Harold Wilson, op. cit. pp. 192–3.

81. Ibid., p. 75.

82. See Norman St. John Stevas's introduction to vol. v of the *Collected Works of Walter Bagehot*, p. 141.

83. J. Mackintosh, op. cit. p. 533.

84. The phrase is explained in S. E. Finer op. cit. and the argument further explored in N. Johnson, op. cit.

85. See pp. 157–80.

2 The Changing Base of British Conservatism

John Ramsden

The proverbial space traveller, returning to Britain after twenty years, would be surprised by many facets of our political life, but perhaps by none so much as the change which has come over the Conservative Party. He would remember from the 1950s a party that had made a surprisingly successful recovery from the catastrophe of 1945 and which had returned to government in 1951 with much of its old assurance. He would know what had been done to modernise the party's appearance during those years of recovery, but—if he were old enough—he would also remember in how many ways the Conservative Party of the 1950s was a direct continuation from the one that had been led by Baldwin and Chamberlain in the years before 1939. Exterior appearances might have changed somewhat, but in the fifties the party was still drawn from the same parts of the country, still built its success on the same social foundations, and enshrined attitudes of which Stanley Baldwin would have approved.

A cursory glance at the seventies would soon convince him that this time a real transformation has been made.[1] The party's area of support has certainly shrunk from what it was twenty years ago, while most of the social bases on which its post-war revival was built have either ceased to exist or ceased to be the preserve of the Conservatives. The most surprising discovery would be that the party had consciously rejected its own past, deliberately snapping the frail cord of continuity on which previous Conservative history had relied.[2]

Geographical patterns of support are the easiest to delineate. The most obvious change in Conservative support is to be found in the outermost parts of the United Kingdom. It is in fact through challenges to the United Kingdom itself that Conservative strength has been eroded. In Ulster, a hundred-year tradition of electing a solid bloc of Conservative allies disappeared overnight. It was by their identification with the Union that Conservatives were able to claim the political allegiance of the majority in Ulster and it was when a Tory Government tried to demonstrate that the responsibilities of Union must work in both directions that the Ulster Unionists threw over the Conservative alliance. Perhaps the Ulster leaders were never Conservative for more than they could get out of it, most of all the preservation of the Union on their own terms, but recent changes in the leadership in Belfast and in London certainly exacerbated the problem. Ulster's political leaders had been predominantly the representatives of the old Protestant ascendancy, old families, business and professional men who fitted in well with the Conservative MPs that they met at Westminster. Since the beginning of confrontation in Ulster in the 1960s, the two groups have moved far apart; the Ulster Protestants have become increasingly militant, with their political centre of gravity shifting from the estates of County Fermanagh to the streets of East Belfast, while the Conservative leadership has become less tolerant, less easy-going and less politically pragmatic about Ireland. The Protestant Workers' Council strike that brought down Brian Faulkner's Ulster Government in 1974 was the political death-blow to the further co-operation of Conservatives and Ulster protestants because it destroyed once and for all the position of the old Ulster leaders who had brought the two together. Conservatives no longer felt able to do what their local supporters in Ulster wanted and so the men who represented co-operation were swept away. It was more than just a gratuitous insult to the Conservative Party when Enoch Powell was elected to Parliament as an Ulster Unionist, but without the Conservative whip, in October 1974. It was a symptom of the change that had come over Ulster politics. Powell's populist political style was more in keeping with the political demands of Belfast than were the more traditional methods and attitudes of the Conservative leadership. The consequence was a regrouping of the forces of the right in Ulster; refusal of the Conservative whip became a sign of Ulster's independence and Faulkner's attempts to build a new bridge between the parties were ineffective. In Parliament, the ten or so MPs who had supported Conservatives for a century suddenly ceased to be available, and the consequence was immediate. With continued support from Ulster, Edward Heath would have been leader of the largest party after the February 1974 General Election and so would have remained Prime Minister.

In terms of the numbers of MPs elected by the parties, the Conservative loss of support in Scotland became obvious only recently, but the erosion had been going on steadily for twenty years. It is now possible to detect over two decades the 'radicalisation' of Scotland, such as occurred in Wales in the late nineteenth century.[3] It was the Scottish National Party that exposed the frailty of Scottish Conservatism, but it was the Labour Party that had been sapping away at the foundations for a generation. The best Conservative performance in Scotland since the war came in 1955, when they not only won 36 of the 71 Scottish seats, two ahead of Labour, but also polled half of the overall vote in Scotland. Individual results at that time were even more impressive: Conservatives won seven of the fifteen seats in Glasgow and were within a couple of hundred votes of winning the eighth. They made an almost clean sweep of the rural counties and came close to victory in such unlikely places as Greenock, Stirling and Falkirk, Bothwell, Motherwell, and in both of the Dunbartonshire constituencies. Had there been a swing to Conservative in Scotland in 1959, as there was everywhere else, then the Conservatives would have taken a large majority of the Scottish seats. But it was in 1959 that the rot actually set in; while improving their position everywhere else, Conservatives in Scotland lost ground everywhere. Every Scottish region registered a swing to Labour and five seats were lost, a pattern that was repeated pretty well continuously until 1974.

TABLE 2.1   Conservative performance in Scotland

Year	% of total vote	Seats won	Net change
1955	50.0	36	+1
1959	47.6	31	−5
1964	40.6	23	−8
1966	37.6	20	−3
1970	38.5	23	+3
1974, February	32.9	21	−2
1974, October	24.9	16	−5
1955−74	−25.1		−20

Table 2.1 tells the story effectively enough – a continuous loss of support, a net loss at five out of the last six elections, and the recovery of 1970 being based on a tiny revival in the popular vote. Over twenty years, the Tory vote has fallen by half and the number of seats won has fallen by an even larger margin. The nature of individual results within this overall pattern is predictably gloomy. By 1974, Conservatives could win only one seat in Glasgow and one in the rest of Clydeside; in the industrial seats of West Scotland, Conservatives scarcely managed even a second place, and meanwhile the Tory strongholds in the counties had fallen to the SNP. The story is effectively told by reference to Kinross and West Perthshire, as typical as any constituency of the old type of Tory ascendancy in Scotland. Held quite easily in the 1950s, it was comfortably retained by Sir Alec Douglas-Home in 1963 in a highly contentious by-election. In 1974, on Sir Alec's retirement, the new Conservative candidate held on by just 53 votes after a recount. If such a traditionally Tory constituency – and in such a profoundly *conservative* part of the country – could be in danger, then no seat could be considered safe. But the change tells another story too; Sir Alec was a perfect candidate for the constituency and such candidates have been increasingly rare. Scottish Conservatives have not been able to find

good new candidates from the old Scottish ruling class. Traditional and religious ties have been weakening, but English businessmen and other carpet-bagging candidates have been all too frequent and especially badly suited to deal with the erosion of support. The low calibre of Scottish Conservative MPs over the past generation, and the failure of attempts to recruit from outside, gives at least a partial explanation of the decline of Scottish Conservatism. This may also explain why some areas have escaped the deluge; in Edinburgh and Aberdeen, the party remains quite strong, partly because politics in those cities has remained under the control of the two old parties, but partly also because Conservatives there have been better organised, closer to the people that they represent, and more able to throw up appropriate candidates. The same point can be seen at Glasgow Cathcart, where Teddy Taylor had the smallest Conservative majority in Scotland in 1966; as a popular MP with strong local roots and a good local organisation, he has survived when many MPs with 'safer' seats have gone down. The future, bound up as it is with the devolution debate and the subsequent role of the SNP is a matter of the most speculative sort, but it is difficult to imagine the party restoring its morale sufficiently to get back to its position of 1955 again.

A similar pattern can be found in London and the English cities. Here a comparison with 1950 is instructive, for Conservatives won exactly 252 English seats both in 1950 and in October 1974; within this, as Table 2.2 shows, the pattern was very different.

TABLE 2.2   Conservative seats in England

Area	1950	% won	Oct 1974	% won
Inner London	12	28	6	17
Outer London	33	60	33	60
14 largest provincial cities	24	30	8	11
Rest of England	183	56	205	60

The divergence is clear; losses in Inner London and the cities have been made up with gains in small towns, suburbs and in the counties. Part of this switch is to be explained by the effects of two redistributions of parliamentary seats, which have taken seats from the inner cities as the balance of population has changed. But the pattern remains: in 1950, the Conservatives won 29 per cent of the seats in London and the largest cities, in October 1974 only 13 per cent. In fact, the position in the cities is even worse for the party than this would suggest, for not only have seats been lost but the number of safe seats has been almost entirely obliterated. In 1950, Conservatives piled up majorities of 10,000 or more in more than thirty constituencies in the largest cities, in 1974 in only seven. Where at one time every provincial city had at least one safely-Conservative suburban seat, in 1976 only West Bristol and Sheffield Hallam could be counted really safe. The flight of middle-class voters from the cities and the redistribution of electors within the cities by council building have thus removed another bastion of Conservative strength. Without a secure base of safe seats, the local Conservative organisation is more stretched and the battle for the critical marginal seats has become correspondingly more difficult for the party. In the 1920s, it could be said that Baldwin could make a majority for his party in the suburbs, but that is now Labour's opportunity rather than the Conservatives'. Within this general decline, some areas have been more marked than others, and the collapse has been greatest in Liverpool, whereas in Glasgow generations of traditional voting habits along the lines of religion broke down suddenly in and after 1964. The subsequent rise of municipal Liberalism in Liverpool is a testament to the breaking of the foundations of local politics there, and the bewilderment of local Conservatives after their winning appeal of over a century had melted away. The Tory decline in Manchester is at least partly attributable to the same cause.

In the rest of England, the Conservative performance has been more mixed. In the West Midlands there was a secular trend towards the right from the 1950s until 1970, founded on the Conservative identification with affluence in an area that had done especially well from the boom years of the 1950s, and founded too on the spectral influence of Enoch Powell. Gains were made in 1959, further gains against the national trend in 1964, and large gains in 1970, with only a small loss of ground in 1966. The same tendency to the right was shown when Dudley registered the largest by-election swing against Harold Wilson's government in 1968.[4] All these advances were then swept away by an equally violent lurch to the left in the two elections of 1974, with all of the foundations of Conservative success weakened at once; Powell was by then urging West Midlanders to vote Labour, the Conservative Government was identified with the austerities of the three-day week rather than with prosperity, and the Conservatives' immigration policy (especially over Asians from Uganda) antagonised the extreme right. The same trend to the right and then back to the left can be traced in Leicester, and is to be explained by the same causes. The net effect is to leave the Tory position in the Midlands only slightly better than twenty years ago, in some places worse.

Against these sorry catalogues of decline can be set some areas of relative success, attributable in the main to the movement of population and to the unpopularity of rivals. The continued expansion of seaside resorts has left them as even safer strongholds than before, although this is offset by a weakening of the Navy connection in ports like Plymouth, Portsmouth and Chatham, producing a similar weakening of Conservatism there and the loss of three hitherto safe seats. The general drift of Conservative voters towards the coast has helped to bolster Conservative positions in the South-West and in East Anglia, and in both of these areas the trend has been reinforced by the continuing decline of political nonconformity and by the reduced employment on the land. Conservatives are now doing better in Norfolk, and the Labour Party worse, than in the 1920s; before the war, Labour could hope to win seats dominated by a labour-intensive farming industry, but Conservatives have gained benefits from mechanisation and the relative prosperity of farming since 1945. The same factors—movement of population from declining industry, weakening of nonconformity, and new industrial prosperity—explain the relative success of Conservatives in Mid-Lancashire and the West Riding. These towns of Northcote Parkinson's 'Left Riding' have been better territory for Conservatives in the 1970s than ever before. The final area of Conservative success contains all of these explanations and more; in October 1974, the Conservatives were stronger in Wales than for over a hundred years. In Cardiff and in rural Wales, the party has done especially well. The drift from the land and the decline of nonconformity explain part of this, but the nature of Plaid Cymru applies too. The Plaid is more radical and more nonconformist in its roots than the SNP, so that it appeals more to Labour voters than to Conservatives.

The conventional summary of these geographical trends is the assertion that Britain is being polarised between a predominantly industrialised, Labour-voting North and West, and a predominantly rural or suburban, Conservative, South and East. But the figures do not bear out such a simple interpretation, and within every region there are divergent trends that must be explained. The regional variations are outlined in Table 2.3.[5]

TABLE 2.3   Conservative electoral performance, 1955 – 75

Declining badly	Declining	Little change	Improving
Liverpool	Inner London	Outer London	Leicester
Manchester	Coventry	Birmingham	Cardiff
Glasgow	Hull	Bradford	Black Country
Rural Scotland	Leeds	Bristol	East Anglia
	Newcastle	Edinburgh	South-West
	Sheffield	Nottingham	West Riding
	Tees-side	Stoke-on-Trent	Wales
	Merseyside	North England	East Midlands
	Tyneside	S.E. Lancs	
	North-West	South-East	
	Clydeside	West Midlands	

The net effect is *not* that the parliamentary Conservative Party is drawn from the South and East to an extent that it has not been before. In 1950, there were 298 Conservative MPs, 113 of whom sat for seats north and west of the Severn-Humber line. In February 1974, there were 297 Conservative MPs elected, 98 of whom came from the same area. That suggests only a slight change, most of which was caused by the changed status of Ulster Unionists. The real trend is more complex, involving an increased Conservative reliance on rural and suburban seats in every area except Scotland, and a universal falling away of Conservative strength in the most working-class constituencies. If there is a polarisation, then it has been social rather than geographical.[6]

The last generation has seen changes in British society that have been fairly designated as a social revolution.[7] These changes that occurred in the course of the fifties and sixties have not benefited the Conservative Party and some have been positively harmful. A generation ago, Conservatives could still pose as the political arm of a traditional ruling class, and could do so quite convincingly. The gradual absorption of the professional and business classes into an older landed society had created one identifiable economic and social élite which was almost entirely Conservative in its politics. Many in the fifties deplored its continued power and some no doubt underestimated its resilience, but none doubted that it was there. The Conservatives might not be universally accepted as the natural governing party, but they did at least constitute the yardstick by which other potential governments would have to measure themselves. Churchill after the First World War had doubted whether Labour was 'fit to govern' and Ramsay MacDonald had said much the same thing at the time; the accepted criterion of fitness to govern, which MacDonald practised as well as preached, was the readiness of a potential government to look and act like a Conservative one.[8] The election in 1945 seemed to have shattered the whole of this political balance, so that many Conservatives no doubt agreed with Sir Hartley Shawcross when he claimed that Labour were the masters, not only then 'but for many years to come'. The revival of Conservatism after 1945, however, did much to restore the older view of politics, and by the mid-fifties Conservatives were more confident and assured than at any time since the twenties. By the end of the fifties, Labour MPs and commentators were asking gloomily 'Must Labour Lose?', and Professor Beer was speculating on the possibilities for democracy in a one-party Conservative state. Hugh Gaitskell took the same lesson to heart when he concluded that Labour's defeats had been due to its 'cloth-cap' image, which he set out to change to one more in keeping with the Tory spirit of the times.[9] Once again, the criterion for acceptability seemed to have become resemblance to the Tory Party. In these years, under Harold Macmillan, the Conservatives themselves bathed in a glow of self-confidence, added very little to the political debate and apparently thought very little about it either. They looked and felt like a governing party, and that was enough.

This successful recovery from 1945 had been based on the putting together of a winning coalition of social forces, partly in reaction to the work of the Attlee Government, partly by re-establishing old ideas and values that had been temporarily damaged by the Second World War. The result was that the Conservative Party of the fifties bore a remarkably close resemblance to that of the thirties, especially because the re-establishment of the old had been more easily carried out after 1945 than the evolution of the new. So for example in matters of personnel; the Maxwell Fyfe reforms were intended to create more opportunities for young men without personal wealth than had existed before, but there was no rapid displacement of Conservative politicians of the more traditional type.[10] Churchill's new Government in 1951 contained as many peers as had any this century, and had a distinctly old-fashioned look. There was always an intention to promote the new men, but there was an inevitable delay while they gained their experience of Parliament, after winning seats for the first time in 1950 and 1951. The character of the Party's highest ranks therefore changed only a decade after the return to power in 1951, and in the meantime continuity rather than change seemed to be the keynote. Anthony Sampson's *Anatomy of Britain*, first published in 1962, drew heavily on this situation; the much-quoted table in his book, showing how many Conservative Ministers and MPs were related to the Duke of Devonshire, was very apt but very misleading. Sampson's picture was drawn at the very moment when a major change was taking place – it described the Toryism of the fifties rather than the sixties. The position of Macmillan and Home as leaders of the party until 1965 disguised the change and allowed Harold Wilson to capitalise brilliantly on Sampson's picture with his caricatures of the Conservatives' 'grouse-moor image'. Until 1965, then, tradition and continuity at least appeared to be the dominant feature of Conservatism.

Rhodes Boyson has written of the importance of tradition in the fostering of a communal Conservatism in Lancashire between the Wars, painting a strong and convincing picture:[11]

> I grew up in a Lancashire cotton town that was traditionally working-class Tory and it is interesting to analyse why the Conservative Party dominated its life. Ordinary people found it easier to identify with the Conservatives in the 1930s because they were the party of tradition, law and order, and of established institutions, including the Empire. People gained pride from their voting which linked them, even in economically depressed years, with a sense of greatness.

What is perhaps not so clear is the extent to which this picture was *not* destroyed by the Second World War. In the early fifties, Britain still ruled the second largest empire in the world, second only to the Soviet Union;

India had been given up and some colonies were being prepared for ultimate self-government, but this was still thought of as a reason for national self-congratulation rather than shame. The army was still a major force in the national life, larger in numbers than any peacetime British army had ever been before and admired for its successes in Korea, in Malaya, in Kenya and in the Second World War itself. Moreover, the influence of the army and the Empire had always been a delayed-action sort of impact, felt by the nation at second-hand. Retired soldiers and colonial administrators had been a sizeable proportion of the traditional élite at home, partly at least because the army itself had been stationed abroad. Journalists, the writers of fiction and the script-writers of films had given a view of the army and the Empire that was always out of date and was virtually timeless in itself. In the Empire of fiction and films, it was always the 1890s. In the fifties, this popularisation of empire went on much as before and a new cycle of epic films about the Empire produced some of the most memorable and least realistic of the entire genre – 'Zulu', 'Lawrence of Arabia', '55 Days at Peking' and many more. How could the British public, brought up to believe in the Empire, fail to identify with David Niven at Peking, Charlton Heston at Khartoum, or Stanley Baker defeating the Zulus? This popularised Empire remained long after the reality had faded, perhaps filling a deep need in the nation's psychology, a need for escapism and reassurance. No doubt it also helped to prolong domestic political attitudes that had been based on imperial power.[12]

Similarly, the return of officers, soldiers and colonial administrators did not begin to stop until the end of the fifties, with the simultaneous reduction of the army after the abolition of conscription and the rapid running down of the colonial service. Until then, the old political attitudes in Conservatism were continuously re-created as before, even given a new lease of life by the triumphant outcome of the Second World War. Realists might have seen how far the popular empire was out of step with reality—but then it always was. The high point of imperial jingoism was reached in the 1890s, only when the frontiers were being closed; in the 1920s, novelists like John Buchan and Edgar Wallace wrote of Britain's power while British Governments were conscious only of her weakness; in 1962, British audiences who watched Peter O'Toole as Lawrence of Arabia must have been jerked back to reality by the shots of the Suez Canal.

In other national institutions, as well as the army and the empire, the Conservatives were able to preserve their traditional identification. In the law and the other old professions, identification with Conservatism was almost complete; there were and had always been a radical fringe amongst barristers, teachers and journalists, but only a fringe that served to demonstrate the solidarity of their colleagues. The universities, still the preserve of a small minority, were a positive haven of Conservatism by comparison with what was to come in the next twenty years; it was fashionable to support the Right in the fifties, as it had been in the twenties, just as the Left had been fashionable in the thirties and forties. The doctors had demonstrated in their recent dispute with Bevan that they remained a highly conservative force in society and that their views and interests coincided with those of the Conservative Party itself.[13] The Party still made regular bows towards organised religion, most of all through the Church of England, and a Christian motivation was assumed by Eden, by Macmillan and by Home. Industry was solidly Conservative after the experience of ten years of state control after 1940. Businessmen were not afraid to identify with the party, industry contributed heavily to party funds, and through front organisations helped to carry on the battle against Labour. Like the Party itself, business was confident that it could do well in the opportunities of the post-war world, asking only to be left alone to get on with its job—an attitude that linked well with Conservative philosophy.[14]

The traditional Conservative link with the national institutions was thus preserved and the party derived both satisfaction and prestige from their strength and confidence, but the party's success was nevertheless fragile and based heavily on two other factors too, the mass media and the political attitudes of the working class. The fragility of success can be shown easily enough; although in Government for thirteen years after 1951, the Conservatives never won half of the popular vote and was never more than a few per cent ahead of Labour. Indeed, opinion polls and by-elections showed that they were usually behind. Labour had polled more votes in 1950 and 1951 than in its victory of 1945, and in 1951 it even polled more votes than the Conservatives. It seems then inherently unlikely that the Conservatives converted many ex-Labour voters in their return to power, rather that they pulled in their own maximum vote and many ex-Liberal voters too. After 1950, the middle-class vote went solidly to the Conservatives, more so than ever before (for Liberals had always claimed a share of it before the war). Conservatives won about four-fifths of the middle class vote in the fifties, a solid base on which to build a majority, but a base that was vulnerable to periodic revivals of Liberalism, as in 1962 and 1973–4. But however solid the base, support amongst the middle class and establishment groups was never adequate as an election-winning formula. Half of the Conservative votes were always provided from the working class; Table 2.4 shows the normal class pattern of voting, as surveyed by Mark Abrams in 1958.[15]

Although only a third of manual workers voted Conservative, their votes made up half of the total Conservative vote. This support was consolidated after the war by a shrewd appeal by the Conservatives to the self-interest and extra-class identity of many workers. These two sides of the Conservative appeal were noted by sociologists who investigated the deviancy of these working-class Tories, men and women who did not vote as their class would seem to dictate.[16] Some such voters supported Conservatives from a sense of deference – a term that covered a wide range

TABLE 2.4 Voting and social class

Class	% Conservative	% Labour
Solid middle	85	10
Lower middle	70	25
Upper working	35	60
Solid working	30	65

of attitudes from actual forelock-tugging to a readiness to support the Tories as the party of Church and Queen, of Empire and world power. There can in fact have been little of the instinctive deference to local landowners or mill-owners, common enough in the previous century, and there were few if any coercive means left available to the élite that would force their tenants and employees to defer. But the habits of generations would take a long time to fade away and, as long as Churchill or Macmillan remained at the helm, the Conservatives were able to pose as the party of Britain's greatness, for something more than, wider than, class interests. One of his first acts after becoming Prime Minister following Suez showed that Harold Macmillan appreciated this point: he derided the view that recent events had shown Britain's weakness and concluded that 'this is a great country'. To such an appeal, many voters responded as they had always done. None of this is to suggest that only Conservative supporters were patriotic men and women with interest in the Empire, for that would be equally true of Liberal and Labour voters in large numbers. Rather it is suggested that nobody voted Labour or Liberal *because* they took a patriotic view of Britain's position but that this was a major motivation for voting Conservative.

The second group of working-class tories identified by sociologists were the 'seculars' or 'pragmatics', those who voted for the Conservatives not for what they were but for what they did, from a rational calculation of self-interest. Home-ownership in the 'property-owning democracy', affluence in the boom years of the 1950s, education of the children at a grammar school under the Act of 1944 – all such factors were used to cement the Tory vote and the Tory tradition. Here again, the party did not have to create a new area of support from nothing, merely to reactivate traditional family views and to tie them to the events and personalities of the fifties. Local variation of social custom and structure explain the variation of voting habits: in mid-Lancashire, a traditionally high level of working-class Conservatism was re-established in the fifties in an area of widespread home-ownership. In Liverpool, Manchester and Glasgow, local religious divisions were again used to underpin the other determinants of voting habits and to strengthen Conservatism through the Protestant and anti-Irish connection. In the West Midlands, the continued weakness of trade unionism linked with the political traditions of the Chamberlains to re-create an impressively strong Conservative organisation and a high level of working-class Toryism. The common factor was the Conservative appeal to those in the working class who found their main point of identity outside the conception of class that prompted most working-class people to vote Labour. To the deferentials, the point of identity was the nation and its leadership rather than social class, to the pragmatics it was the family or individual. To some, the point of identity might be a religious group, the status confered by a house or car or television set, or employment in a small workshop or trade where trade unionism had not yet organised 'us' against 'them'. In every case though, the Conservative success was based on the continuation of traditional feelings and the non-existence of working-class solidarity.

The final factor in Conservative success was the remarkable restraint and self-control exercised by the press and by broadcasters, amounting almost to self-censorship. The papers of the fifties were not much more restrained than today in their general outlook, but there was a very heavy bias to the right in Fleet Street. All of the popular dailies except three were steady supporters of the Conservative Government; of the others, both the *Daily Herald* and the *News Chronicle* were failing rapidly, and the *Daily Mirror* was not noticeably concerned with politics anyway. The broadcasters were determined to be uncontroversial, so much so that television did not even cover general election campaigns seriously until 1959, and then only with self-conscious decorum and restraint. The howls of rage that greeted Kingsley Martin's 'The Crown and the Establishment' in 1962, or Malcolm Muggeridge's irreverent comments on the monarchy in 1958 show how narrowly were set the limits of acceptable social comment; both would be considered almost hagiographical today. The prevailing trend of comment was optimistic and the voices of protest were either suppressed (like Muggeridge who was banned by the BBC) or treated with the amused tolerance that is redolent only of the most assured and confident of establishments.[17] British industry was booming, the civil service, the great national institutions and the professions were happily confident, the Empire-Commonwealth was about to become a magnificent new experiment in international relations and the envy of less happier lands. And after six years of war and six of austerity, was it not all gloriously deserved? All this contributed to Tory success in the fifties because all of it was popularly associated with them. It took the Second World War to bring 'Attlee's Consensus' into being, but once established it rebounded more to the benefit of the Tories than Labour.[18] This winning coalition had been put together after defeat in 1945, carried the Tories to power and kept them there; but it was not to last, and neither were any of the foundations on which it had been built.

The clearest cracking of the foundations came through the position of Britain in the world, with all that this implied for domestic politics. The

Suez fiasco briefly lifted the curtain to show the realities behind the apparent glories of Empire and, although Harold Macmillan gained much support for his refusal to admit a defeat, the wound to the national pride was a deep one. 'Suez' was a hecklers' cry at Conservative meetings for years and, by the changes of their colonial, defence, and foreign policies, the Conservative Government showed that they had learnt their lesson – whatever they might say.[19] Henceforth, international affairs were to provide for Britain only humiliation (as over Rhodesia), ridicule (as over Anguilla and the attempt to mediate over Vietnam), and irrelevance (as at the 1960 Summit or in the Nigerian Civil War). The scramble to get out of Africa and the upholding of native rights against colonial governments on the way out did much damage; such a policy could be defended as necessary steps towards a free and multiracial Commonwealth, but this defence would not impress voters who had regarded the Empire simply as a source of pride, proof of Britain's strength and greatness. Decolonisation gave great satisfaction to those who had always disliked the imperial idea and who wanted to see a Commonwealth based on morality rather than power, but few such people had ever voted Conservative; it was a shattering blow to those who had derived pride from the greatness of Britain. At the same time, the gradual running down of the armed forces and the colonial service meant that there would be a steady reduction in the numbers of those within Britain who had personal experience of Britain as an international force. Men who joined the army to see the world were likely by the seventies to spend their service in Aldershot or Catterick, with trips no further than Belfast or München-Gladbach. They were not likely to return home and spread the word about Britain's greatness and might.

Dean Acheson's jibe that Britain had 'lost an Empire and not yet found a role' was angrily refuted by Conservative leaders precisely because it was too near the bone, too uncomfortably true to be admitted. The Macmillan-Heath strategy to meet this situation was a commitment to Europe through entry to the EEC, but this strategy was slow to pay any dividends in domestic political terms. The popularity of the Common Market in Britain, as measured by opinion polls, rose only when Britain had little chance of joining and waned alarmingly whenever Britain actually applied for entry. Some groups in the country certainly found a new faith in a new European ideal, but these have never been more than an intellectual and commercial minority. Public opinion at large could not be expected to forget quickly the legacy of two world wars, and the reluctance of the EEC even to allow Britain to join made an emotional commitment rather difficult to justify. To Edward Heath, Europe would give Britain at least a chance to participate in a shared greatness, thus at once finding a focus for British foreign policy and an international point of identity for the ordinary citizen that would replace the Empire. But the point of the Empire, in its appeal to the baser human instincts, was its age and tradition, and the fact that its attraction was founded on the family and personal connections of millions of individual Britons. So Robert Blake has argued:[20]

> Within six years Africa, which had absorbed so much of the mental and spiritual, as well as the financial, capital of the Conservative-minded classes, disappeared entirely from British rule. I believe we greatly suffered from this process. It won us no votes, and it lost us the hearts of a great many people who still believed in Empire. It may have been unavoidable, and no-one could have done it more skilfully than Mr. Macmillan. But I am not surprised that the first election which we lost for 13 years should have been in the aftermath of that policy. It was a recipe for electoral trouble.

Europe could provide a focal point for British diplomacy at once, but it would take time before Europeans were regarded with the same affection as Australians and Canadians. In the meantime, there was no faith to replace the one that had been so urgently and so unceremoniously destroyed. The change was noted by Rhodes Boyson. In the thirties,[21]

> most families boasted relatives who populated the Empire, all were royalists and Tory meetings always had the Union Jack draped over the platform table. It is perhaps significant that when I wanted a Union Jack on my table at election meetings [in] October [1974] in Wembley, I was told by one of my members that this was the flag of the National Front.

In the seventies, the Conservative Party has indeed been outflanked on the right for the first time in its history. Labour used its resistance to the EEC in order to appear as the patriotic party, and the National Front has taken over the Union Jack (and the outspoken patriotism that goes with it) which was a Tory monopoly in every previous generation. The result has been an erosion of the party attitudes that went with patriotism in the minds of many voters, and in particular a drift of working-class voters away from Conservatism. Up to 1974, the National Front had not proceeded very far in drawing off Conservative voters, but it had already done better than Sir Oswald Mosley at the height of his success. Indeed, had a German or Italian party of the extreme right done as well as the NF did in East London in October 1974, the world's press would have been full of the danger of a reversion to fascism. The pattern of NF candidates in that election gives a clue to the source of their support; their worst three results were all in middle-class and suburban seats, where the effect of their intervention was only slight, a mean swing to Labour of 0.9 per cent. In their eight best constituencies, however, the mean swing to Labour was 3.5 per cent and these were working-class constituencies in a belt across North-

East London. It was clearly the defection of working-class Conservatives to the NF that swelled their vote and at the same time increased the apparent swing from Conservative to Labour. Private Conservative polls from 1974 apparently showed also that it was among working-class voters everywhere that the party was losing the most ground. Since 1974, the NF have made further headway, although it is impossible to say how much because the press seem determined not to publicise their activities. There is evidence of Conservative defections to the NF, including in some towns ex-councillors and ex-candidates; there is no doubt that the NF have built up a position of considerable strength in Blackburn, Bradford, the West Midlands, East and West London. In July 1976, the National Party and National Front candidates together polled more votes than Labour in a municipal by-election at Deptford, with the Conservative coming a poor fourth with only 12 per cent of the vote. The imperial challenge has then been taken up by the NF with consequences that Conservatives would do well to consider.

The second reason for working-class Conservatism also took a battering in the sixties and seventies. The failure of Conservative Governments to deliver the goods, in material benefits, could be expected to decrease the propensity of the working-class pragmatists to vote Conservative. Similarly, the controversy over the Industrial Relations Act of 1971 encouraged voters to think on class lines and to see the Conservatives as inherently opposed to the Unions. Any such influence that polarised class identification and encouraged the working-class voter to vote as such could only harm the Tory position. At the same time came the culmination of the consolidation of industry, away from the family firms and the small workshops to the monoliths and giants of today. Rhodes Boyson, again on the thirties:[22]

> Many of the working class voted Conservative because free enterprise was real to them. Big business was historically linked with the old Liberal manufacturers, but many ordinary workers saved up to buy two houses whose rents would provide for their old age while their cousins often started small businesses. As Co-operative members, they equated profit with the 'divi' as a goal to be lauded, while the early unions pioneered self-help in welfare. As employees they knew cotton spinners and weaving masters who had started at the mule and the loom. Capitalism for them represented thrift and investment, not faceless financiers whom they never met.

Capitalism could look more human and more acceptable when seen at close quarters and when the responsible authority was clearly in view. The process of consolidation was a long one, but it accelerated when industry ran into difficulties in the sixties and after. Another factor that had helped to break down class solidarity – self-interest and the refusal to think in the economic terms of class – was thus broken down.

Over this same period, the Conservative Party became much less clearly the representative of the establishment, although the changing social character of the party was slow enough to be far from obvious. The leadership actually seemed to have taken a step backwards, with the top job occupied in turn by Churchill (heir of the Marlboroughs), Eden (the country gentleman), Macmillan (scion of the House of Devonshire) and finally the 14th Earl of Home. Beneath the surface, though, the new generation of candidates selected after 1945 and elected first in 1950 was of a distinctly lower social level than their predecessors. Indeed a new career norm became visible in the sixties, with many candidates fitting it like an identikit. Tory MPs were now almost certain to have interests in finance rather than in one of the older professions or in manufacturing industry. Table 2.5 demonstrates the change.[23]

TABLE 2.5   The Backgrounds of Conservative MPs (% of total number of Tory MPs)

	1914	*1939*	*1964*	*1970*	*Oct 1974*
Education					
Public schools	68	59	77	50	63
of which Eton	30	26	21	18	17
Grammar, technical etc.	12	16	17	17	22
Universities	57	55	66	69	76
of which Oxbridge	49	46	54	53	55
Occupation					
Barristers and Solicitors	32	21	25	20	21
Regular forces	22	16	5	—	—
Landowners and farmers	23	10	14	12	8
Journalists, writers, publishers	3	5	10	12	13
Businessmen and company directors	22	42	32	50	50

In the seventies, for the first time in its history, the Conservative Party has more MPs from grammar schools than from Eton and half of its MPs occupied in business. There have been inevitable short-term fluctuations, but the long-term trends that have emerged have been the gradual extinction of the ex-officers on the backbenches and the rise of the businessmen at the expense of farmers, landowners and lawyers. A greater concern with image-building (with which this paper is concerned) and with communication, has provided openings for writers and journalists as never before. These changes are to some extent occasioned by developments within industry and society—in industry, a new generation of public companies and corporations requiring a new, technocratic, managerial class. As a result, many of the political arguments about industry have ceased to be arguments about ownership and become debates about management and administration. No longer, who should own the steel industry?; but how can investment in the industry best be managed in the national interest? Industries that after the war had asked merely to be left alone now beg for government intervention as a source of public money. Conservative MPs, increasingly representative like Peter Walker of this new attitude of industry, have become less sure about the correct line of demarcation between the role of the state and the role of the individual industry, company or citizen. There were important political consequences; financial and commercial ownership had been in themselves reasons for deference by the electors – as one working-class Tory told Robert McKenzie, 'I always go by money. If you haven't the money it's no good, so you have to go to the party with capital'.[24] This new generation of Conservative MPs is the first such generation to come into politics without some source of independent authority outside. In the past, it might have been achieved through landowning, wealth, writing, a brilliant legal career, each of them a source of status and authority outside politics. From the sixties, many Conservative MPs have been professional politicians in the sense that they have made a name in nothing else and have no external source of authority. A politician known as 'the Grocer' to friends and colleagues as well as to satirists might be respected and admired for what he had become, but he could not expect to be deferred to for what he had been, or for what he symbolised. The leaders of the middle class finally came into their own in the Conservative Party in the sixties, and the result was a style of party that appealed less and less to the traditional working-class voter. The thread of continuity was deliberately snapped by the party. The Edward Heath Government of 1970 contained fewer members whose fathers had been politicians than the Wilson Government that it succeeded; in one sense at least, Labour had become more of a party of tradition and establishment than the Conservatives. The retirement of Robin Turton from Thirsk and Malton and of Jasper More from Ludlow marked the end of generations of family service to the same county constituencies; the old guard, recognising the spirit of the times, seem to have bowed out.

Over the same period, all of the great national institutions with which the Tories had successfully linked themselves have come under fire. The dominant note in writings about Britain in the sixties was not the celebration of success, but a questioning of the viability of everything in sight, and a readiness to look abroad for new models. The Treasury, the civil service, parliament, education, the trade unions, industry, the people themselves – all were investigated and all were deemed to need urgent and sweeping reform. The mania for investigation was typified by a seemingly endless series of Penguin Specials, all entitled 'What's wrong with . . .?'[25] The economic climate of the sixties and the national self-doubt that characterised the post-colonial era were clear enough reasons for the national mood, but again the consequences were profound. The establishment was in every case derided as old-fashioned, fuddyduddy, out of touch. The Conservative response under Edward Heath was to leap aboard the reform bandwagon.[26] Conservatives thus fought the 1966 election with a programme as radical as any produced by a modern British political party. But the institutions were not only more criticised, but also less inherently conservative in themselves; in the universities, the professions, in industry and in the media, a process of radicalisation took place that shook the foundations of Conservatism. The satire boom, *TW3* and *Private Eye* were one example; the ferment in the universities was another. It was increasingly common for industrialists to appear as Labour sympathisers and increasingly rare for them to nail their colours to the Tory mast. Edward Heath's reprimand to 'the unacceptable face of capitalism' and Campbell Adamson's comment that a Tory victory would not solve Britain's problems in the election of February 1974 were both symptoms of the increasing estrangement between the party and British industry.

The social revolution of the 1960s is clear enough to those who have lived through it and has been brilliantly charted by Christopher Booker.[27] Its net effect in British politics has been to discredit conservatism as an attitude and the Conservative Party as a political choice. In the process, respect was reduced for all of the intermediary institutions with which conservative attitudes were linked. So the decline of the family and the advent of the permissive society may have contributed as much to the process as the satire directed against Tory politicians.

In retrospect, many of the recent developments can be seen as a revival of the liberal Centre Radicalism that destroyed Baldwin's Conservatism during the Second World War. After the war, in the period of national reconstruction and prosperity, the pace of change slackened and a new consensus emerged which the Conservatives made their own. So the stock of the party fell again with the social conservatism from which it had profited for a generation. It would be unprofitable to speculate on the future – few would have predicted in 1945 that Britain was heading for either prosperity or for a generation of social and political conservatism. There are signs at least that Conservatives are becoming increasingly aware of the scale of the problem and an intellectual debate is taking place about the party's future that has no real precedent in the post-war years. Nor should these symptoms of long-term decline be taken as suggesting that the Conservative Party will not win elections in the future as in the past. Conservatives won in 1970 despite the existence then of all the trends that this essay has outlined and could in any case do so again merely because of the greater unpopularity of the other parties.

But if Conservatism is to recover again, then much has to be done to repair the effects of the past generation on the foundations of the Party's support. The Conservative Party has no God-given right of ultimate survival, any more than had the Gladstonian Liberals—who at least believed that God was on their side—and the history of party is littered with the political corpses of politicians who awaited the swing of the pendulum that never came.

NOTES

1. The new mood is evidenced well enough by the content – and the title – of John Biffen's 1976 Conservative Political Centre Lecture, *A Nation in Doubt* (CPC, 1976).

2. Robert Blake, *Conservatism in an Age of Revolution* (1976). I have looked at this aspect of the party's history myself in Lord Butler (ed.), *The Conservatives* (1977).

3. John Vincent, *The Formation of the British Liberal Party* (Penguin ed., 1972) p. 89; Michael Kinnear, *The British Voter* (1968) p. 136.

4. C. P. Cook and J. A. Ramsden (eds), *By-Elections in British Politics* (1973) p. 250.

5. Calculated, as are the other tables of results, from the various Nuffield College Election Studies of the past twenty-five years.

6. This was of course also a major finding of David Butler and Donald Stokes in *Political Change in Britain* (Macmillan, 2nd ed., 1974).

7. See for example Christopher Booker, *The Neophiliacs* (1969).

8. Ralph Miliband's *Parliamentary Socialism* (1961) is one of many books to suggest this.

9. Stephen Haseler, *The Gaitskellites* (1969) p. 143.

10. J. D. Hoffman, *The Conservative Party in Opposition* (1964) p. 126.

11. *The Times*, 31 December 1974.

12. Jeffrey Richards, *Visions of Yesterday* (1973) p. 6 and *passim*.

13. Peter Jenkins' 'Bevan's Fight with the B.M.A.' in Sissons and French (ed.), *The Age of Austerity* (1964) pp. 240–66.

14. Nigel Harris, *Competition and the Corporate Society* (1972) pp. 149–53. This was of course the time of the 'new Elizabethans', when the buccaneering salesmen of the new Queen Elizabeth would take Europe by storm just as Drake and Hawkins had done for Queen Elizabeth I.

15. Quoted in Jean Blondel, *Voters, Parties and Leaders* (1963) p. 57.

16. Eric Nordlinger, *The Working Class Tories* (1967); Robert McKenzie and Alan Silver, *Angels in Marble* (1969).

17. Malcolm Muggeridge, *Tread Softly for you Tread on my Jokes* (Fontana ed., 1968) p. 178.

18. Paul Addison, *The Road to 1945* (1975) p. 280.

19. Robert Skidelsky's 'Lessons of Suez' in Bogdanor and Skidelsky (eds), *The Age of Affluence* (1970) pp. 168–91.

20. Robert Blake, *Conservatism in an Age of Revolution* (1976) p. 19.

21. *The Times*, 31 December 1974.

22. Ibid.

23. Taken from the 1964, 1970 and 1974 editions of the *The Times Guide to the House of Commons*. Figures for 1914 and 1939 derived from J. M. McEwen, *Conservative and Unionist MPs 1914–1939* (University of London PhD thesis, 1960), which used similar sources. The earlier figures are not in exclusive categories and so are not directly comparable to the later ones, but they give an indication of the trend. Such figures are in any case useful only for outlining general trends.

24. Robert McKenzie and Alan Silver, *Angels in Marble* (1969) p. 109.

25. Also by the number of investigating Royal Commissions appointed to consider major British institutions.

26. Robert Blake, *Conservatism in an Age of Revolution* (1976) p. 20.

27. Christopher Booker, *The Neophiliacs*.

3 Labour since 1945

Iain McLean

Every political party is a complex organism. The Labour Party, like any other, has three main interdependent elements: the parliamentary leadership, the paid-up members outside the parliamentary elites, and the mass of ordinary Labour voters. But for the last of these, neither of the others could exist; but the relationship between the three is far from straightforward. Party membership does not vary directly with electoral support (between 1945 and 1974, for instance, the Labour Party has lost, proportionately, far more members than voters) – and, still more important, the three levels of the party may differ sharply among themselves on the issues and personalities of the day. It is customary to study the Labour Party in terms of conflict *within* its elite: fights between left- and right-wing factions to control the parliamentary party or the National Executive, for instance. But it is worthwhile to extend the study to relations *between* the elements of the party. Politicians are in business to win elections (though the Labour Party has never lacked expressivists for whom a gesture – a big demonstration or a conference resolution—matters more than getting things done). So they must adapt their policies to what the voters want, or persuade voters to support their policies, or a combination of both. In this they may be helped or hindered by voluntary workers up and down the country who provide door-knocking labour and some campaign finance.

Real-world party politics are more complex than this simple model,[1] largely because the actors lack perfect information. Electors often do not know what politicians are doing; and politicians are often surprisingly ill-informed about what electors want. It is not easy for either side to obtain this information, and there are further psychological barriers. Knowledge of electors' wants is made more imperfect than it need be by the tendency to wishful thinking amongst politicians. People in politics do not always wish to admit that others supporting the same party disagree with them. So they refuse to face up to any evidence which points this way. Labour politicians' attitudes to immigration and race relations provide a good example. For many years, Labour leaders refused to accept the obvious fact that many of their own supporters were actively hostile to coloured immigration. (This is not to say that if Labour voters are racialist, Labour leaders should be racialist also; merely that they should be aware of the fact.) The two commonest problems in the relationship among the tiers of Labour support have been: *firstly*, mistaking the views of party activists for those of the electorate; and *secondly*, appealing to the electorate over the heads of party activists, without allowing for the effect on party cohesion and effectiveness of doing so.

Aneurin Bevan, resigning from the Labour front bench in 1954 because he could not endorse the American action in setting up the South-East Asia Treaty Organisation, made a fierce attack on Anthony Eden which illustrates the first of these points.

> Is the Minister aware that the statement which he made today will be deeply resented by the majority of people in Great Britain? Is he further aware that it will be universally regarded as a surrender to American pressure?[2]

This was passionately sincere nonsense. There is no evidence that the majority of people in Great Britain either knew or cared one iota about American policy in South-east Asia. Bevan had mistaken the views of the majority of his friends for those of the electorate. On many (but not all) subjects it was Bevan's great rival Hugh Gaitskell who had a much clearer view of what the electorate really thought about politics. Many MPs in marginal seats, he complained in 1947,

> are most unrealistic about the Left Wing character of the electorate . . . identifying their own keen supporters – politically conscious and class-conscious Labour men – with the mass of the people, who are very much against austerity, utterly uninterested in nationalisation of steel, heartily sick of excuses and being told to work harder, but probably more tolerant of the Government and appreciative of its difficulties than many suppose.[3]

But if Gaitskell avoided the first trap, he charged into the second with all banners flying. His attempt to remove the notorious Clause IV from the Party Constitution in 1959 arose from his conviction that its stress on nationalisation was an electoral liability. He might as well have tried to persuade Christian fundamentalists that they need not believe in God. In attacking a basic belief of so many devoted party activists, he had caused an entirely unnecessary and damaging row.

The changes in Labour policy since 1945 which it is the task of this chapter to examine emerged from a complex interaction between the three levels of Labour support, and between the Labour Party as a whole and the outside world. Before examining the substance of party conflict, we should look at the changing social base of the Labour Party at every level.

The Labour landslide of 1945 resulted from the greatest leftward shift of voting since mass party politics began. Though concealed by the wartime party truce, the shift took place between 1941 and 1944. Working-class voters came to blame the miseries of the Depression on the Conservatives. There was massive public support for the Beveridge Report and its aim of vastly extending the scope of state welfare services. The war had shown that physical planning and rationing of scarce goods could work, and work fairly. Those who remembered the brief boom and long slump after the First World War were determined not to see it happen again, and many believed that a continuation of wartime controls was the only way to prevent a repetition of the slump into mass unemployment. The Labour Party was far closer to public opinion than the Conservatives on all these points, and it won an overwhelming majority of seats in the 1945 general election. Its lead in votes was not so impressive; but 1945 nevertheless ushered in a period of two-party politics with a very strong association between class and party. Most working-class people voted Labour and most middle-class people voted Tory. The general elections of 1950 and 1951, in which the Liberal vote almost totally vanished, marked the peak of class-consciousness in British voting behaviour. In these elections, turnout rose to record levels, so that the number of Labour votes cast actually rose, although their share of seats declined, because of a faster rise in the Conservative vote.

The Conservatives won the general election of 1951, although Labour got more votes, and increased their lead in 1955 and 1959. After Labour's third successive defeat, writers began to suspect that the working-class base of Labour support was being eroded. Were voters forgetting the miseries of the 1930s and being captivated by Harold Macmillan's effective, if crude, slogan 'You've never had it so good'? An influential group of academics, to whose theories Gaitskell was an early and disastrous convert, argued that growing affluence meant the end of Labour unless it widened its class appeal to embrace the new middle classes.[4] Later research showed that the workers, though affluent, were still none the less workers. The trappings of prosperity at home did not conceal the fact that at work they were still the underdogs, subject to many influences that were liable to keep them loyal to Labour.[5] Labour need not lose, as its victories in 1964 and 1966 showed. But the prophets of gloom were right in a way. In the last ten years, working-class support for the Labour Party has become much less solidaristic and more conditional. In the early days of the party, its pioneers were missionaries preaching the word with religious fervour. In many working-class communities, especially close-knit ones like mining villages and shipyard towns, voting Labour became not so much a rational political choice as a religious act of affirmation. But the society which produced this solidarity has vanished. People no longer spend their days watching political rallies (the Durham Miners' Big Meeting is the last attenuated relic of an old tradition) and their evenings attending branch meetings. Greater affluence has led to more private life-styles. Today's voters go on family trips in their private cars and watch television at home. Traditional social ties have weakened, and that includes ties of working-class solidarity. Voters now are more likely to vote for a party they think will deliver the goods and less likely to vote for the party all their neighbours support simply because their neighbours support it. This has affected both the traditional class parties, the Conservatives as well as Labour. In the 1970 election, their joint share of the electorate's votes continued to decline slowly from the peak reached in 1950 and 1951, because there was a steady decline in turnout. This trend was reinforced in 1974. The general election of February 1974 seemed to be fought on issues of acute class polarisation. The miners' overtime ban and strike against the Conservative Government's incomes policy had led to drastic power cuts and a three-day working week, and eventually the Conservatives were forced to call an election. In circumstances which seemed to one side like justified revenge for 1926, and to the other side like an intolerable exercise of economic power against the public interest, one might have expected a resurgence of class politics in the mould of 1950–1. But it did not occur. True, a higher proportion of the Labour vote came *from* the working class than before. Middle-class Labour supporters seem to have been frightened off by the circumstances surrounding the election. But the proportion of the working class whose votes went *to* the Labour Party was the lowest since the Second World War. This is so unexpected, paradoxical even, that it has barely been recognised. But the fact is that in February 1974 only 44 per cent of manual workers voted Labour; 25 per cent of them voted Conservative, 14 per cent Liberal, 3 per cent nationalist, and 14 per cent did not vote.[6] Both main parties were damaged by the rise of third and fourth parties—the Liberals with six million votes in February 1974 and five million in October, the Scottish and Welsh nationalists, and the Ulster 'loyalists'. It is impossible to say whether the Liberals will retain their vote, but the Welsh and (especially) Scottish nationalists have done lasting damage to the major-party vote, and there is no particular reason why the Labour Party should hope to regain the ground it has lost.

These recent results draw attention to the little-known fact that the social base of the Labour Party is not as secure as the election results might indicate. Butler and Stokes have thoroughly established that demographic change has at least as great an impact on electoral fortunes as voters' changes of party.[7] Since at least 1959, the Labour Party has benefited from the dying-off of a predominantly Conservative generation of electors and the coming-of-age of a predominantly Labour generation. Voters who came of age before the Labour Party became a national challenger for power in 1922 are much less likely than younger men and women to have become Labour voters. As that generation dies off, the Labour Party gains relative to the Conservatives. But its gains from this source must be diminishing with the number of electors whose political socialisation antedates 1922. Furthermore, although Labour retains a comfortable lead *over the Conservatives* among the youngest political generations in the electorate, young voters are much more likely to support the Liberals or Nationalists than their elders. Therefore Labour's gains from demographic change seem likely to slow down. But it can also be shown that during the 1960s Labour was losing ground among constant members of the electorate.[8] The slight net improvement in Labour fortunes between 1959 and 1970 occurred because the demographic changes in Labour's favour just outweighed the net switching of votes, which benefited the Conservatives.

In terms of the simple Downsian model suggested at the beginning of this chapter, the Labour leadership would respond to the steady seepage of their support by either changing their policies to fit public opinion or trying to change public opinion to fit their policies. But their record in doing either is very patchy. Few politicians know (and some do not seem to want to know) the real trends in electoral behaviour, which makes it hard for them to act in a Downsian 'rational' way.

The Labour leadership is often more in touch with the second level of political activity – the rank-and-file membership of the party. Here the decline has been sharper than among the electorate, although it is not necessarily evident in published membership statistics. According to the NEC's Annual Reports, membership of the Labour Party rose from 3,038,697 in 1945 to a peak of 6,582,549 in 1957, whence it declined to 6,073,196 in 1973. But as is well known, most of these members are affiliated to the party by virtue of paying a political contribution to their trade union. In 1946, when this payment was changed from 'contracting in' to 'contracting out', affiliated membership rose in one year from 2.6 million to 4.4 million. This strongly suggests that many trade unionists are Labour Party members from inertia rather than conviction. And the membership numbers on which unions affiliate have been known to be manipulated for political reasons; for instance, in 1955 the TGWU and the NUGMW between them increased their affiliation by over 400,000 simply in order to increase the right-wing voting strength at Annual Conference.

Thus the only true measure of Labour Party membership is the roll-call of individual members of the party. According to official statistics, these numbered 487,047 in 1945, rose to a peak of 1,014,524 in 1952, and declined again slowly to 665,379 in 1973. But even these figures are exaggerated. No individual constituency may affiliate on the basis of fewer than 1000 members – and the vast majority affiliate on precisely that number. The actual membership of these parties is certainly far smaller. Informed guesses at the real individual membership of the Labour Party put it at around 150,000 to 200,000.

Why has the individual membership of the party declined? The Bevanites and their successors on the left have never been in any doubt: because the party had watered down its socialist commitments and disappointed the hopes of the rank and file.[9] In a sense they are right, although they have usually failed to accept the corollary that if the leadership *did* pay more attention to the rank and file, 'we could say goodbye to any Labour Government being elected again in Britain'.[10] This is because of the gap between the views of the electorate and those of party activists. People become individual members of the Labour Party because they are passionately concerned about something – most commonly because they are concerned about social injustice and convinced that only socialism can remedy it. But not all aspects of 'socialism' are equally popular with the electorate. Survey evidence shows that voters are proud of some aspects of the welfare state, such as the NHS or the payment of old age pensions, and would like to see more public spending in these areas. But they are deeply suspicious of other items on the socialist programme. Nationalisation of industry is a good example. A large majority of the electorate, and a majority even of Labour voters, are hostile to proposals to extend public ownership. If the Labour Party chooses a policy to suit its activists, it may well offend the electorate, and vice versa.

There seems to be no way of escaping this dilemma on issues where opinion ranges along any sort of spectrum. If two parties are competing for the support of 100 voters ranged along an ideological spectrum, the first party to declare itself ought to take its stance at the position occupied by voter number 50. It is then assured of at least half the votes; the best the other party can do is to come as close as possible to the same position, say to voter number 51. This would ensure a dead heat. But if a party adopted the ideology of (say) voter number 33, the other party need only take that of voter number 34 in order to win two-thirds of the votes cast. It follows that it will always be in the interest of political parties to converge in the centre of the ideological spectrum. If the views of the party militants are expressed by voter 20 and voter 80, they are bound to be brushed aside in the rush to occupy the middle ground.

Of course, this model is grossly oversimplified,[11] and vulnerable to two main criticisms: that electors' ideologies are not in fact ranked on a left-right scale, and that parties which converge on the middle ground risk losing their militant supporters either to new extremist parties or to abstention. Both objections have value. But the Labour Party has clearly not lost any electorally significant support in the drift towards the centre. The votes won by far-left candidates in British elections are both derisory and diminishing (the Communist Party, for instance, got 0.3 per cent of the votes in 1950, 0.2 per cent in 1966, and 0.1 per cent in 1974). And, although abstention has increased, very little of it is what might be called 'principled abstention' – abstention on the grounds that the Labour Party is insufficiently socialist (or the Tory Party insufficiently conservative). That the concept of the middle ground is real enough can be seen by looking at the fate of candidates who abandon it, the most spectacular instances being the American presidential candidates Barry Goldwater (Republican,

1964) and George McGovern (Democrat, 1972). Both took stances which satisfied their party militants; both were crushed in the ensuing election. It is hard to see how the Labour Party can avoid the problem. If it wants to win elections, it must disappoint party militants; but if it disappoints them again and again, it can hardly expect them to keep on paying their subscriptions, let alone pound the streets door-knocking and leafletting on the party's behalf. Hence the steady decline in individual membership.

The social base of the third level—the parliamentary elite—has also been changing. In its early days, the Parliamentary Labour Party consisted largely (though never exclusively) of manual workers. But the proportion of middle-class Labour MPs has been rising as fewer and fewer of each successive intake of new MPs come from working-class jobs. The crude statistics can be misleading, however. What matters politically is not the occupation an MP had before entering Parliament, but the class he identifies himself with. An MP may be the son of a miner who went to a grammar school and Oxford. But this in itself tells us nothing about his political views, or about whether he perceives himself as working-class. Are we talking about the Rt Hon. Roy Jenkins (son of a miners' agent, educated at Abersychan County School and Balliol College, Oxford) or about Mr Dennis Skinner (former miner, educated at Tupton Hall Grammar School and Ruskin College, Oxford)? This problem cannot be entirely avoided; but careful research[12] has shown that there are systematic differences between the ideologies of different groups of backbenchers (workers, university-educated professionals, and miscellaneous in-betweens, for instance). The two central issues within the Labour elite since 1945 have always been foreign affairs and economic policy. Left- and right-wing positions on these two sets of issues are not always closely correlated; an MP may be, say, left-wing on economic policy and totally indifferent to foreign policy issues. Broadly speaking, from 1945 to 1961 foreign policy and defence issues dominated internal debate among Labour MPs; here the Left found its strongest support among middle-class, non-union-sponsored MPs. Since 1961, economic policy has come to eclipse foreign policy as a source of internal dissension. Increasingly, the Left has been identified with a new set of issues. It is more insular, more interested in economic issues – and more working-class. In the 1950s, a coterie of right-wing trade union bosses told the middle-class dissenters on foreign policy to shut their gobs.[13] In the late 1960s the union chiefs themselves attacked the party leadership from a left-wing stance. They were far more interested in government economic than foreign and defence policy, and from 1964 onwards one central issue emerged slowly to eclipse all others, namely the validity of enforced restraint of incomes as a weapon against inflation. These issues were the successive epicentres of conflict in the PLP, the NEC, and Annual Conference.

It is not always easy to decide what constitutes a left-wing attitude to foreign policy. Since at least the time of Gladstone, the British Left has been dogged by an internal contradiction in its foreign policy views. Should the dissenters stress their opposition to militarism, armaments expenditure, conscription, and entanglement in other people's wars? Or should they press for Britain to end injustice and oppression in foreign regimes of which they deeply disapproved? The logical difficulty of holding both of these views at once seems rarely to have been a constraint. A classic example was the attitude of many members of the Labour Party in the 1930s to the rise of Hitler and Mussolini. For several years, the leadership opposed both Fascism and any steps the British Government might take to stop it. The brutal, but necessary, destruction of George Lansbury by Ernest Bevin at the 1935 Annual Conference ('It is placing the Executive and the Movement in an absolutely wrong position to be hawking your conscience round from body to body to be told what you ought to do with it')[14] was a first step towards consistency. Bevin did not get any gentler as he got older. As Labour's Foreign Secretary from 1945 to 1951, therefore, his views were a standing provocation to the generous but not always logical minds on the left of the Labour Party.

The conflict between hostility to repression and hostility to the means to prevent it was not always manifest. A more prominent issue in the early post-war years was the attitude Britain should take to the Soviet Union. Many on the left were uncritical admirers of the USSR in 1945; any pre-war doubts about Stalin had been submerged by admiration for the Red Army, which had done more to defeat Hitler after 1941 than Britain could possibly have done. But Bevin was no friend of the Soviet Union. Successive Soviet acts of repression, such as the overthrow of the Czech social-democratic regime or the Berlin blockade, both in 1948, brought most of the PLP into line behind Bevin, but a small left-wing group remained to oppose Britain's agreement to the NATO pact in 1949, or her support for the UN forces in the Korean War in 1950. But the only possible leader of the Left was Nye Bevan, who was no Soviet apologist or even an anti-NATO neutralist. As long as he was in the Cabinet, left-wing protest on foreign policy was limited to sporadic sniping by a pro-Soviet or neutralist minority. His resignation from the Cabinet over NHS charges in April 1951 heralded the only period since 1945 when the foreign-policy Left was effectively and cohesively led. It was to last for just over six years.

Up to Bevan's resignation, the issue between himself and his colleagues was the fairly narrow one of Health Service charges. But he soon raised his sights to a broad-based attack on Gaitskell's budget of 1951. This contained a £4700 million armament programme occasioned by the Korean War. Paranoid fear of the Soviet Union was at its height, but Bevan did not share that fear. His opposition to the armament programme was based on two main arguments. First, we could not afford it. It was not just a matter of the £4700 million; it was also that other nations' (especially the USA's) stockpiling of arms was taking too much of scarce world resources like steel; the result would be scarcity-fuelled inflation. Second, Bevan never shared the popular fear of Soviet might, even during Stalin's lifetime. The USSR, he wrote in 1953, 'in coming so far into the West—particularly into Czechoslovakia – . . . overran her sociological frontiers. She could occupy but she had not been able to digest.'[15]

On the first point Bevan was certainly right. On the second, though 1948 and 1968 have shown that the USSR remains determined to 'digest' Czechoslovakia, he was far ahead of his time in recognising that it would make no serious moves to digest any of the rest of Europe. Bevan was no simple-minded pro-Soviet apologist, and his leadership gave the Left a great boost.

This was demonstrated at the notorious Morecambe party conference of 1952, when the Bevanites suddenly discovered that they could win almost all of the seats on the NEC that were controlled by constituency parties rather than trade unions (12 out of 28). The right-wing union bosses of the day, led by Arthur Deakin of the TGWU, were appalled at the Bevanites' presumption, and three years of bitter internecine strife ensued as Attlee doodled. In 1954 there was an acrimonious row over German rearmament, in which the Bevanites were joined in opposition by some politicians of the right, such as Hugh Dalton with the simple atavistic slogan 'No guns for the Huns'. In March 1955, Bevan had the Labour whip temporarily withdrawn, and the NEC was widely expected to expel him from the party, though in the end he was saved by one vote. But Deakin died suddenly in May, and no other union leader shared his single-minded determination to crush Bevan. Matters improved again when Attlee at last resigned in December 1955. Gaitskell won the leadership with 157 votes; Bevan got 70 and Herbert Morrison 40. Though Gaitskell and Bevan were never close friends, they were not such bitter enemies as they were often depicted. Gaitskell recognised Bevan's talents, and in 1956 appointed him shadow foreign affairs spokesman. The Suez affair, which united the whole PLP in hostility to Eden's expedition, also helped to mend fences.

But one allied issue still threatened to tear the party apart – the hydrogen bomb and the problem of nuclear disarmament. Britain's first H-bomb tests were announced early in 1957, after both the Americans and the Russians had started their testing programmes. Before long, a strong movement had arisen on the left calling for unilateral nuclear disarmament by Britain and withdrawal from nuclear-based alliances, including NATO. The unilateralist argument tapped deeply-felt pacifist sympathies in the Labour Party, especially among individual party activists. The old conflict between a desire to do good in the world and a passionate hatred of armaments re-emerged. The issue was bound to come to a head at the Party Conference held in Brighton that year, at which the unilateralists looked hopefully, but a little uncertainly, for a lead from Bevan.

Nye Bevan's speech at the Brighton conference was the greatest turning-point in the post-war history of the Labour Party. He not only deserted the unilateralists; he turned on them with burst after annihilating burst of oratory.

> If you carry this resolution, . . . you will send a British Foreign Secretary, whoever he may be, naked into the conference chamber. Able to preach sermons, of course: he could make good sermons. But action of that sort is not necessarily the way in which you take the menace of this bomb from the world . . . [A cry of 'Do it now']. 'Do it now', you say. This is the answer I give from the platform. Do it now as a Labour Party Conference? You cannot do it now. It is not in your hands to do it. All you can do is pass a resolution. What you are saying is . . . that the British Labour movement decides unilaterally that this country contracts out of all its commitments and obligations entered into with other countries and members of the Commonwealth – without consultation at all. And you call that statesmanship? I call it an emotional spasm.[16]

The rebel Left had lost its leader. It has never since regained one. Like Bevin's brutality in 1935, Bevan's in 1957 did the party much more good than harm. Brighton ended factionalism for three years. Bevan did not even oppose Gaitskell's abortive attempt to get rid of Clause IV in 1959. This harmony was shattered by Bevan's untimely death in July 1960, and Gaitskell was left to face the most notorious party conference in post-war history without him. After their overwhelming defeat in 1957, the unilateralists regrouped in order to capture a number of major trade unions. The TGWU's weight had already shifted markedly to the left, not because its members had become more radical, but because Deakin's death was quickly followed by that of his heir-apparent, Jock Tiffin. Tiffin was succeeded by Frank Cousins, a left-winger both on defence and on economic affairs. The second biggest union, the Amalgamated Engineering Union, was still under right-wing control (and was to remain so until 1967). But its highly democratic constitution allows the leadership to be overruled on conference votes, and the AEU also took the unilateralist side.

With the two biggest unions and many smaller ones behind them, the unilateralists came to Scarborough in 1960 determined to force the hand of the Parliamentary leadership, who were backed by the majority of the PLP. Gaitskell knew he was bound to lose the vote, because the votes of a number of unions commanding more than half the conference's votes between them were mandated in favour of unilateralism. His speech ended with a bitter, even contemptuous peroration, delivered amid a chorus of hostile interruptions.

> The vast majority of Labour Members of Parliament are utterly opposed to unilateralism and neutralism. So what do you expect them to

do? Change their minds overnight? To go back on the pledges they gave
to the people who elected them from their constituencies? And
supposing they did do that. Supposing all of us, like well-behaved sheep,
were to follow the policies of unilateralism and neutralism, what kind of
an impression would that make upon the British people? . . .

There are some of us, Mr Chairman, who will fight and fight and fight
again to save the Party we love. We will fight and fight and fight again to
bring back sanity and honesty and dignity, so that our Party with its
great past may retain its glory and its greatness.[17]

Gaitskell carried out his promise. He spent most of the ensuing year
persuading Conference delegates to change their minds. An anti-
unilateralist pressure group called the Campaign for Democratic Socialism achieved more by intrigue than Gaitskell did by confrontation, but
the result was what both wanted: the verdict of Scarborough was reversed
a year later at Blackpool.[18]

The foreign policy battles of the years 1957 to 1961 were decisive. There
was only one later fight that mattered: over British membership of the
EEC, which was not inherently a left-right issue. On the central dispute
which had divided the Labour Party ever since the Russian Revolution,
the leadership was never again seriously challenged. Gaitskell did not live
to enjoy the supremacy he had established in the party by 1962, because he
died in January 1963. However, both of his successors have continued his
policies, though neither has had Gaitskell's relish for seeking open
confrontations with fundamentalists. Harold Wilson faced sustained left-
wing opposition over Britain's role in the Vietnam war. But the opposition
was as ineffective as it was noisy. The left's only possible leader was Frank
Cousins. But from 1964 to 1966 he was shackled by being in government.
When he did resign in July 1966, it had much less impact than Bevan's
resignation in 1951; Cousins was no parliamentarian, and in any case was
more worried about government economic than foreign policy. When the
leadership was defeated on Vietnam at the 1967 Party Conference, Wilson
brushed it aside. The incident merits two lines in his 1000-page memoir of
his premiership.[19] Wilson's judgement was sound. Ultimately, Vietnam
mattered not in the slightest to Britain. We were not fighting there; we had
no interests to defend there; and the general public (as opposed to
constituency activitists) could not have cared less. Here lies another reason
for the decline of foreign affairs as a divisive issue in the Labour Party. It no
longer matters very much what Britain does or says, and this has become
increasingly clear even to Labour Party members. Even in Bevin's day,
Britain had not the resources to be a world power, but it did have the
prestige. But the prestige faded – quite a lot disappeared at the time of
Suez—and eventually, though not until the Defence Review of 1966, the
British Government stopped pretending even to itself that it could have the
resources. What the Labour Party thought of the American actions in

Vietnam was therefore of very little interest to the rest of the world.

Britain's attitude to the European Common Market was a different matter. When the Macmillan Government first proposed entry in 1961, Gaitskell led most Labour MPs to a stance of malevolent neutrality: joining the Common Market would entail weakening Britain's links with the Commonwealth, and flying in the face of 'a thousand years of history', in Gaitskell's phrase. In 1967, however, the Wilson Government decided to make a second application to enter, and managed to carry with it a majority both in the PLP and at Conference. In opposition once again, the party had to decide how to respond to the third try, made by the Health government in 1970–2. In an attempt to reconcile the deep division between the pros and the antis, a package of measures for a future Labour Government was proposed: renegotiation of the terms of entry; a special Party conference to decide if it approved of the renegotiated terms; and a national referendum. There was much that was constitutionally unclear about this (whose word was to count for most—the electorate's, or Conference's, or MPs'?), but as a device for preserving party unity it was remarkably successful. Labour took office in March 1974, and the renegotiation was concluded just over a year later. The Government naturally endorsed the renegotiated terms it had secured, but the special conference, backed by a substantial minority of Labour MPs, rejected them. This might have caused trouble had not the referendum result been a two-to-one 'Yes'.

The Common Market saga illustrates the difficulty of satisfying the three levels of Labour support. Most active party members were anti-Market—partly because the Common Market was identified as another device to keep capitalism alive. With the Left almost wholly anti-Market and the Right divided, the party majority as a whole was thus firmly anti. But mass opinion was highly unstable. The EEC was not a salient issue for ordinary voters, and their views on it as expressed to opinion pollsters were unstable over time. Even if two successive polls showed, say, 40 per cent of the electorate in favour of the EEC, this figure was merely the sum of self-cancelling movements of individual voters in both directions. On a remote issue like the Common Market, people tend to take their cue from the political leaders with whom they identify. Hence Labour voters tended to be anti-Market in 1962, pro in 1967, anti in 1972, and pro again in 1975. Voters were much more likely to take a lead from Harold Wilson than from the Labour Party Annual Conference, however. Thus an issue which had looked as if it might split the party from top to bottom has left it virtually unscathed. Not for the first time, there was an alliance of two elements of the Labour coalition (elite and electorate) against the third (party activists). But no lasting damage was done to the coalition. Unlike Gaitskell over Clause IV and unilateralism, Wilson did not challenge the hostile verdict of Conference; he simply ignored it. On a key issue like *In Place of Strife*, to be discussed later, this could be damaging. But on the EEC no harm was done, because opposition to it could not be effectively sustained once Britain was in. Left-wing opponents of incomes policies have continuing sanctions against the government that introduces them—they can support strikes for wages higher than the policy allows, for instance. But anti-Marketeers can do little more once Britain is in than Jacobites after 1745. They may refuse to recognise the new regime, but this does not have much impact on the outputs of government. A far more serious, and growing, threat to the cohesion of the Labour Party has been the handling of economic policy by Labour governments, and since 1964 the central question has been incomes policy.

All parties of the left – perhaps all parties of any sort—face a conflict arising out of 'the lack of a budget constraint among voters', as Samuel Brittan has put it.[20] Ordinary voters may welcome higher pensions but resent the taxation needed to pay for them. On a more sophisticated level, party activists may condemn a Labour Government for failing to carry out its election promises, while claiming that a more uncompromisingly socialist approach would by-pass what the politicans claim to be harsh economic realities. Only the politicians themselves are forced to observe budget constraints. Indeed each post-war Labour Government has had to operate in severe economic circumstances usually dominated by balance-of-payments or foreign exchange crises. The Attlee Government, for instance, had to face huge American debts between the end of Lend-Lease in 1945 and the beginning of Marshall Aid in 1948, and home consumption had to be fiercely restrained in order to increase exports. These were needed to finance imports previously paid for by invisible exports and overseas investment income which had been swept away by the Second World War. On such highly technical matters the failure of Labour Governments to satisfy their supporters often turned. This was a much more serious problem after 1964 than between 1945 and 1951 because expectations were so much higher in more recent years. The gap between voters' expectations and politicians' ability to live up to them became extremely wide in the mid 1960s, and indeed the Wilson government touched depths of unpopularity in the opinion polls and by-elections of 1968 and 1969 never reached by any other modern government. Some pessimistic commentators such as Brittan claim that the gap between expectations and the capacity to deliver the goods must grow so wide that it is dubious whether liberal democracy can survive. Voters, it is argued, have political expectations unrestrained by budget constraints. They look for full employment, steady prices and a stable currency without allowing for the near-impossibility of achieving all of these at the same time. Meanwhile, because politicians are in a Downsian competition for votes, they must emulate each other in their claims that they can achieve the impossible. Hence growing disillusion and, ultimately, the collapse of the system.

There is some evidence that the system is more resilient than this suggests. The Labour administration of 1974 has faced economic problems at least as severe as those of 1964, and it would be a brave man who claimed that it had conquered them. But voters may have toned down their excessive expectations. The 1974 administration has not slumped nearly as badly as its predecessor in by-elections, opinion polls, or local elections. Possibly voters are coming to have a better appreciation of what politicians can and cannot do in the real world.

The harshest test is bound to be incomes policy. A policy of holding back incomes in order to restrain inflation presents peculiar difficulties to a party of the left. For one thing, it will be criticised by its own left wing on the grounds that holding down the workers' wages merely swells the capitalists' profits. But Labour leaders can ignore their left-wing critics; they cannot ignore trade union opinion. Before looking at successive crises in the Labour Party over incomes policy, we ought to try to understand this particularly acute dilemma.

If I am a trade union leader, I am paid by my members to get them the best wages and conditions obtainable. Does this mean I should organise strikes in pursuit of the highest possible wage rises? Not necessarily; because if everybody else does the same, the only result is runaway inflation. Should I then restrain my members' wage claim in the public interest? Again, not necessarily; unless I can be certain that everyone else is doing the same, I shall be in the worst of all possible worlds. My members will be left behind in the wages race, and I shall have failed in the job I am paid to do. 300 years ago, Thomas Hobbes put the point concisely:

> For he that should be modest, and tractable . . . in such time, and place, where no man els should do so, should but make himselfe a prey to others, and procure his own certain ruine.[21]

The incomes policy problem is a classic case of one of the most puzzling conundrums in social science, the 'prisoners' dilemma'.[22] Let us imagine a world consisting of two union leaders deciding whether or not to make an inflationary wage claim.

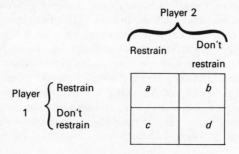

There are four possible outcomes: *a*, where both players restrain their wage claims; *d*, where neither does; and *b* and *c*, where one does but not the other. Everybody prefers *a* to *d*. That is, everyone agrees that universal restraint is better than a universal free-for-all. But—and here is the catch—for each player the best possible outcome is that in which he does what he likes while his opponent exercises restraint; and the worst possible is where he, like Hobbes's 'modest and tractable' man, exercises restraint when nobody else does so. Player 1, therefore, prefers *c* to *a* to *d* to *b*. Player 2 prefers *b* to *a* to *d* to *c*.

Suppose now that a Labour Prime Minister comes along to ask each union leader for his co-operation in a voluntary policy of pay restraint, like Sir Stafford Cripps's pay freeze of 1948, George Brown's incomes policy of 1964, or Harold Wilson's 'Social Contract' of 1974. If I am Player 1, I have to consider what Player 2 will do. If he holds back, I will get the payoff in *c* by not restraining and in *a* by restraining – *c* is better for me than *a*. Therefore I should not restrain. If Player 2 goes for a free-for-all, I will get *d* by not restraining and *b* by restraining. As I prefer *d* to *b*, it again follows that I should not hold back. Thus, *whatever I expect the other player to do*, it can never be in my interest to agree to pay restraint. But the reasoning is symmetrical for Player 2. Hence both players seem inevitably to home in on outcome *d*, *even though they both know* that outcome *a* is better for each of them. This seems to show that a voluntary incomes policy is a will-o'-the-wisp, and that only one backed by coercion could work. Only if I know that other people's breaches of the policy will be punished could it be in my members' interest for me to offer to hold back.

The first effort at an incomes policy was in some ways the most successful. In February 1948, the Chancellor of the Exchequer, Sir Stafford Cripps, proposed a wages and prices freeze as an anti-inflationary measure. This was accepted by Vincent Tewson, the General Secretary of the TUC, and also by the leaders of the biggest unions. This was important, because it is a peculiarity of modern producer-group politics that it is conducted by bargainers who cannot necessarily deliver their bargains. The TUC makes bids and receives offers, but it has no binding powers over its member unions, and union general secretaries have diminishing control over what goes on the shop floor. It is therefore necessary (though not sufficient) for the success of an incomes policy that it should be supported by most of the leaders of individual large unions. The Cripps wage freeze was agreed at a special congress of the TUC by five million votes to two million; it lasted until it was swamped by the Korea-induced inflation of 1950–51.

Two unique factors helped the Cripps freeze to succeed. One was the self-evident honesty and austerity of its creator; the other was the gratitude of union leaders to the Attlee government for not only maintaining full employment after the war, but also laying the foundations of the welfare state.

The Conservative government elected in 1951 at first made no attempts to introduce an incomes policy. When it did, in 1956 and 1961, its attempts were ham-handed, and no serious effort to gain the TUC's co-operation was made. But as Labour was in opposition, no rift was opened between the parliamentary leadership and the trade unions. Although Gaitskell, characteristically, said, 'We should never stifle the still small voice that whispers to us, "Yes, but what would you do if you were the Government now?" ',[23] he never provoked a confrontation on this issue.

In 1964, Wilson split economic management between the Treasury and the new Department of Economic Affairs, and George Brown at the head of the DEA made incomes policy one of the cornerstones of his policy for economic growth. This had the moody assent of George Woodcock, the TUC general secretary, but he was much less closely aligned with individual union leaders than Tewson had been. Perhaps the most important change was the succession of the left-wing Hugh Scanlon in place of the old right-wing hierarchy of the AEU in 1967. Scanlon and Jack Jones (Cousins' successor at the TGWU) became the chief opponents of the Government's incomes policy, which became a total freeze in the crisis measures of July 1966, to be followed by what was officially called a 'period of severe restraint'. The incomes policy worked with steadily declining success through 1967, 1968, and 1969, but its fate was sealed by the sorry drama of *In place of Strife*.

Harold Wilson and Barbara Castle, who was Employment Secretary, became convinced that the Government must reform the structure and operation of trade unions. They were worried about strikes allegedly called by militant and manipulative shop stewards against the wishes of those they represented, and by the widespread layoffs caused by strikes in interrelated plants—a notorious problem in the motor industry. They were convinced that their proposals were more socialist than an un-regulated free-for-all of inter-union relationships; the title of their White Paper, *In Place of Strife*, echoed (surely deliberately) Nye Bevan's personal testament, *In Place of Fear*. They knew that public opinion, even among Labour voters, massively favoured 'something being done about the unions'; their proposals had the initial approval of George Woodcock.

For all that, they were repeating Gaitskell's blunder of 1959. It is one thing to have the electorate on your side; it is quite another to assume thereby that you can count on those on whose votes you depend in Parliament. For union leaders to accept incomes policy, they had to swallow extensive interference with their essential functions; it was asking far too much to expect them to swallow compulsory union reform on top of incomes policy. Many backbench Labour MPs, including union-sponsored members who had been the loyalist backbone of the party in the Bevanite era, were deeply unhappy. They found a leader in James Callaghan, who, although a member of the Cabinet, voted in the NEC against accepting legislation based on *In Place of Strife*. As Party Treasurer, Callaghan knew how totally the Labour Party depended on the financial aid of the trade unions, and he saw no reason for gratuitously offending them. Wilson continued to take a tough line with the union leaders. One exchange allegedly ran thus:

Scanlon: Prime Minister, we don't want you to become another Ramsay MacDonald.

Wilson: I have no intention of becoming another Ramsay MacDonald. Nor do I intend to be another Dubcek. Get your tanks off my lawn, Hughie![24]

But when Wilson's chief whip told him he could not provide the votes to pass *In Place of Strife* into law, Wilson and Mrs Castle had to capitulate. On 18 June 1969, they announced a face-saving formula in which the TUC General Council gave a 'solemn and binding undertaking' that member unions would observe the TUC's own guidelines on regulating unofficial strikes. Solemn it may have been, but binding of course it could never be, as the TUC General Council has no powers to bind anybody.

When Labour went into opposition in 1970, the predominant mood was 'never again'. This applied not only to industrial relations reform, but also to incomes policy, which had become tarred with the same brush of interference in the private affairs of trade unions. This mood was strengthened by the activities of the Heath Government. Their own version of *In Place of Strife* was the Industrial Relations Act of 1971. This encountered no problems in parliament, but insuperable ones in implementation. A compulsory strike ballot turned out to be the best possible way to encourage wavering trade unionists to fall in behind their union's strike call; and the saga of the five dockers briefly jailed for continuing an unofficial strike in defiance of the procedure laid down by the Act vividly demonstrated why every government desperately tries to describe its compulsory incomes policy as voluntary. The Heath Government was brought down by the miners' overtime ban and strike in early 1974 after the miners refused a pay offer of the maximum they were allowed under 'Phase III' of the then incomes policy.

The miners' strike, illustrating the vast power of a group of workers in a vital economic position, caused some unease on the Labour right. Was there anything socialist in the miners' use of their economic strength to climb to the top of the pay ladder at the expense of other groups such as postal workers, who merely lacked the ability to shut down hospitals? Nobody remembered that in 1949 Gaitskell, then Minister of Fuel and Power, had sent in troops to run the power stations during a strike. 'The Government', he said, 'ought really to face up to the issue of Power Station strikes, and decide whether they can afford to treat them as ordinary industrial disputes. In my view they cannot.'[25] However, the period since 1974 has seen a greater acceptance at every level in the Labour Party that naked industrial power may have to be curbed in the public interest than would have been believed possible in the light of events between 1969 and 1974.

In March 1974 Wilson and Len Murray, the new General Secretary of the TUC, pinned their hopes on a voluntary Social Contract to restrain inflationary wage increases. It did not work. In a prisoners' dilemma, it can never be in my interest to restrain my wage claim unless I am absolutely certain that everybody else will do likewise. Without that certainty, the outcome of the Social Contract was a level of wage settlements far above the level of price increases as each group strove for the self-defeating objective of keeping ahead in real terms as well as in money terms. With startling suddenness, the Wilson government then turned back in mid-1975 to the measures they had sworn they would never reintroduce. A £6 a week pay limit was introduced, backed by rather obscurely described (and never implemented) sanctions. Jack Jones and, more reluctantly, Hugh Scanlon joined Murray in ensuring trades unions' acceptance of the new incomes policy which has been remarkably comprehensive up to mid-1976. Despite the circumstances of its introduction, the current pay policy has had more union acceptance than the 1964 policy and as much as the pioneering efforts of 1948–50. Why? Partly because people were shocked by the 30 per cent annual inflation of 1974 and 1975 into supporting it more wholeheartedly than before; partly because communications between the Government and the unions are better than in 1969.

The future remains uncertain. Labour has some assets: for instance, its demographic advantage over the Conservatives, and the perception that only a Labour Government can deliver an enforceable pay policy. But it also has problems. The complex of issues related to Scottish nationalism and devolution, on which there has been no room for comment here, is not the only threat to the Labour coalition. The parliamentary and union leadership are closer than at any time since the death of Arthur Deakin, but individual party members have fallen further out of line. Most constituency parties are dominated by the left, sometimes the far left; defeats at Conference for the party leadership are now too common to attract much notice; as the NEC becomes more left-wing, Wilson and Callaghan have paid less attention to it. This has two noteworthy consequences. First, it cannot halt the long-standing decline in individual party membership; it is more likely to accelerate it as members find themselves conspicuously ignored. So they are more likely to use the one power they undoubtedly retain: selection of candidates for general and local elections. The new Labour MPs of 1970 and 1974 are clearly more left-wing than their predecessors. But it is too early to say whether their views will be tempered by contact with harsh economic reality (or corrupted by the influence of the Westminster club, depending on one's point of view).

Finally, has the Labour Party arrested its steady decline in elections?

Again, the evidence is mixed. Party managers ought to be studying events in Scotland with alarm, and busily calculating how much Labour would lose from any electoral reform; but the steadiness in the Labour vote in polls since October 1974, coupled to a decline in the Liberal vote, must encourage them. There is no shortage of willing authors of the Labour Party's obituary; but, on balance, their efforts may be premature.

NOTES

1. Whose debt to A. Downs, *An Economic Theory of Democracy* (New York: Harper & Row, 1957) should be obvious.

2. Quoted in L. Hunter, *The Road to Brighton Pier* (London: Arthur Barker, 1959) p. 72.

3. Gaitskell's diary for 12 August 1947, quoted in P. M. Williams, *Gaitskell* (forthcoming). I am most grateful to Mr Williams for allowing me to see and quote from this work.

4. See especially M. Abrams and R. Rose, *Must Labour Lose?* (Harmondsworth: Penguin, 1960).

5. J. H. Goldthorpe, D. Lockwood *et al.*, *The Affluent Worker: Political Attitudes and Behaviour* (Cambridge: Cambridge University Press, 1968).

6. Statistics from I. Crewe, B. Sarlvik, and J. Alt, 'The Election of February 1974' mimeographed, Essex University, 1974.

7. D. E. Butler and D. Stokes, *Political Change in Britain*, 2nd ed. (London: Macmillan, 1974) esp. chs 10 to 12.

8. See Butler and Stokes, op. cit., 2nd ed., Table 12.11, p. 267.

9. For the most sophisticated recent version of the argument see B. Hindess, *The Decline of Working-class Politics* (London: McGibbon & Kee, 1971).

10. The words are Bevan's—written after his assault on the unilateralists in 1957. M. Foot, *Aneurin Bevan 1945 – 1960* (London: Davis – Poynter, 1973) p. 579. Bevan was never a Bevanite; he knew, unlike his followers, that politicians must win elections as well as conference decisions.

11. Grossly oversimplified even in comparison with Downs, op. cit., ch. 8.

12. H. B. Berrington, *Backbench Opinion in the House of Commons 1945–55* (Oxford: Pergamon, 1973) and S. E. Finer, H. B. Berrington and D. Bartholomew, *Backbench Opinion in the House of Commons 1955–59* (Oxford: Pergamon, 1961).

13. 'Shut yor gob' was the reported retort of Sir Will Lawther of the NUM to a heckler at the Annual Conference of 1952.

14. A. Bullock, *The Life and Times of Ernest Bevin*, vol. 1 (London: Heinemann, 1960) p. 568. The official report has '*taking* your conscience', but eyewitnesses say that Bevin actually said 'hawking'.

15. Foot, op. cit., p. 404.

16. Labour Party, *Annual Conference Report, 1957*, p. 181.

17. Labour Party, *Annual Conference Report 1960* p. 201.

18. For details, see P. M. Williams and K. Hindell 'Scarborough and Blackpool', *Political Quarterly*, 1962.

19. H. Wilson, *The Labour Government 1964–70*, Penguin ed 1974, p. 557.

20. S. Brittan, 'The Economic Contradictions of Democracy', *British Journal of Political Science*, V 2 (1975) p. 139.

21. T. Hobbes, *Leviathan* (1651), ch. xv (Penguin ed., ed. C. B. Macpherson, p. 215).

22. For more details, including an explanation of the title of the game, see any textbook on games theory, e.g. R. D. Luce and H. Raiffa, *Games and Decisions*, (New York: Wiley, 1957).

23. Williams, *Gaitskell*, ch. 7.

24. P. Jenkins, *The Battle of Downing Street* (London: Charles Knight, 1970) p. 140.

Wilson's own account of the meeting blandly notes, 'It was friendly throughout, but tough' (Wilson, op. cit., Penguin ed., p. 822).

25. Gaitskell's diary, 7 January 1950, quoted in Williams, op. cit., ch. 4.

4 Economic Debates

Peter Sinclair

What constitutes a trend in economics may sometimes be hard to identify. The movement of some economic variable is examined between two dates; but unless the dates are rather far apart, history often shows that such apparent movements merely reflect temporary rises or falls, followed by movement at an altered pace – or even by movement in the opposite direction. Prediction, the chief exercise for which identifying trends is a necessary preliminary, is peculiarly hazardous in economics. Since the actors on the stage are human, their scales of preferences are fickle, and perceptions of their environment incomplete. How, and when, they respond to events can rarely be foreseen accurately. In economics, everything is, at least in principle, capable of influencing everything else; and the past can be a treacherous guide to the future. But some changes in the contemporary British economy are readily discerned. It is to the analysis of the policy issues some of these changes provoke that this chapter is devoted.

We begin by investigating these changes, over the past 20 or 25 years. In the macroeconomic field, perhaps the most conspicuous change has been the sharp rise in the speed of inflation. The twentieth century has witnessed the greatest rise in prices in England's recorded history, and much of this inflation has occurred in the past ten years. After a six-fold rise in prices in the sixteenth century, England experienced a horizontal trend in prices—no inflationary trend—for the three centuries up to the First World War. The sterling price of gold, for example, which had been set by Sir Isaac Newton at £3 17s 10½d, lasted until 1931, and the silver value of the pound had remained unchanged from 1601 to 1816. The period 1914 – 20 saw prices rather more than double in Great Britain, but they fell back somewhat in the next 15 years. The 42 years from 1935 have seen prices rise each year; but until the late 1960s, the annual rate of inflation averaged little more than 3 per cent, and between 1952 and 1965 prices rose annually at slightly less than this. By 1970, however, inflation reached 10 per cent per annum, and the pace quickened sharply after 1973 to culminate in 25 per cent inflation per year in 1975. Between 1973 and

1977, prices will have doubled. If this quadrennial rate of inflation continues, the index of retail prices will rise fifty-fold between 1977 and 2000: the median dwelling in Britain will therefore change hands at the turn of the century for approximately half a million pounds, and a daily newspaper will cost about £5 per copy. If the speed of inflation continues to accelerate as it did between 1960 and 1975, prices in the year 2000 will be vastly higher still. These changes are mesmerising. But this should not blind one to the fact that inflation has surprisingly few, and trivial, effects on a country's overall real standard of living. Real resources may be wasted, to some extent, in otherwise needless activities, like printing new price lists. Companies and individuals are driven by the fear of future inflation into cutting back their holdings of depreciating cash. If governments are unwise enough to keep insisting that loans should be negotiated in paper terms, and not expressible in guaranteed purchasing-power terms, the flow of funds within the economy may become gravely distorted, or even seize up, with serious potential consequences for Britain's productive capacity, and the welfare of those (for example) who contribute to and draw from pension schemes. But most people's real incomes will continue broadly as they would have done in the absence of inflation, and Government has at its disposal devices (indexation of tax thresholds, welfare benefits, and Government debt; devaluation of the external value of sterling) which can neutralise many of its effects.

Another readily discernible trend since the 1950s has been a pronounced rise in the level of unemployment, when averaged across the up-swing and down-swing years of the business cycle. That this should have accompanied the acceleration of inflation is paradoxical: most theories of inflation emphasise that high aggregate demand—influenced, perhaps, by rapid increases in the money supply in previous quarters—should generate inflation or, indeed, accelerating inflation; and high aggregate demand for goods and services is likely to be reflected in a high level of demand for labour and, consequently, in a low level of unemployment. In the 1950s, unemployment sometimes fell to little over 1 per cent of the labour force, and averaged about 2 per cent. The 1970s have (thus far) seen it average one million (about 4½ per cent), and in the winter of 1976/7 it reached over 6 per cent. The rise in unemployment has been associated with a fall in employment of even greater magnitude. The consequences of high unemployment are only too clear: aggregate output, and hence national income, are less than they could otherwise be; the extra leisure that the unemployment represents is not, of course, valueless, but it is very inequitably distributed over the labour force, and may well be valued by its recipient at much less than the social value of the goods he could otherwise have produced, had he been working. The sharp rise in unemployment from winter 1973/4 to winter 1976/7 largely reflects the severe international slump between these years, and similar movements have occurred in all major Western developed economies. But this cannot explain the rising trend of unemployment, the first signs of which occur a decade, or even more, earlier. There are several contributory factors at work here. Structural changes within the economy have become more frequent since the tranquil period of the 1950s; if some sectors expand and others contract more quickly, more people will be changing jobs; and at any instant a still photograph of the labour force will display more people temporarily out of work. Well-intentioned but often counter-productive policies of suppressing rents and regulating tenancies in the interests of existing tenants have made it progressively harder for much of the work-force to move house. Steady increases in the effective marginal rate of tax on incomes—particularly in the lower wage groups—and increases in the ratio of unemployment benefit to after-tax wages—have made it more attractive for the unemployed to spend longer before accepting any new job offered. The increasing cost of hiring labour borne by firms—including the employer's national insurance contributions, and his potential liability for redundancy payments—have made industry more cautious in expanding employment. This has been particularly pronounced in the lower skill range. Some trade unions have understandably reacted to the loosening labour market by pressure to extend entry barriers and other devices to protect their own members' jobs; any repercussions this has on other workers can only be unfavourable.

The rise in unemployment has stimulated some sharply divergent policy recommendations. The Labour Left has argued that the increasing gap between the potential labour force and actual number in work calls for measures to reflate aggregate demand: tax cuts (particularly for those with below-average incomes), and rises in government expenditure (particularly in education and the social services). Since they recognise the potential threat to reflation that would be posed by the additional imports that have so often in the past overwhelmed the balance of payments in previous British booms, they call for import controls that would freeze the existing volume of imported manufactures. In this way, they argue, the balance of payments could be insulated, and the multiplied effect of reflation on national income and employment at home would be greater.[1] Price controls could be applied to check inflation; but even if higher inflation were to result from reflation, it would (in their view) probably be a price worth paying.

The Conservative Right has maintained that it is the reduction of inflation to which first priority should be given. In their view, this is only possible if the growth of the money supply is checked, and reduced. High unemployment will be a consequence—but only a transitory effect; it will ensure that wage increases are modest (whether there is an incomes policy or not); the fall in wage rises will bring down the actual and expected speed of inflation, and employment will then begin to rise back to its 'natural' rate. The natural rate of unemployment depends, in their judgement, on the rate of job turnover, and the various sources of friction (tax distortions, monopolistic practices, deficient information) which impair the smooth functioning of the labour market. The only effective method of cutting long-run unemployment, they maintain, is to reduce those sources of friction.

These two explanations of rising unemployment, and sets of policy recommendations, exemplify a wider disagreement among economists about how successfully economies operate in the absence of intervention by the state. The disagreement also extends to the question of what form (if any) state intervention should take. Two polar positions can be identified: optimism and pessimism about the ability of the free market economy to generate a social optimum. These two positions represent the opposite ends of a spectrum along which most economists' views may be placed.

The optimists maintain that, if left to themselves, economic agents (households and firms) will so arrange their patterns of sales and purchases that it would not be possible to make all of them better off by allocating economic goods between them in any other way. This contention rests upon a number of assumptions. Everyone must be properly informed of the prices at which they can buy or sell, and of the characteristics of what they buy and sell. The market must have a large number of participants, none of whom can influence the prices they face by unilateral action or collusion. No third party must be affected directly by any activity or transaction undertaken by others. Prices must be free to change, and succeed in clearing the markets for everything, so that demand and supply are in balance everywhere. If these conditions are met, it does indeed follow that if individuals all pursue their own interests, a social optimum results; but a social optimum in the restricted sense that no intervention, or alternative set of allocations, could improve the lot of all of them. This result provides the intellectual basis for the *laissez-faire* tradition and continues to permeate much Conservative thinking on economic matters today.

For the pessimists, the price system works too slowly on its own to remove disequilibria (shortages or surpluses). In some cases, prices may not even be relied upon to move in the right direction, and violent disturbances may arise. The way in which the market distributes income between families and individuals is thought to be arbitrary, and to conflict with the canons of justice and equity. Labour may be regularly exploited by the owners of capital, and fail to receive the full true value of its work in the wage packet. The threats posed by imperfect information, the power of monopolies, and third-party (or 'externality') effects may be so severe as to constitute an overwhelming case for Government regulation of prices, production and investment. The facts of the world are therefore felt to falsify the premises on which the optimists' contention rests. This pessimistic view of the market economy is a central tenet of Socialism.

That experience of contemporary Britain invalidates the optimists' assumptions in their strictest form is beyond doubt. No one has perfect perception of his economic environment, and only the haziest of guesses are possible about the future. The mere existence of advertising testifies to the incompleteness of information on the consumers' part; and although advertising may improve information, it can also pervert it by mendacious claims. Technical indivisibilities in production and sales make it inevitable—and desirable—that most commodities should be made and sold by rather a small number of firms; this makes it likely that the firms have at least some monopoly power. Largely as a result of takeovers and mergers, Britain has witnessed a considerable increase in industrial concentration,[2] and this has been especially pronounced since the early 1960s. The markets for industrial products are increasingly dominated by a few large firms. The merger movement has been partly a defensive response to falls in the rate of return on capital; when measured before tax and after depreciation and stock appreciation, these falls have been little short of astonishing since the mid-1960s.[3] The real effects of this have been masked somewhat by Government attempts to switch the burden of taxation away from the corporate to the household sector, and establish new channels of finance to industry to prevent investment drying up (Finance for Industry, and the National Enterprise Board). The labour market has also seen a rapid growth of trade union membership, and some significant trade union amalgamations, in these years; these developments and recent legislative changes (such as the Closed Shop provisions in 1976) represent further growth in monopolies. See Chapter 5.

Perhaps the most serious defect in the market system is the third party (externality) effects. The case for the existence of the state—and the explanation of its evolution—is based on the phenomenon of public goods.[4] In their strict form, these are goods which can be consumed collectively, and from which potential consumers cannot be excluded. A market system will generally underprovide public goods, since individuals will be able to consume what others provide, and will tend to ignore the benefit to others that their own provision confers. Examples abound: national defence; the legal system, and police force; public health services (particularly when they contain contagious illnesses); lighthouses; certain types of information provision and education (particularly broadcasting). Some form of government is clearly needed to decide the appropriate level of provision of these goods, and to levy coercive taxation to defray the costs.

The British Conservative Party readily concedes these arguments, and its adherents clearly support some state intervention to check the distortions that spring from monopoly power, to repair deficiencies in information, and to secure satisfactory levels of provisions of public goods. Furthermore, the British Labour Party is usually gradualist and selective in its reforms and, *de facto* if not *de jure*, remains committed to retaining a large privately owned industrial sector. Nevertheless, there are substantial disagreements between the major parties about how far state intervention should go – and disagreements within them, as well. Most of these disputes can be shown to turn on the issue of *laissez-faire* v. *dirigisme*. Two examples:

the Labour Party has been divided since 1975 on the question of import controls, opposition to the suggestion coming largely from the party's right. The classical argument against any type of tax or quota on international trade (of which import controls are a special case) is that such devices must break the link (the equality that would be observed in a small, perfectly competitive economy) between domestic prices and the true social marginal benefit or cost of international trade: resources will therefore come to be allocated in a wasteful manner and the price ratios that home residents face between importable goods and other (domestically produced) goods will be unequal to the ratios at which these two sets of goods can be exchanged on international markets. Since the beginning of the decade, the Conservative Party has been divided on the question of whether slow growth of the money supply, or controls on the growth of money wage rates, is the better means of containing inflation. The case for the former (argued by the party's right) rests, again, on the optimistic paradigm: an ideal competitive economy will display a tendency towards automatic full employment, so that the pressures built up from an increase in the money supply on total demand can only find a vent in increases in the price level; while controls on money wage rises can only serve to distort the allocation of labour between industries and to frustrate the proper functioning of the price mechanism. If wage rises do occur (faster than the rate of about $2\frac{1}{2}$ per cent per annum, at which overall labour productivity goes up) when the money supply is fixed, they argue, unemployment will go up as workers price themselves out of their jobs; and this must eventually curb the wage rises, as the 'excess supply' of labour exerts a dampening influence on the strength of labour's bargaining position against employers. The opposition to free trade in the Labour Party, and to 'monetarism' in the Conservative Party, is motivated in each case by scepticism about the rapid and successful working of the price system.

The most profound area of dispute between optimists and pessimists, between right and left, concerns the distribution of income and wealth between individuals. The statistical evidence on changes in inequality in contemporary Britain is not clear-cut: much depends on which of many possible indices of inequality is selected, and on which statistical sources are tapped.[5] But there cannot be much doubt that the distribution of both incomes and wealth has shown some trend towards greater equality in post-war Britain. We shall investigate the question of what might constitute an optimum distribution, and how economic policy towards it should be formulated. First, however, we must attempt to define the object of economic policy in general.

Economic policy has one overall objective. This may be called the maximisation of the economic welfare of a society, subject to constraints imposed, for instance by technology and the endowment of resources. But this definition is unhelpful as it stands. So broad that it cannot be disputed, it provokes questions rather than answers them. How is the welfare of society related to the welfare of the individuals who comprise it? How are we to decide upon the relative social desirability of different 'states of the world', if individuals' interests clash? What information do we have about the effects on *any* individual's welfare of various policy options—devaluing the currency, for example, or building a hospital, or raising unemployment benefit, or lowering the sales tax on motor cars?

Society's economic welfare must depend upon the economic welfare of the individuals within it. Individuals' economic welfare will, in turn, depend partly upon their wealth (or income). It will probably also depend upon other factors – their range of choice, their access to 'public goods', the welfare of their relatives and friends, and so on. Economic welfare is, moreover, only one constituent element in total welfare (whether for society or its individuals); but because of other elements, like health which may (to some extent) be purchased, as well as having repercussions on earning power, the domain of economics is hard to define. The reader is begged to suspend his scepticism, and consider a society composed of n egocentric individuals whose welfare varies only with their own wealth. The community's total wealth is taken to be a given number, and equal to the sum of individuals' wealth. Social welfare is defined to be S,

$$\text{where } S^c = \sum_i^n a_i W_i^c$$

W_i is the ith person's welfare; a_i is some positive number (corresponding to the weight social welfare places on the ith person's welfare when $c > 0$ and on its reciprocal when $c < 0$); and c (which ranges from $+1$ to $-$ measures society's aversion to inequality. When all the as are equal, for example, different individuals' levels of welfare are perfect substitutes if $c = +1$, and society has no preference for any one distribution of welfare levels over any other – provided that the sum of everyone's welfare does not alter. If c tends to minus infinity on the other hand, society becomes very strongly averse to any departure from a unique optimum distribution of welfare levels, and if the as are all equal, society will insist upon complete equality in the distribution of welfare.

Given our assumptions, this simple equation can help us to frame answers to perhaps the most important of the questions of economic policy; how should society distribute a fixed total sum of wealth between its members? Usually, all that is needed in addition is a knowledge of how everyone's welfare level is related to his wealth, and the stipulation of values to the as and to c. But the results—which can all be framed as imperatives – are highly sensitive to the numbers we impose upon the as and c, and to what we assume about individuals' wealth-welfare relationships. The second point can be clarified by introducing the concept of the marginal welfare from wealth. Let us call m_i the effect upon the ith person's welfare of a tiny change in his own wealth; we presumably can take it that m_i is positive. A selection of the results we can derive are presented in Table 4.1.

Several cells in the matrix of Table 4.1 correspond to recogniseable political positions, as set out in Table 4.2

The extreme liberal will not concern himself with the distribution of wealth between people; he will, however, be anxious to make sure that the aggregate value of everyone's wealth is as high as possible—assuming of course that the generation of extra wealth carries negligible costs. It is the extreme liberal's approach to economic policy problems that underlies traditional cost-benefit analysis, as we shall see later. That it has been applied so widely (and all too often implicitly) does not of course serve to justify it.

The traditional utilitarian approach is to redistribute wealth until its subjective marginal value is the same to everyone. If it so happens that everyone has the same wealth – welfare relationship, this of course implies an equalisation of wealth. But it can be only anti-equalitarian if some people are less efficient 'welfare-machines' than others. If the old or the blind cannot derive as much welfare from their thousandth pound as the young and the sighted, then the utilitarian rule requires us to transfer wealth away from them. The opposite prescription emerges from, for example, IIIB; and the utilitarian may rescue himself from this objection if he places high enough *a*s on society's less fortunate members.

Perhaps one would not expect IIA to have many adherents. Yet if society were ruled by an egocentric autocrat, he would impose the condition that social welfare and his own welfare were synonymous, and give himself the highest *a* (everyone else's *a* would be set at zero). In practice, despots will probably allow their subjects some positive wealth, as an 'efficiency wage' to maximise their work-productivity, or to stop them dying or rising in rebellion. Fortunately IIA is hardly applicable in contemporary Britain, but one may suspect that it is not entirely wide of the mark as a description of economic distributive policies pursued in one or two countries in the Third World.

Cells IIIA and IIIB are an interesting contrast: if individuals are deemed to have different wealth-welfare relationships—or in other words 'different needs'—the optimum policy will be IIIB rather than IIIA, and some inequality in wealth distribution will be required. IIIA will be imposed if and only if everyone is deemed to have identical needs. IIIA and IIIB correspond with Socialist or Marxist political positions. The British Welfare State, which evolved from nineteenth-century and earlier origins and reached approximately its present shape under the Attlee Government of 1945 – 51, enshrines IIIB in the principle of universal and (usually) free access to the education and health services administered by the State.

Cells VA and VB can be traced back to a special case of the value judgement of Vilfredo Pareto, which underlies many theorems in welfare

TABLE 4.1

	I	II	III	IV	V
	$c = +1$ *a*s equal	$c = +1$ *a*s unequal	$c \to -\infty$ *a*s equal	$c \to -\infty$ *a*s unequal	$c \to -\infty$ reciprocals of *a*s represent the existing distribution of wealth.
SPECIAL CASE (A): m_i are constant equal for everyone.	Ignore the distribution of wealth: It does not affect social welfare.	Give everything to the person(s) with the highest *a*.	Equalise the distribution of wealth.	Equalise the weighted distribution of wealth.[1]	Freeze the existing distribution of wealth.
GENERAL CASE (B): (assuming that m_i diminishes as is wealth increases)[5]	Equalise everyone's *m*s.[2]	Equalise everyone's weighted *m*s.[3]	Equalise the distribution of welfare.	Equalise the weighted distribution of welfare.[1]	Freeze the existing distribution of wealth.[4]

[1] The reciprocals of the *a*s provide the weights.

[2] This entails the equalisation of the wealth distribution, if and only if everyone has the same wealth – welfare relationship; and the rule itself may break down if there are large enough disparities in individuals' wealth – welfare relationships.

[3] The *a*'s provide the weights. To be sure of this result, we must be sure that there exists no pair of individuals j and k such that $a_j m_j$ is less than $a_k m_k$ when j's wealth is negligible and k's wealth approaches societies entire-wealth.

[4] If the reciprocals of the *a*s represent the existing distribution of welfare.

[5] The condition that m_j diminishes as i's wealth increases is not needed when $c \to -\infty$

TABLE 4.2

I	II	III	IV	V
A Extreme liberal	Extreme supporter of plutocracy	Extreme equalitarian (pecuniary)		Extreme conservative
B Traditional utilitarian		Extreme equalitarian (welfare)		Extreme conservative

economics, and can generate some surprisingly powerful conclusions. Pareto maintained that it was not possible to say that society as a whole would gain by pursuing a particular policy, if some individuals were worse off as a result; nor could society be held to have lost as a whole, if some individuals gained. If this principle is strengthened by assuming that society loses whenever at least one of its members loses, we effectively give everyone a veto. While Cell IA implies that the existing distribution of wealth is as good as any other, Cells VA and VB imply that the existing distribution is better than any other. As formulated, the assumptions behind V produce a conservative, but not a reactionary prescription. The reactionary would insist that the reciprocal of the as represent some previous distribution of wealth or welfare. While generally consistent with right-wing policy recommendations, there are elements of VA and VB in some policy measures introduced by recent Labour Governments: legislation to insulate tenants from eviction or employees from dismissal (without substantial compensation) could be interpreted as instances. Furthermore, although socialists and conservatives will disagree about the as, they will tend to agree that c is less than 1. Trade unions sometimes invoke VA and VB (or some reactionary version of them) when they maintain that their members' position in the wage hierarchy must not sink, or must be restored to some previous level.

A few remarks may be made about the policy imperatives that emerge from other cases. If c exceeds minus infinity but falls short of $+1$, the IIIA, IVA and VA rules still stand (provided that the ms are constant and equal for everyone). If c is zero, our equation for S shrivels up into the unhelpful statement that the as sum to one, and is replaced by the entropy or 'Cobb-Douglas' equation:

$$\log S = \sum_i^n a_i \log W_i$$

and this states that social welfare is (some multiple of) the weighted geometric average of individuals' level of welfare. If the weights (the as) are equal, of course, this will also imply an equalisation of wealth when everyone has constant and identical ms. If c were allowed to exceed $+1$, society would become averse to equality in (weighted) welfare levels, and would positively seek to achieve inequality of wealth under most conditions.

Powerful as our equation has been on exposing the assumptions on which so many economic policy recommendations rest, it must not blind us to the many difficulties that have been side-stepped. First and foremost, there can be no *objective* justification for dismissing certain values of the as and c, and selecting others. If I announce that I believe that the social welfare equation places equal weights on everyone's welfare levels, and that increases in equality lower social welfare beyond some point, I express a personal subjective judgement, and no more. As has been seen, the policy recommendations vary very greatly, according to the value judgement inherent in the choice of these numerical values. Second, it is hard to see how the ms could be measured for any one individual – to establish for example whether m diminished as wealth rose – let alone how they could be compared for different individuals. Any method of making inter-personal comparisons among the wealth – welfare relationships which was proposed would fall victim to the sceptic's request for independent corroboration. It has long been suggested that individuals do betray some information about how their m changes with their wealth in their gambling behaviour: opting for comprehensive rather than third-party motor insurance, holding safe assets or different assets with low mutual co-variance in expected returns, or refusing to play card-games for high stakes may all be cited as evidence of diminishing m as wealth increases. But even if this be accepted, there is still no way of telling whether one person's m exceeds another. Other problems with the analysis concern the fact that real-world phenomena like generosity and envy have been ruled out by the assumption that everyone is egocentric (where do families fit in?); that semi-economic and non-economic elements in society's or individuals' 'welfare' have been ignored; and that wealth, rather than income, has been taken as the determinant of welfare (are we to include 'human wealth', the capitalised value of future income from work, which constitutes by far the greater part of national income – and if so how?)

Probably the gravest difficulty of all, however, attaches to the assumption that the sum of individuals' wealth is fixed. This is patently unreasonable. Saving augments wealth; dissaving reduces it. Measures to reduce inequality will involve taxation on principal, interest or both. This will blunt the incentive for thrift. It may well lower total savings (although this is not necessarily true if redistribution is sufficiently unexpected, sufficiently gradual, or sufficiently counterbalanced by saving by the state). A fall in present savings will permit a rise in current consumption; but it entails a cost in future consumption forgone. Whether this exchange of more jam today against less jam tomorrow is desirable depends on several factors; how society weights its present members' consumption against future consumption by them or their successors, on how large a permanent stream of future consumption is sacrificed by an act of extra consumption now, how quickly the population is expected to grow, and the speed with which technical progress, inventions, and the like are expected to raise living standards. Wealth redistribution via inheritance taxes entails restrictions on the freedom to bequeath, which society may or may not deem important.

A more clear-cut effect of redistribution on total wealth operates on individuals' choices—if they are free to make them – between leisure and work. Work is generally assumed to be disagreeable, and to be undertaken solely for the consumption expenditure that earnings sustain. If individuals differ in earning power or preferences as between leisure and consumption, and wages paid vary with hours or intensity of work, the distribution of income will in general be unequal. Attempts to equalise it must involve a positive marginal rate of income tax, at least across some belts of income. The proceeds of the income tax rate will then be distributed, in whole or part, as a lump-sum 'social dividend' or 'reverse tax'. The equalitarian will probably wish to see an equal reverse tax paid to everyone. Under these conditions, as the marginal tax rate rises, the individual's leisure becomes more and more of a public bad, and a private good for the person concerned. The marginal hour he does *not* work involves steadily smaller sacrifices of consumption for the individual, and steadily greater sacrifices of consumption for everyone else. If the marginal tax rate were 100 per cent (this is necessary to equalise incomes except in trivial cases, or if people's freedom of choice is infringed), no one would choose to work; and, if land and any surviving machinery could not produce output on their own, there would be no output; so everyone would have an income of zero. Unless we are prepared to clutch to the Protestant ethic as a description of reality—to believe that individuals treat leisure as a private bad—we are forced to conclude, sadly, that the cost of equality is servitude or indigence. Society faces an awkward, three-dimensional maximisation problem: how to choose the most desirable combination of liberty, wealth and equality in the distribution of wealth. The Marxist will place stronger emphasis on the last two of these than on liberty; or he may agree with Lenin that reducing disparities in earned income takes second place to the elimination of capitalist ownership of the means of production, and accept some roles for incentives in the labour market. The liberal will place more emphasis on the first two than on the third, and may even adhere to the view that we saw the extreme liberal take in Cell IA: that inequality does not matter. The Conservative may be prepared to surrender some liberty to preserve the existing distribution of wealth and keep its aggregate high; he may also oppose attempts to dismantle the structure authority in businesses, which he will view as providing the stick (if not the carrot) for productivity. Turning to contemporary Britain, it is hard to discover any evidence that

Governments have thought through the implications of greater job security and increasing effective marginal rates of taxation for the liberty-wealth-equality triangle; an economy that refuses to espouse either commands or incentives will not produce very much.

A recent solution to the dilemma has been proposed by Rawls.[6] Liberty is taken to be a primary good, which must be set no lower than some critical value. Granted this, national wealth (or income) is now considered to vary with the degree of inequality: as inequality falls, national wealth may at first rise, but must eventually start to decline. A particular group—the poorest group—is now defined. Their wealth rises steadily as inequality falls, but only as far as a given level; after that, further falls in inequality will lower the wealth of the poorest group, as the disincentive effect of marginal tax rates on everyone begins to dominate and depress their wealth; the cake diminishes faster than their share of it rises. Rawls seeks a contractual non-Utilitarian resolution of the optimum distribution problem. He asks this question: if everyone were placed behind a veil of ignorance, so that they did not know into which socio-economic class they would fall, to what distribution of wealth (or income, or welfare, or justice) would they assent? His answer is that if they are sufficiently risk-averse, they would be so horrified of the possibility of landing in the most disadvantaged group that they would agree to whatever distribution of wealth (income, justice etc.) maximised the wealth of that group. This Rawlsian 'maximin' solution is to redistribute until the absolute wealth of the poorest group is maximised, but no further. If people are envious of each other, there might be a case for further redistribution; if people are neutral to risk, for accepting more inequality. Utilitarians may take comfort from the argument that Rawls can be said to assume implicitly that m diminishes as wealth increases, when he maintains that individuals are strongly risk-averse. There are difficulties of defining the 'poorest group', and in using the Rawlsian criterion to split the remainder of the cake between the other members of society. It may also be objected that the poorest group can have even higher wealth than Rawls allows them, if the citizenry behind its veil of ignorance is prepared to trade off some liberty. Is it necessarily worse to be a prosperous serf than a pauper?

We have seen that the optimum distribution of goods between individuals depends, in part, or what one assumes to be their marginal benefit. No distinction was drawn between wealth and income. This section will explore the distinction, and set out another central and difficult area for economic policy—the appropriate division of resources between present consumption and future consumption.

Wealth is a stock, income the flow to which it relates. Income is what an owner of wealth can keep spending without suffering a reduction of his wealth. Income is the recurrent yield from wealth. If you consume more than your income, your wealth is cut and you must, sooner or later, accept a fall in your own or your beneficiaries' consumption. If you consume less than your income, your future consumption possibilities are expanded.

How much of its income should society refrain from consuming? How should the benefits of present consumption be weighed against the consumption of present or subsequent generations in future? These are perhaps the most difficult and important questions a society has to face. The difficulties are obvious: we can never know our future scale of preferences; posterity is not present to inform us of its preferences; the character and speed of technical progress can never be foreseen; what present saving implies in terms of additions to future consumption cannot be known; we have imperfect knowledge of stocks of raw materials, and future technological requirements.[7]

Under certain extreme conditions, our questions are answerable. For example, if capital lasts for ever, technology is stagnant, production requires no natural resources, and there is perfect competition, a society's consumption should equal its wage-bill, and profits should be equal to savings—if society wishes to achieve the highest (constant) value of consumption per person. The benefits in future consumption afforded by saving should be discounted by the rate at which the population increases. If technical progress—an increase in the output of industries, for given inputs – occurs, and is known to recur, consumption can be a still higher proportion of income without threats of declining consumption per head. If industry makes use of land, however—and, worse still, of non-replenishable resources like fuels and metals—intergenerational equality calls for much more abstemiousness. History may be an unreliable guide to the future; it suggests that technical progress (in the broadest sense) has displayed a gently accelerating trend over the past two or three centuries, with long periods of stagnation before that. In particular cases, shortage and necessity mothered invention: scarcity encouraged economy, miniaturisation, the search for alternatives. In others, scarcity has meant starvation. History permits no generalisations about the extent to which resource shortages stimulate breakthroughs in knowledge, and still less about the speed with which this occurs. It could even be that technical progress is sometimes inimical to posterity; technical advances in some industries will boost the community's real income, and hence its demands for other goods and services where progress has not occurred. As in most other aspects of economic policy, the views of experts can be located on a continuum ranging from optimism to pessimism.[8] The optimists argue that there is no case for checking the level or growth of consumption; if certain non-replenishable resources are run down appreciably, the price mechanism will work to encourage substitution into other, more plentiful resources, to stimulate technical change which economises on the scarce resource, and to promote greater recycling; growth in income, they maintain, is needed to provide the wherewithal to combat the adverse effects of industrial production on the environment; and if population growth appears to threaten living standards because capital and labour are complementary in production, there will tend to be a low mean age in the population and a high share of savings in national income to compensate, since the dissavings of the retired will be more than offset by the savings of those in work.

The pessimists maintain that our ignorance of future demands and supplies, and the unreliability of the scarcity – technical progress mechanism, make it very imprudent to allow world consumption to continue to grow at post-war rates (which have averaged about $3\frac{1}{2}$ per cent per head per year in the world's advanced countries). Many of the alarmist projections made by the pessimist school have turned on strong—rather unreasonably strong—assumptions, about the inability of economies to switch between resources or obviate supply restraints by improved technology. But it should be remembered that *some* technical progress is needed even to sustain a *constant* long-run level of total consumption, given that production techniques continue to erode finite stocks of fuels and metals. A still faster technical progress rate is required if population is expanding and consumption per head is to keep constant, while increases in both population and consumption per head will only be possible in the long run if technical progress occurs yet more rapidly. Another reason for not dismissing the pessimistic view is the fact that if the pessimists' recommendations are followed and proved wrong, the damage that occurs will presumably be much lighter than if the reverse occurs. There is, indeed, some meagre but accumulating evidence that the pessimists may not now have to exercise so much persuasion. All developed countries have seen a marked fall in birth rates (in the UK the fall has been one-third since 1964) which began in the middle 1960s. In many countries, the share of consumption in households' disposable income has fallen appreciably over the same period, if not longer. The first half of the 1970s has seen a sharp (if erratic) rise in the price of fuel and most metals and primary foodstuffs relative to manufactured goods; this has induced an increased awareness of the need to conserve scarce stocks, and of the fragility of advanced economies devoted to converting raw materials into finished manufactures. Most significant of all (although it may still be far too soon to say), the trend growth rate of real income seems to have fallen appreciably since the late 1960s in many advanced countries – this is especially true of West Germany, but apparently detectable, too, for the UK, the USA and France. Perhaps the great post-war boom will prove to have been a mere quarter-century interlude, succeeded by a period of cautious consolidation.

For Britain, the most pressing problem in this regard is what to do with North Sea oil.[9] There are two related, but distinct aspects to this: when to extract it, and what to buy with the proceeds. If all the known oil could be extracted at once, its disposal value as exports would represent (at present prices) perhaps ten or eleven months of national income, or some £2500 per person in the British Isles. A generous allowance for future discoveries and for conservative estimates of the size of existing fields might allow one to double these figures. Of course, instantaneous extraction is technically impossible, and very slow extraction is also ruled out by the heavy fixed costs of drilling and pipelines. Technical considerations prescribe an optimum steady extraction rate of between 5 per cent and 10 per cent of recoverable reserves each year, for most of the North Sea fields. Approximate extraction trajectories have in fact already been determined for the majority of fields. On existing plans and known reserves, Britain can expect to be self-sufficient in oil for about two decades, from 1981 onwards The characteristics of the oil will make it necessary to continue importing certain grades; these imports will be offset—or more than offset – by exports. Only history will tell whether it will, in retrospect, have proved wise to begin extracting the oil at once: the fact that world oil reserves are finite implies that its price (in terms of other goods) may rise over time – perhaps by the real rate of interest, perhaps even faster—and delayed reactions throughout the world to the fourfold increase in oil prices between 1972 and 1974 may induce a temporary energy glut in the 1980s. In this event, oil may turn out to be rather more valuable in the 1990s than in the 1980s. On the other hand, the pace of technical developments – in nuclear fusion, wave and solar power for example—cannot be foreseen, and it is clearly possible that industrial and commercial demand for oil could fall substantially by the end of the century. Since Britain will be roughly self-sufficient in oil until 2000, fluctuations (up or down) in the relative price of oil between now and then will have a negligible immediate effect on her real income; but if oil proves to be very expensive after 2000, when she will most likely have to start being a net importer again, she will have cause to regret not having deferred extraction until then. Also, it will be advisable to pass on any increase in real oil prices that occurs before 2000 to domestic users, so that the full value of the lucrative exports can be reaped. Since the extraction programme has already largely been set, one can only hope that oil will be a cheaper commodity in the twenty-first century than in the closing decades of the twentieth.

It is the second question—what to buy with the proceeds of North Sea oil – that is the more pressing and probably the more important. It is here that the authorities in London (or Edinburgh, or Lerwick?) still have considerable discretion. One possible course of action is to devote the funds to consumption, whether private or public, over the twenty-year period. If wholly applied to increasing consumption, the wealth of the North Sea could raise the level of consumption by between 5 per cent and 10 per cent, once and for all, over these years. But in this case, nothing would be left for future consumption, after the year 2000. It would be hard to justify such profligacy, unless Britain could be assured of similar windfalls in subsequent periods – which of course she could not be. The opposite policy would be to convert all the wealth of the North Sea into investment goods – physical capital in buildings, plant and machinery, or invisible capital in technical education, research and development – which would permit future rises in national output and consumption. Perhaps the fairest policy would be to treat present and future generations equally, and so to split the extra national expenditure which the North Sea permits between consumption and investment, so that there is an approximately equal increase in consumption per head, once and for all, for *all* subsequent years. If the present value of the North Sea oil (net of the debts incurred to drill for it and extract it) is put between £100,000 million (conservative) and £200,000 million (generous estimate), population growth is ignored, and the real rate of interest – which measures the real reward from investment, per year, over an indefinite horizon – is put at 2 per cent, the permanent increase in consumption per head turns out to be between 80p and £1-60 per week, or between £2-50 and £5-00 per week per household. If the existing ratio of private to public consumption is retained, roughly one quarter of these sums would be withheld by the state to finance enhanced provision of current services in education, health, and other social amenities.

This policy would imply that almost all—all but about 2 per cent—of the 'income' from the North Sea would be invested. It would require governments to display much more courage and foresight than they have tended to display in the past. The political pressures to raise private and public consumption would be considerable; posterity cannot place its mark on the ballot paper, or form itself into an articulate interest group. Even if the temptation to yield unsustainable increases in consumption is overcome, governments will be confronted with other dangers. Some low-productivity industries make substantial losses, some part of which—but hardly all of which – may be justified on grounds of optimal pricing or˙ social costs. The railways are a prominent example. Despite four major debt write-offs, and in addition to other explicit or disguised subsidies, British Rail loses over £350 million per year. Perhaps 75 per cent of the households in Britain pay more in tax to finance these losses than they do in rail fares. There are nearly fifteen employees per kilometre of track, which is considerably more than for most other sizeable railway systems in the world, and it is difficult to escape the conclusion that British Rail's losses are traceable in large measure to just this. Motor assembly, shipbuilding and the docks provide further examples of very low productivity by international standards, and have required the infusion of public funds to sustain operations (although British docks have the good fortune to be largely immune from foreign competition, and can pass on high unit labour costs in high charges quite easily). In some instances, low productivity may be attributed to antiquated or small-scale plant; substantial investment may then be called for. But there is a grave danger that North Sea oil may enable Britain to postpone necessary increases in productivity, to preserve its museum economy, and to continue indulging the myopia and Luddism of so many of its managements and unions.

Underwriting losses is the very antithesis of productive investment.

No less insidious may be the Bonapartism of the heads of some high-technology industries, and even more perhaps of the high priests of technical research on their periphery. Concorde appears to be an unmitigated commercial disaster without historical parallel in the British Isles. The British share of the present value of development and production costs, net of the rather nugatory sales receipts, may prove to exceed £1000 million on 1977 prices. The aeroplane has been plagued by ill-luck for which its promoters cannot fairly be blamed—the marked deceleration in the growth of passenger air travel, the sudden vociferousness of environmental lobbies inside the USA and elsewhere, technical obstacles to abating noise and emissions—but, even despite this, it is impossible to envisage circumstances in which the project could ever have been a financial success. The tragedy of Concorde is the story of blind optimism in the economic value of high-technology projects; of the credulous acceptance of woolly and fallacious economic arguments about the disproportionate social benefit of additional exports, or the huge size of investments already made justifying further expenditure to complete the programme; and of the Prisoner's Dilemma of heavy cancellation charges payable to the other if one of them withdrew, into which both Britain and France had ensnared themselves.

Concorde may be egregious in the scale of its losses, but it does not constitute the only victory of technological ambition over commercial sense. The Post Office's decision, over two decades ago, to by-pass an intermediate system of telecommunication has proved highly questionable in retrospect. Britain's heavy investment in nuclear power since the mid-1950s only begins to show a profit if one assumes that the true cost of alternative energy sources is much higher than it has turned out to be in most of the period since. Concorde itself is only the most recent of a long string of aircraft projects, some of which (the Brabazon, the Britannia and the RB211 engine, for instance) have also turned out to be misconceived or gravely underpriced. Britain's escapades in space rocketry have been happily curtailed by lack of funds at an early stage, but not before some significant losses had been incurred. Against all of this, there are clearly dangers—commercial as well as strategic—in adopting too negative an attitude to all advanced technology projects: the decision to suspend development of the vertical take-off jet fighter for several years in the late-1950s (an aeroplane which has now emerged as a major success by all criteria) seems to have been quite unwarranted. It is probably inevitable that some errors of commission and omission will be made. But there can be no controverting the lesson of so much of Britain's post-war experience—that a careworn Cabinet and an embattled Treasury have been unable to ensure an adequate scrutiny of the prestige ventures submitted to them. The speed, nature and costs of the fruits of technical research can never be quantified in advance. But there is a strong case for adopting zero-base budgeting, or sunset laws, whereby a particular research institution or research project will be terminated automatically at a specified date, unless enough concrete evidence of success is forthcoming to persuade Parliament to renew its lease of life. The British Government must be alive to the risk that the fruits of the North Sea will be usurped by expensive flights of engineering fancy; it is essential that investment projects of this nature should be carefully screened.

Maximising the return from the investments that the North Sea can provide will prove a forbidding task. It will be expedited somewhat if certain distortionary features of Britain's fiscal and financial systems are removed. There is at present a substantial incentive for individuals to save through house-purchase rather than acquiring equity in companies or corporate debentures. Mortgage interest is tax-deductible: this cheapens the nominal cost of borrowing for house-buyers by at least 35 per cent and up to 83 per cent, depending on their marginal income tax rate. The real cost of borrowing (when one subtracts the allowance for inflation inherent in 'nominal' or paper rates of interest) generally receives a subsidy of over 100 per cent. By contrast, anyone who borrows to buy shares cannot set his interest charges against tax. When one examines the taxation levied on the income from different sorts of asset, one notices that the rent a house-owner avoids having to pay to someone else is not liable to tax in the UK, and that household rates – which do tax this – are much lighter than the 52 per cent Corporation Tax implicitly charged on corporate dividends. Dividends are taxed even more heavily for high-income households. When shares are sold for a profit – even a paper profit, which may easily fail to compensate for the fall in the value of money during the period over which the shares were held – Capital Gains Tax is levied, at 30 per cent or half the vendor's marginal income tax rate; but capital gains on disposing of one's (primary) residence, if sold at least two years after purchase, escape Capital Gains Tax completely. These major fiscal distortions may go some way to explaining why industrial capital per worker is more than double the British figure in France and West Germany, while the average standard of housing appears to differ little between the three countries.

Further assistance to the proper functioning of capital markets could come from allowing British companies to borrow by issuing indexed debentures. A fully indexed debenture issued, for example, in January 1978 for 20 years would promise its holder in January 1998 not £100 in cash, as at present, but £100 multiplied by the ratio of some price index in January 1998 to its January 1978 value. The fixed-interest payment or 'coupon', payable each year between the two dates, would also be inflation-proofed in similar fashion. The major advantage of this scheme would be that the lender would be insured against the chance that inflation over the period could proceed unexpectedly fast, and the borrower against the chance that it could proceed unexpectedly slowly. Unexpected inflation redistributes arbitrarily from lenders to borrowers, while unexpectedly slow inflation redistributes in the other way, if lender and borrower negotiate loans in paper terms. Limiting companies to borrowing in unindexed debentures is rather likely to reduce the overall level of investment (below what it would be – and probably should be – otherwise), since companies are typically risk-averse. Another advantage from indexation is that it would allow borrowers to spread the real costs of servicing debt more evenly over the life of an investment project, and thus avoid the problem of 'front-loading' which occurs when inflation is expected.

Removing tax distortions against borrowing by private industry, and the uncertainties and complications of inflation from industrial borrowing, would undoubtedly achieve a more satisfactory balance of investment outlays in Britain, and increase the returns from investment. There is, indeed, a case for extending indexation to all categories of loans. But the transition to a more rational basis for capital markets would have to be controlled carefully. In such an arthritic economy as the United Kingdom, rapid changes of rules can produce serious disturbances. The besetting characteristics of so much government economic policy in the past two decades have been excessive mercuriality, excessive concern with immediate and direct effects, and inadequate attention to the subtler and longer-run consequences of decisions taken.[10]

Government will clearly have to continue guiding and tempering the outcome of the market system. But one can only hope that it will do so with greater long-sightedness, patience and ability than it has too often displayed in the past. The last two decades of the twentieth century provide Britain with an unparalleled opportunity to arrest the long relative economic decline since the Second World War. Whether the opportunity is grasped or allowed to slip by will depend on several factors: whether sensible measures are taken to correct the distorting and uncertainty-inducing effects of inflation; whether the rising trend of wasted labour—unemployment—can be reversed by imaginative combinations of microeconomic as well as macroeconomic policies; whether the ideological debate between the optimists who espouse *laissez-faire* and the pessimistic *dirigistes* can be confined to central empirical questions of detail, and illuminated by first-class statistical research; whether the complex trade-offs between liberty, equality and efficiency can be identified, and consequential social choices resolved with the minimum political and social disruption and disharmony; whether the fruits of the North Sea, and other reserves of minerals and coal, can be applied to productive investment and the raising of labour productivity for the benefit of future and present generations. One can only hope.

NOTES

1. See W. Godley and R. M. May, 'The Macroeconomic Implications of Devaluation and Import Restriction', *Economic Policy Review*, March 1977, for an interesting exploration of the effects of import controls. The case for import controls is, nonetheless, controversial: an eloquent attack on the proposal can be found in W. M. Corden, I. M. D. Little and M. F. Scott, *Import Controls versus Devaluation and Britain's Economic Prospects* (Trade Policy Research Centre, 1975).

2. See, for example, S. Aaronovitch and M. C. Sawyer, *Big Business*, 1975; L. Hannah and J. A. Kay, *Concentration in Modern Industry*, 1977; S. J. Prais, *Giant Corporations*, 1976; G. Meeks and G. Whittington, 'Giant Companies in the United Kingdom 1948 – 1969', *Economic Journal*, vol. lxxxv, December 1975, pp. 824 – 43.

3. See J. S. Flemming (with others), 'Trends in Company Profitability', *Bank of England Quarterly Bulletin*, March 1976, pp. 36 – 52. A rather more sanguine picture (up to 1972 – 3) emerges from M. A. King, 'The United Kingdom Profits Crisis: Myth or Reality?', *Economic Journal*, vol. lxxxv, March 1975, pp. 33 – 54.

4. P. J. N. Sinclair, 'The Economic Roles of the State', in Lord Blake and J. Patten (eds.) *The Conservative Opportunity*, 1976, contains a slightly less skeletal account of the problems posed by public goods.

5. For an excellent textbook on all aspects of this subject, see A. Atkinson, *The Economics of Inequality*, 1975. Some of the theoretical and methodological problems are explored very carefully in A. K. Sen, *On Economic Inequality*, 1974. Recent statistical evidence is reviewed by M. C. Sawyer, 'Income Distribution in OECD Countries', *Organization for Economic Cooperation and Development Occasional Studies*, July 1976, Economic Outlook.

6. John Rawls, *A Theory of Justice*, 1972.

7. Hywel G. Jones, *An Introduction to Modern Theories of Economic Growth*, 1975, has an excellent account of this difficult issue in chapter 9.

8. Wilfred Beckerman, *In Defence of Economic Growth*, 1974, presents a powerful case for a qualified version of the optimistic view. The pessimistic case is presented by Jay W. Forrester, *World Dynamics*, 1971. Forrester is reviewed critically in W. D. Nordhaus, 'World Dynamics: Measurement without Data', *Economic Journal*, vol. lxxxiii, December 1973, pp. 1156 – 83.

9. The February 1977 issue of the *National Institute Economic Review* contains an interesting comparison of three recent sets of forecasts of some of the effects of North Sea oil. See pp. 51 – 7.

10. See R. W. Bacon and W. A. Eltis, *Britain's Economic Problem: Too Few Producers*, 1976, for a detailed case that increased provision of non-marketed goods by the Government—motivated partly by a desire to reduce unemployment in the short run—has had serious adverse long run effects.

5 Scapegoats for National Decline: the Trade Unions since 1945

Robert Taylor

Ever since the end of the Second World War, Britain's trade unions have sought to achieve what are two incompatible aims in a declining economy: enjoy a decisive influence over government economic policy and preserve their freedom to bargain unhindered by any form of state interference. It is this curious amalgam of collectivism and *laissez-faire* that has dominated the outlook of most unions over the past 32 years.

By their very nature, unions remain highly defensive organisations that rarely innovate except under great pressure. Custom and practice are strong forces for conservatism within their ranks, particularly in those of our own. As H. A. Turner has observed, 'British trade unions, more than those of most countries perhaps, are historical deposits and repositories of history'. Nobody who ever visits the annual conference of a major British union and observes the often archaic rituals and procedures can ignore the deeply rooted respect for tradition and past achievements, the sense of pride and sobriety handed down from one generation of trade union activists to the next. The old precepts have come under attack in the post-war years, but it would be foolish to anticipate our unions will rapidly acquire the professional progressivism of their counterparts in Sweden or West Germany. Inertia and the maxim 'what is is best' hamper change. So do sectionalism and inter-union rivalry.

Our unions are often portrayed as over-mighty subjects with a lust for tyrannical power and a contempt for individual freedom. 'British trade unionism has become a formula for national misery', intoned Paul Johnson in an article in the *New Statesman* (16 May 1975). Samuel Brittan, economic commentator of the *Financial Times* suggested the unions 'are not the Robin Hoods they are supposed to be on every television programme. They are the robber barons of the system'. (Institute of Economic Affairs' pamphlet 14, 1974.) Strong or weak, the unions have become popular scapegoats for national decline. They are blamed for making excessive wage demands which produce inflation and resisting technological progress in defence of labour-intensive methods of production.

On the other hand, when union bosses try to make a deal with a government over pay and prices, as they did successfully in 1975 and 1976, their critics accuse them of wanting to run the country through the establishment of a corporate state. No union leader has received more venomous abuse than Jack Jones of the Transport and General Workers, who was the effective architect of Labour's social contract with the unions between 1972 and 1977. Caricatured as a Czar, Jones did more than any other man (for good or ill) to educate the trade union movement in the harsh realities of Britain's economic plight. But those who run the unions at the top are not autocrats who can order their well-drilled, passive members into militant action at the drop of a cloth-cap. They can only lead and influence, just as far as their fickle rank and file will tolerate their behaviour. In the last resort, no man can hope to carry weight in his union or with government if he no longer speaks for those he claims to represent.

The persistent, worrying theme of the last 32 years in the tangled relationship between the unions and government has been the wide, often uncomprehending gap between what union leaders see as being in the national interest and the restless, more prosaic but far more vitally immediate interests of those who pay their union dues and have little political or collective persepective. It is the lack of union solidarity, the absence of cohesion, which has bedevilled the weak, divided ranks of British trade unionism since the war.

'What are we here for?', asked that despairing realist George Woodcook, who led the Trades Union Congress from one disappointment to another as general secretary from 1960 to 1969. He never heard a satisfactory answer to his pertinent question through all those years. There is no doubt what those who favoured union reform wanted to see—a highly centralised TUC with the power to make bargains with government and the discipline over affiliate unions to ensure the majority voice prevailed. It has been the avowed aim of Walter Citrine, TUC general secretary from 1926 to 1946, to make the TUC an estate of the realm, which no government could ignore. He wanted to win for the trade union movement the 'power to act on policy issues in a cohesive manner'. To a very large extent, he succeeded. During the Second World War, the TUC was a vital force on the home front in the achievement of total victory. Between the formation of the Churchill coalition in May 1940 and July 1945 a real social contract was forged between the unions and government. Its fruits were seen in the creation of the welfare state and the post-war managed economy, in the 1944 White Paper with its pledge to full employment in peacetime and the Beveridge plan for social insurance. The General Council reports of those years read as though the TUC had become an arm of government. No wonder an optimistic Citrine could tell his last Congress in 1946 that the movement had passed from the 'era of propaganda' to that of 'responsibility'. And this had been achieved without any direct state intervention in voluntary collective bargaining. Central control of wages and prices was not an essential element in the war effort. It is therefore not surprising that the TUC laid great stress on the need to preserve the voluntarist principles in the years of peace.

But in the difficult economic conditions of the late 1940s the Labour government felt compelled to reach agreement with the TUC on wage restraint. Reluctantly – far more from a sense of political loyalty than economic conviction – union leaders agreed in March 1948 to a virtual freeze on all wage increases. It held over two years, despite mounting rank-and-file frustration and government inability to keep prices down, before the dam burst in 1951. The close personal and political ties between the union bosses and the Labour cabinet ensured the temporary success of the wage restraint policy. As Gerald Dorfman has written, 'There was displayed a strong feeling of identity by the general council members with the Labour government. It was "their" government. It had delivered on promises of economic and social reform. It had kept its pledge to sustain full employment, even against some very powerful arguments in favour of deflation in 1947'.

Once again, between October 1964 and June 1970, the TUC found itself making sacrifices for the well-being of a Labour Government, with even initial consent to a highly regressive statutory wages and prices policy. It is true that as early as 1967 Labour could only rely on the 'reluctant acquiescence' of the TUC. But the inability of the TUC itself to control wage demands through its own machinery in 1965–6 made it easier for the Government to impose a pay restraint policy of its own. Again, this was only a a temporary affair.

The 1969–72 wages explosion was in part the result of three years of severe controls on the level of pay settlements. In the words of Leo Panitch, 'In four out of the six half yearly periods between Labour's 1966 election victory and the summer of 1969 workers experienced declining real incomes *before* tax'. Turner and Wilkinson at Cambridge University calculated the net real income of an average male manual worker, married with two children, rose by a derisory 0.5 per cent a year during Labour's time in office, despite the achievement of an annual growth rate of around 3.0 per cent.

A further effort was made at voluntary pay restraint between Labour and the unions between July 1975 and August 1977. This time union leaders took the initiative – to the obvious surprise of Harold Wilson and the Treasury. The £6 flat rate policy of 1975–6 and the 5 per cent pay deal of 1976–7 worked remarkably well and helped to reduce the rate of inflation, which had reached a frightening figure of 25 per cent a year in the early summer of 1975 with wage settlements climbing to over 30 per cent. Of course, neat and crude pay formulas mask the complexities of the wages system and store up intractable pressures and problems for the future, but for two years the TUC demonstrated an impressive unity in holding the line on pay, despite mounting unemployment, periodic cutbacks in public expenditure, a crippling level of direct taxation on manual workers, and a real cut in everybody's living standards for the first time since the war.

But union leaders are not in business as the policemen of pay restraint on behalf of any government, whether its political attitudes mirror their own or not. Most believe their function is to better and safeguard the pay and conditions of the membership. Some aspire to a bigger voice in the making of public policy. And here there have been immense strides since Citrine's heyday. No public body or Royal Commission is complete without a union worthy sitting on it. Ability or experience are not the only desirable qualifications. Despite a reputation for ruthlessness, the trade union movement is soft-hearted and sentimental. The rule of Buggins's turn is a strong one. Union muscle also counts for a great deal as well. The longer a union boss sits on the TUC General Council, the more he gets laden down with extra jobs, which usually carry more social prestige than money with them.

It is hard, in retrospect, to trace the positive influence of the unions on post-war Britain, but the TUC decision to serve on the newly-founded National Economic Development Council (Neddy for short) in 1962 was of crucial importance in pulling trade unionism out of its old negative attitudes. This proved a singular success for George Woodcock. As he told the 1962 Congress: 'We must not as a trade union movement give the impression that we are claiming absolute, unfettered, unqualified freedom to do what we like and to hell with the rest. This is not trade unionism, never has been. The whole point and purpose of trade unionism is for people to get together and collectively come to a common policy.' Neddy was seen as an instrument to make the unions more responsible, by taking, in Woodcock's words, 'a completely impartial, coldly analytical view of all our problems'. The TUC's Neddy Six work as a team, serviced by the TUC's own secretariat and answerable to the General Council. Reporting back is essential. They have become the holy of holies, the group whom Chancellor Denis Healey negotiated with over pay in 1976.

The TUC has never pulled out of Neddy. The senior union bosses have turned up every month to council meetings, even during the June 1970–June 1972 period of non-cooperation between the TUC and the Heath Government. Whether the union involvement in Neddy has proved successful is problematic. With its commitment to tripartism and consensus, Neddy has a reputation for being a talking-shop with no power of executive decision-making and the unions have always insisted on keeping pay and collective bargaining off the Neddy agenda. Yet in areas of weak unionism such as retail distribution, hotels and catering and textiles, the Little Neddies have achieved some success.

In retrospect, we can see the 1962 TUC decision to join Neddy was crucial, though it was not until the middle seventies that the trade union movement actually welcomed close involvement with the workings of the state. The deep antipathy to law and the courts in the unions has a long history going back to the Combination laws and the Tolpuddle martyrs. The very origins of the Labour Party stemmed from adverse legal judgments that threatened free trade unionism in the 1890s and the Taff Vale case of 1903 stimulated union commitment to the need for a separate political voice in Parliament. Until very recently unions always resisted the idea that the state could be used to better industrial relations. The limited aim of the law was to widen union freedom and autonomy and nothing more. Union leaders proved articulate, effective champions of voluntarism, so there was not even consistent pressure on governments to legislate over contracts of employment, working hours and holidays. These were to be left to the bargainers. The 1963 Contracts of Employment Act was a clear breach with the past. So was the 1970 Equal Pay Act. But the cause of enlightened labour law suffered setbacks in the late sixties and early seventies. The 1969 White Paper—In Place of Strife – contained a number of positive proposals to strengthen unions. Unfortunately union leaders also believed the attempt to fine and punish unions for the wildcat behaviour of unofficial strikers was a direct threat to their own freedom to act in their own best interests. The Labour cabinet was compelled to retreat in June 1969 before the powerful alliance of the unions and their allies in the Parliamentary Labour Party.

In June 1970 Edward Heath won an unexpected election victory and came to power with a determination to force through a reform of the unions by legislation. The 1971 Industrial Relations Act was the result. The national industrial relations court under Sir John Donaldson was to administer the new law, which brought the trade union movement firmly within a legal framework which clearly defined the limits on their behaviour. The depths of opposition among union leaders to the 1971 Act took many people by surprise. For once, the TUC managed to establish a solid and effective policy to boycott the Act, though individual unions were allowed to defend themselves before the court. Under the 1971 Act, all unions had to register, if they intended to enjoy the legal immunities and privileges of *bona fide* unions. Thanks to the militant stand of the Amalgamated Union of Engineering Workers in 1972, the TUC agreed to 'instruct' all its affiliates to deregister. Twenty-two refused to do so for a variety of often plausible reasons and they were expelled from the TUC for their pains. Luckily for trade union unity, none of the larger unions stayed on the register, though it was touch and go with the Electricians, the General and Municipal Workers and the National and Local Government Officers Association (NALGO).

The repeal of the 1971 Act was a foregone conclusion with the return of a Labour Government. It became one of the first urgent tasks of the minority administration in the spring of 1974, but Labour did not return the legal position to the pre-1971 situation. Under the 1974 Trade Union and Labour Relations Act (amended in 1976) and the 1975 Employment Protection Act, the law has provided a new stimulus for the unions to behave in a constructive way. These measures widened trade unions rights in areas such as dismissal and redundancy, maternity leave and provision of time off work to carry out union duties. An Advisory, Conciliation and Arbitration Service (ACAS) was established to act as an independent body in solving industrial disputes and bettering industrial relations. Its first chairman is Jim Mortimer, former general secretary of the draughtsmen's union, DATA.

New voluntary legal bodies such as the Central Arbitration Committee and the Employment Appeal Tribunal have been created to help in the working of the labour laws. Trade unionists are playing an active part on those bodies. Jack Jones called the Employment Protection Act 'a workers' charter', though its provisions only help bring British standards on the shop floor up to the level of our European neighbours and the body of case law may help to dilute their impact on the power of managers to run their enterprises regardless.

Trade unionists at national as well as local level are also active on the Manpower Services Commission, established in 1974 to streamline the country's employment policies. There is close union involvement on the Health and Safety at Work Executive, which is chaired by Bill Simpson, former leader of the Foundry Workers. The Equal Opportunities Commission—to further sex equality – also contains its trade union nominees. In an *ad hoc*, unplanned way, the unions are acquiring collective responsibilities, if they are willing to take them.

Union officials co-operated with the industrial training boards from their beginnings in 1963, but the promotion of Hugh Scanlon, AUEW president, to the chairmanship of the Engineering Industry Training Board in 1975 was the first time that any union leader had accepted that ultimate responsibility, and in a sector renowned in the past for restrictive practices and controls on apprenticeship entry and the dilution of skills. Although only a part-time job, running an ITB is a good way for a union leader to widen his perspective. There is no doubt that the TUC'c counsels were helped on unemployment and training by the work of their nominees on the statutory agencies.

Of course, not all such jobs are of immediate or obvious value to the movement as a whole. Having a QUANGO office (quasi-non-government organisation) is often provided as a reward for years of long service in the movement or a lubricant to smooth personal relations and reward an old friend. Ever since the war union bosses have been enmeshed in the patronage system and many proved adept at lobbying their own interest. You will find union leaders on a diverse range of QUANGOs from the Community Relations Commission to the Press Council, from the British Overseas Trade Board to the Metrication Board, from the BBC to the

National Water Council. It is often unclear who appointed them and why, and most are not regularly answerable to the TUC for their actions. Until recently the TUC has displayed little interest in the idea that trade unionists should be directly represented on the boards of the firms they work for. Union nominees do sit on the boards of most of the nationalised industries, though almost all of them come from unions who do not have members in that particular sector. For example, Derek Gladwin of the General and Municipal Workers sits on the Post Office Board and Alan Fisher of the National Union of Public Employees on the board of Harland Wolff, the shipbuilders. Neither have direct union interests in those concerns.

In 1966 the TUC changed its attitude to the issue of worker representation in industry in its evidence to the Donovan Royal Commission where there was a call for a more flexible, modified form of worker participation:

> There is now a growing recognition that at least in industries under public ownership provision should be made at each level in the management structure for trade union representatives of the workpeople employed in these industries to participate in the formulation of policy and in the day to day operation of those industries.

Donovan took no notice and the TUC pursued the issue with desultory concern until the early seventies. A number of sporadic attempts were made to convince government that certain jobs should go to workers in the industry concerned and not to outside union worthies, but they made no impression. Worker directors at top level in the renationalised iron and steel industry after 1967 were not an obviously radical departure and only enjoyed limited influence. As a Warwick University study said of the British Steel scheme:

> The directors had no effect on the decision-making process because the board was not really the place where it occurred; even if it had been things would have changed little; management has a monopoly of knowledge, of language and of authority; the worker directors were individuals with no sanction and no powers.

Under TUC pressure the Labour Party began to examine the industrial democracy issue in the early seventies. In 1974 the TUC came out in favour of equal representation for trade union and employer nominees on the boards of all private and publicly owned firms. The general secretary, Len Murray, made it clear that this was seen by the TUC as 'a logical development of what we have established in collective bargaining'. A committee of inquiry was created in 1975 under the chairmanship of Alan Bullock, the Oxford historian, to examine industrial democracy and the

TUC's proposals in particular. It reported within a year with a divided set of recommendations. The majority backed the idea of parity for employee representatives alongside those representing shareholders on unitary boards for Britain's top private firms with over 2000 workers on their pay-rolls. A minority report from the employer members of the Bullock committee poured cold water on any such idea, going no further than the suggestion that workers in a firm could have minority representation on a supervisory board. The hostile response of Britain's employers to Bullock and the equally critical views of some major unions, notably the Engineers, the General and Municipal Workers and the Electricians, suggest that no government will move drastically into action, though the industrial democracy debate is now no longer concerned with whether it is a good idea but with the pace at which it will come and in what form. Bullock supporters in the unions argue that the movement needs the outside stimulus in order to reform itself. Since the middle-1960s the old negative attitude to worker participation in the unions has begun to erode. It will take time for enthusiasn about industrial democracy to reach the shop floor.

The important new laws of the middle seventies, giving unions the opportunity to extend their power and influence, were the direct result of the political alliance between the unions and the Labour Party, which entered a new phase in 1970. The two partners remain indissolubly linked by emotion and self-interest, the product of history. The unions have always provided the financial muscle, which turned Labour into a mass national party. Ross McKibbin observed of Labour in the early 1920s: 'The Labour Party always needed the unions; the unions did not always need the Labour Party.' But even in the formative years, there were tensions between unions and party over economic policy. Should Labour reflect the interests of the unions or should it embrace a wider concern for the nation as a whole? That question has remained to trouble the party ever since, and it has never been decisively answered.

Today the unions are vital for the financial health of the party, with over 80 per cent of its income derived from union sources. With the rapid decline in individual membership, union affiliation has grown relatively more important. In 1975 trade unionists accounted for 5,750,039 out of Labour's total membership of 6,468,874. Around 80 per cent of votes cast at the Labour Party Conference come from the unions. The unions hold 12 seats on the National Executive outright and the bloc votes help elect five women members, the Young Socialist and the treasurer. As many as 40 per cent of Labour MPs are directly sponsored by a trade union (October 1974). Until very recently, union bosses made a clear distinction between union and political work and a tacit understanding kept the two spheres of influence separate. The union bloc votes were used to buttress the Labour leadership from left-wing attack in the constituency parties and in turn the party leaders kept well clear of any criticism of the way the unions behaved. The union bosses were instrumental in thwarting revisionist efforts to abandon or revise Clause IV of the party constitution in 1959–60, but they could be relied on to turn back the tide of unilateralism that threatened to swamp Labour in 1960.

In Harold Wilson's early years as party leader, considerable efforts were made to play down the umbilical ties between Labour and the unions, in trying to help the party to lose its 'cloth-cap image', which was thought to be electorally damaging. In its 1966 evidence to the Donovan Royal Commission, the TUC stressed the differences not the common interest between the party and the unions.

> Trade unions and political parties perform quite distinct functions and their preoccupations can often be quite different. The growth of the Labour Party to the point where it became the government of the country has entailed a significant divergence of function. The existence of common roots yet distinct functions is therefore the most important feature of the relationship between the trade unions and the Labour Party.

In the TUC's opinion the strength of the alliance now lay 'paradoxically in the looseness of the ties'.

The events of the next few years revitalised the party/union entente at national level. The trauma of *In Place of Strife* and the 1971 Industrial Relations Act made it imperative to cement closer ties between the partners. This led to the creation of the TUC-Labour Party liaison committee in January 1972, which rapidly became a major decision-making body, threatening to usurp the importance of the National Executive itself. The initiative for the committee came from Jack Jones at the 1971 Party Conference. As he explained to delegates: 'There is no reason at all why a joint policy cannot be worked out. But let us have the closest possible liaison. This is not just a matter of brainstorming in the back rooms of Congress or Transport House just before the next election. In the past we have not had the dialogue necessary.' The committee, which meets once a month, is made up of six representatives from the TUC General Council, the National Executive and the Parliamentary Labour Party. All the policy initiatives of 1974–7 were the result of liaison committee work. The close, intimate involvement of union leaders in the inner counsels of the party was a break with the recent past. The last time there was such formal intimacy came after the 1931 debacle, when the TUC virtually shaped Labour policy.

The identity of interest between the unions and Labour was never total and the strains imposed by inflation and economic failure made it very difficult to hold the alliance together. After all, unions are not in business to pull Labour's chestnuts out of the fire. True, union activists share an unquestioning loyalty to the aims of the Labour 'movement'. As Martin

Harrison wrote in 1960, 'No one who has worked among trade unionists could fail to be aware of how often affiliation with Labour is taken as a natural and undiscussed part of union life'. This does not mean to say that rank-and-file trade unionists on the shop floor share a similar opinion about the alliance.

David Butler and Donald Stokes in their 1970 study, *Political Change in Britain* discovered that only 17 per cent of the sample of voters believed there should be a close tie-up between Labour and the unions and as many as 72 per cent thought the unions should 'stay clear of politics'. The 1976 Houghton committee on financial aid to political parties found 51 per cent of their survey sample thought it was 'a bad thing' that the Labour Party should get finance from the unions. Opposition to a formal link between the unions and Labour is even strong among those who are regarded as traditional Labour voters. Stephen Hill in his 1976 study of London dockers found that 60 per cent of his admittedly small sample disliked the alliance.

There is now fairly conclusive survey evidence to suggest that very few workers see either the unions they belong to or Labour as anything more than what Robert McKenzie and Eric Silver called 'defence organisations required to insure the working class obtain their "fair share" '. As they argued, 'Only a few see these organisations as means whereby to transform or radically alter present social and economic arrangements'. To a great extent, the economic views of most trade unionists seem closer to the Conservatives than the Labour Party. A 1976 survey by the Confederation of British Industry found that 86 per cent of the sample of trade union manual workers believed it was important to live in a free enterprise society and 82 per cent disagreed with the suggestion that profit was a dirty word.

Most trade unionists do not see the organisation they belong to as a way of achieving democratic self-government. They fail to share the wider political goals of the activist minority who run the unions at all levels. Members tend to view their union membership card as a kind of commodity, which they pay for in order to gain tangible rewards in better pay and working conditions. In the words of John Goldthorpe and his colleagues, whose survey of Vauxhall car workers in Luton in the early sixties remains seminal, they practice 'instrumental collectivism – the achievement of individual private goals outside the workplace'. Just so long as unions appear to be delivering the goods through the bargaining process, members will tolerate the political activities of the minority. But if a union fails to fulfil its primary function, the members are liable to grow dangerously restive.

In his study of the Engineers before 1967 Irving Richter argued 'the unions remain primarily concerned with *more* within the existing framework and political action will be mainly designed to protect their power to achieve that goal'. But this is much closer to business unionism, American style, than what we have in Britain, where ideology still dominates the outlook of many hard-headed union bosses.

The large union affiliation figure to the Labour Party is highly misleading. Under the 1946 Trade Unions Act, trade union members can contract out of paying the individual political levy each year that their union (if affiliated to Labour) pays into the party coffers. This means making a positive decision to refuse payment to Labour and few trade unionists are prepared to make the effort as a matter of principle for such a puny sum of money. Moreover, many have no idea that they contribute anything to the Labour Party. Goldthorpe and his colleagues found a third to a half of the five occupational groups of Vauxhall car workers they interviewed did not know they were paying any political levy at all. Of those who were aware of the levy, a sizeable number did not think their union should be affiliated to the Labour Party. Nearly a third of the craftsmen and setters (the elite at Vauxhall on the shop floor) had in fact contracted out of paying the levy.

In white-collar unions affiliated to Labour, a large number of the members refuse to pay the levy. In 1974 a mere 49,140 out of the 351,000 members of the Association of Scientific, Technical and Managerial Staffs (ASTMS) bothered to contribute the levy to Labour, though this has not stopped that union from adopting a consistently left-wing line over the years. The Technical and Supervisory section (TASS) of the Engineers is a highly militant organisation under the leadership of a Communist, Ken Gill, but in 1974 as many as 65,745 of its 127,999 members refused to pay the political levy. Many trade unionists in craft unions feel the same way. In 1974 as many as 50,493 of the 129,618 members of the Boilermakers contracted out. A mere 26,000 of the 190,473 members of the Society of Graphical and Allied Trades (SOGAT) paid the levy in the same year. It is only in the general and manual unions that the members do not make the effort in large numbers in refusing to pay the levy.

In fact, in 1975 only 61 out of the 110 unions affiliated to the TUC were also formally tied to the Labour Party and their total membership (as affiliated) accounted for under half the rank and file in the trade union movement. This has not stopped unions such as the National and Local Government Officers Association (NALGO), who only joined the TUC in 1965, and the Civil and Public Services Association (CPSA), which recruits in the clerical grades of the civil service, from adopting radical policies, even if they have always rejected any suggestion they should forge formal links with Labour. The last sizeable union to join the party was the Post Office Engineering Union as long ago as 1964, and it looks most unlikely that any others will do so over the next few years.

The existence of a sizeable minority of non-party affiliated unions in the TUC and the growing practice of white-collar workers to contract out of the levy make it difficult for the union bosses and Labour leaders to enjoy a close, working alliance. Yet pressure from below did not wreck the social contract until 1977.

Our unions are not highly centralised, tightly disciplined monoliths where tough bosses bark out orders to an obedient cadre. To a very alarming extent, the very reverse is closer to the truth. Unions at the centre lack power, rather than enjoy too much, and the crisis of authority has grown much worse since the early sixties. It is the shop stewards and staff union representatives who are the direct union presence at the workplace. What order and cohesion still exist in shop-floor bargaining are the result of their efforts. Only since the middle fifties have stewards begun to acquire recognition for their work from the unions. The 1968 Donovan Royal Commission argued that they were 'rarely agitators pushing workers towards unconstitutional action' – quite the opposite: 'Commonly they are the supporters of order, exercising a restraining influence on their members in conditions which promote disorder.' In the words of W.E.J. McCarthy and Stanley Parker in their social survey for Donovan, 'For the most part the steward is viewed by others, and views himself, as an accepted, reasonable and even moderating influence; more of a lubricant than an irritant'.

Contrary to popular belief, stewards are not dogmatic zealots leading a bewildered workforce by the nose. The vast majority are in no sense militants. Nor do they often have party political perspective on industrial relations. The Parker and McCarthy survey discovered that a mere 17 per cent of stewards actually belonged to a political party. Yet these are the men and women who act as the unpaid subalterns of the unions. It is they who have to bear the burdens of the new labour laws. A 1975 TUC estimate suggested there are 291,000 workplace representatives in Britain, about one for every 65 trade unionists and nearly half of them belong to the three biggest unions—the Transport and General Workers, the Engineers and the General and Municipal Workers.

Most are bargainers with management. In his important 1976 PEP study—*Wage Determination in Industry*—W. W. Daniels found an astonishing 90 per cent of all union negotiators in manufacturing industry were predominantly part-timers. As there are only around 2800 full-time union officials in the whole country, this is not perhaps so surprising. Daniels wrote:

> In only about half of the cases was a full-time officer of the union, at any level, spontaneously cited as having been involved in preparing the claim. And in only a quarter of the cases where a full-time officer had been involved was he identified as having had the most influence in the preparation of the case. Thus, although wage negotiations often involved consideration of complex financial, statistical and technical issues, they were very frequently conducted on the union side by lay officers with little or no training and without any expert or professional support or advisory services.

Daniels concluded that over vast areas of private industry trade union bargainers now operate largely independently of their formal union structures and written national or company-wide agreements, so they are far less sensitive to exhortation or pressure from above to follow a particular tactic or line of policy. The extent of decentralisation and fragmentation should not be exaggerated. In the nationalised industries and the service sector, where trade unionism remains traditionally weak, plant bargaining is less important. Nevertheless the trend to greater shop-floor autonomy has grown rapidly since it was first spelled out dramatically by the Donovan Royal Commission in 1968. So far the political implications of a potentially anarchic industrial relations system have not been worked out satisfactorily, but it is undoubtedly going to make it much harder for the politically conscious union minority to exercise control and influence over what happens down at shop-floor level.

To what extent do union leaders in head office and the branches speak for the membership? Lack of interest in the affairs of the union is a common complaint about the rank and file. Attendance at branch meetings is usually very low and voting in union elections often appears derisory. In 1948 PEP calculated no more than 15 to 20 per cent of trade unionists went to their branches, while Professor Ben Roberts suggested the turnout was more like 4 to 7 per cent in the middle 1950s. Joseph Goldstein in his classic study of the Transport and General Workers at the time, in the heyday of Arthur Deakin, claimed TGWU branch attendance never rose much about 15 per cent.

It is probable that rank-and-file involvement has grown less since that period. Goldthorpe and his colleagues found as many as 60 per cent of Vauxhall car workers in Luton in the middle sixties had 'never' attended a branch meeting of their union. In a study of London Transport in 1975, Denis Brooks found only 4 per cent of busmen went to branch meetings and 3 per cent of the station staff. Bob Fryer and colleagues in Warwick University sociology department reckoned 67 per cent of NUPE branches had no more than 5 per cent of their members turning out to meetings. The picture is almost universally bleak, for what goes on at the branch is routine and tedious, attracting only the political zealot or the bureaucrat. Years ago a union branch was a thriving centre of social and intellectual life, but few want to devote their leisure hours away from home to the necessary chores of union administration. In most unions the branch is based on a geographical area, not the place of work. Efforts are being made to reorganise union structures to enable branches to evolve on the shop floor.

Elections usually arouse a similar lack of rank-and-file response. Most full-time union officials never face elections, for they are usually appointed by committees of elected part-timers. In the manual unions the union boss is invariably elected, through usually on small turnouts through the branch system. In the case of the Mineworkers and the Engineers the ballot box is the chosen method. The former vote at the pithead in polls administered by the independent Electoral Reform Society, while the latter since 1972 have had a postal ballot system. Both enjoy substantial participation in their elections, compared with other unions. In most, the annual conference remains the supreme governing body, where delegates (mostly from the activist minority) decide on major policy issues. But the Mineworkers are fond of by-passing conference decisions through a mass ballot of the entire membership on crucial issues such as pay settlements and the decision to strike. During the 1972 and 1974 national coal strikes, the rank and file gave impressive backing to their leaders through the ballot box. There is a widespread assumption that the majority of trade unionists are sound and reasonable people, who if they only took a more active part in the affairs of their unions would swamp the 'extremists', alleged to be manipulating the true voice of the shopfloor. The Conservative Party wants to encourage more unions to democratise their organisations by offering state financial help for the holding of ballots, but it is doubtful whether this will make much dramatic difference.

In May 1972 the Heath Government activated the ballot clauses of the 1971 Industrial Relations Act to test the views of railwaymen, whose unions had decided on strike action. The result was an impressive endorsement by the members of their union leaders. During the late sixties a growing number of unions took practical steps to narrow the gap between their formal structures and the realities of the shop floor. The Electricians and the General and Municipal Workers introduced the idea of industrial conferences, which brings together similar groups of workers to discuss their common problems. As John Hughes argued in a research paper for Donovan,

> As the arrangements fall into an accepted and expected pattern they can be seen as the development of a largely unwritten constitution of considerable significance in the formation of the union's industrial policies. Through these channels the industrial interests of active members are developed. their views are co-ordinated and at the same time the participants can be given a wider view of the union's concerns and a sense of its principles and strategy can emerge.

It is a sensible way of co-ordinating the work of the shop-stewards and making sure the union machine does not lose control of what is going on among the members. Yet this is a perpetual and lasting dilemma, pinpointed as long ago as 1896 by the Webbs in their *Industrial Democracy*.

> Directly the working man representative becomes properly equipped for one half of his duties, he ceases to be especially qualified for the other. If he remains essentially a manual worker, he fails to cope with the brain-working officials; if he takes on the character of the brain-worker, he is

apt to get out of touch with the constituents whose desires he has to interpret.

More elections in the unions of full-time officials (and their need to face re-election) is unlikely to make those bodies any more stable or cautious, but quite the opposite. Rank-and-file moods tend to be fickle. The ultimate test for a union is how successful it remains in improving and safeguarding the living standards of the members. Union democracy (in all shapes and sizes) is a safeguard against oligarchic, ineffective rule, but it remains a necessary second.

Giving the unions responsibility and making them accountable to the 'national interest' is what has preoccupied much of the top level debate about the unions since the fifties. This trend is in direct conflict with the spread of decision-making across the shop floor, that has gathered pace in the intervening period. 'All power to the centre' used to be a favourite slogan of union reformers. Michael Shanks in his *Stagnant Society* (1960) and Eric Wigham in *What is Wrong with the Unions?* (1961) laid particular emphasis on the need to give the Trade Union Congress more authority.

Yet in essence, the TUC remains what it always has been since Citrine's changes in the early 1920s—a loose confederation of autonomous and disparate members, not a centralised unit. An effort at reform was made between 1943 and 1947 but it failed. 'It is one thing to plan an entirely new structure on unoccupied ground; it is another to plan and rebuild where so many institutions already exist. Basic structural changes are impracticable', concluded the 1947 TUC report. 'Practical experience shows that the obstacle to greater cohesion is the tendency to struggle for the union or the theory of organisation, in which members have an interest or a loyalty, rather than the trade union movement as a whole.'

Another attempt at union reform was launched in 1962. George Woodcock gave it his cautious blessing. 'Structure is a function of purpose', he informed delegates. But nothing dramatic emerged from the half-hearted internal effort. As Woodcock explained to the 1963 TUC, 'All unions are equal. All are of equal merit; all of equal value. The problem for the TUC is how to hold together unions free, sovereign and independent in themselves and at the same time make some common step forward'. A reason for the ultimate failure at union reform in the early sixties was the unrealistic interest in the idea of industrial unionism and the virtual neglect of what could be done with the TUC itself. When it became clear that the only way in which Britain could enjoy one union for every major industry was through the break-up of the three big manual unions, there was no chance at all of further progress. Frank Cousins, the abrasive general secretary of the Transport and General Workers (1955–69), suggested at the 1963 TUC that his union provided the best model for change. There were some union mergers and amalgamations, initiated by the TUC, but it was a sad anticlimax for the high hopes of 1962.

The 1970 TUC interim report on structure was well aware of the obstacles to change. As it argued: 'The TUC is primarily concerned with developing policy rather than acting as an executive body. It produces a means through which unions can collectively achieve objectives which they cannot achieve, or which it could be difficult for them to achieve separately.' As the establisher of 'standards of good union practice', the TUC has a role, but not as an executive. 'It would be meaningless for the general council to be given powers to direct and instruct unions unless unions in their turn have the same powers over their members', said the 1970 report. Persuasion and argument were seen as the only way in which to win union willingness 'to abide by decisions to which they are parties'.

This was a sober recognition of the possible in the trade union movement, but it fell short of any major critique of what is wrong, if anything, with the existing system. The gap between the political activists and the union rank and file, between the formal and informal industrial relations structures, threatens to stimulate instability. But the single, overriding cause of friction in the unions stems from their sheer number. In 1900 there were 1323 trade unions covering a membership of 2,022,000 workers. At the end of 1975 there were still as many as 488, representing just under 12,000,000 workers or half the total labour force of the country. Only 111 of those were actually members of the TUC. Of course, the vast majority of trade unionists belong to a handful of unions. A mere 11 have more than 250,000 members and these account for nearly two-thirds of the entire unionised workforce. The mighty Transport and General Workers, with members in almost every occupational group, now boasts nearly 2,000,000 in its ranks.

At factory level joint shop steward committees usually bring together activists from the different unions in the plant where they can try and establish a common cause. These are often *ad hoc*, informal arrangements, the result of custom and practice rather than neat procedures hammered out beyond the factory gates. A major recommendation of the 1977 Bullock committee on industrial democracy was the establishment of a joint representation committee in each private company made up of stewards from the different unions. This body was to be the catalyst for change, which cut right through the archaic lines of union demarcation. We know that 98 per cent of British industry is trouble-free. Strikes remain a rarity, despite the adverse publicity they bring. Moreover the unofficial, short, sharp stoppage, so much a feature of industrial relations in the fifties and sixties, has now become less prevalent. But the widespread existence of multi-unionism in industry does make it more difficult to establish harmony and cohesion. Many employers can use the diversity of unions to divide and rule. The lack of a common strategy can often weaken the solidarity of the shop floor.

A fatal consequence of too many unions without clear spheres of influence is that we get trade unionism on the cheap in Britain. In real terms, a union member paid far more before the war than he or she does now. On the basis of 1974 TUC returns the average annual contribution worked out at £6.99, just over 13p a week or less than the price of half a pint of beer. Competition for members compels most unions to keep their subscription rates low. Most face sizeable labour turnovers every year and find it difficult to stand still. They do not want to lose their attraction to potential members. As a consequence, unions lack a professional expertise to give their members comprehensive servicing. Dislike of bureaucracy is deep rooted in the movement and that is a healthy attitude, but not if it leads to a complacent neglect of union education, so that the bargainers lack the elementary skills when they face their employers over the table to argue about the annual wage claim and company profits. Ever since Citrine's day, the TUC has sporadically shown an interest in becoming the general staff of labour. Cost has dimmed any pretensions of collective power. Most unions are unable or unwilling to insist on realistic subscription rates that even keep up with the rate of inflation.

Of course union monopolies do exist in areas like printing, mining, shipbuilding and the railways. The spread of the closed shop – which has speeded up since the late sixties and especially since the repeal of the 1971 Industrial Relations Act – has restricted the ability of workers to move from one union into another. The TUC 1939 Bridlington agreement is supposed to stop inter-union poaching, but this remains an erratic safeguard. Unions may lay claim to whole tracts in recruitment drives, but they lack any effective sanctions to uphold them against the competition from others. Blurred lines between the unions involve union officials and managers spending much of their time in a duplication of effort. All this weakens union effectiveness.

Yet such problems have not halted the onward march of the unions. In fact, from 1969 until 1974 trade unionism enjoyed one of its major growths, comparable to the explosion in union recruitment between 1918 and 1920 and the late forties. In 1969 only 44.4 per cent of the workforce was unionised; but six years later the proportion had risen to just over half. After a period of relative stagnation, the unions regained the initiative, even though the old traditional centres of power like coalmining, textiles and the railways were in steep decline and the new sectors like banking and insurance lacked any trade union experience. Much of the gain came in the mushrooming public service sectors like local government administration and the health service. Unions like NALGO, NUPE and the Confederation of Health Service Employees enjoyed particular expansion. But figures comparing 1948 with 1974 published in the Bullock report suggest that a substantial cause of union growth was the ability of the unions to extend their recruitment in traditional areas where the manual workers were present. As Professor Bain and Robert Price argued, 'The level of manual union density achieved in 1974 has only been equalled once before, in 1920 at the height of the short-lived boom in union membership following the end of World War I'.

Clive Jenkins's ASTMS was the main beneficiary of the growth in private services. In 1964 ASSET (as it was then called) claimed to have a mere 72,800 members; by 1976 the union boasted 374,000 and it had become the eighth biggest in the TUC. A major expansion took place during the period in female recruitment to the unions. In 1964 only 28.6 per cent of all working women were in unions; a decade later the proportion had risen to 36.7 per cent. As there were 2,209,000 women trade unionists in 1964 and 3,190,000 a decade later, this amounts to a significant expansion. Why, despite the widespread unpopularity of trade unionism, has belonging to a union become more popular over the past decade?

Robert Bacon and Walter Eltis in their influential book—*Britain's Economic Problem: Too Few Producers* (1976)—suggest the reason is the belief among many workers that they need the protection of a union to face the threat of rising direct taxation. As they wrote,

> What has happened since 1963 is that all too often those who sought higher living standards, or the mere continuation of car and home ownership (which have risen in cost far more than prices in general) found that they could only obtain these by making full use of their trade union power, with the result that ordinary workers turned to aggressive union leaders to produce results.

George Bain and Farouk Elsheikh in a recent book, *Union Growth and the Economic Cycle* (Oxford, 1976), highlight the impact of rising prices and wages on union membership expansion. In particular, they argue this is why there was an 'explosion' in union growth in 1969–70.

> Price rises generally have a positive impact upon union growth because of the 'threat effect' – the tendency of workers to unionise in an attempt to defend their standard of living against the threat posed by rising prices – and wage rises will have a similar impact because of the 'credit effect' – the tendency of workers to credit wage rises to unions and to support them in the hope of doing well or even better in the future.

The overwhelming evidence backs the view that people join unions either to safeguard or improve their wages, so we can conclude that the new recruits since 1969 have little sympathy with the calls of restraint inherent in the social contract between Labour and the unions. Strikes can prove effective recruiting sergeants. The militancy from NUPE and the public service unions after 1969 helped to transform traditional anti-union attitudes among many workers in hitherto passive and badly organised sectors of the labour force. Growth was also aided by the growth in the concentration of companies and the decline in small workplace units. The successive round of mergers and takeovers that hit British capitalism from the middle sixties helped the cause of trade unionism. Not only did the growth of large combines like GEC/AEI and ICI encourage union expansionism, it made beloging to a union more attractive to workers, uneasy about their position at a time of radical change.

It is also fair to add that some union growth came as the result of moral coercion by a more systematic use of the closed shop in industry. More positively, the 1968 Donovan Royal Commission and its aftermath created a new favourable climate for union growth and more sympathetic attitude to unions from many employers, who began to see the value of collective bargaining. The Commission on Industrial Relations (CIR) enjoyed only a brief life from 1969 to 1974, being killed off because of guilt by association with the machinery of the Industrial Relations Act, but it preached the virtues of trade unionism with some success.

By the standards of Western European trade unionism, our movement has a patchy record. Overseas observers are impressed by the calibre of our top union leaders, but Britain is a low-labour-cost country with poorer fringe benefits than her neighbours. The fragmented structure of the unions, which often try to transcend the real manual/white collar divisions, generates less awareness of the economic rewards and privileges enjoyed by different groups of workers. Pay differentials and relativities remain hallowed by custom and practice and they bedevil the creation of a rational industrial relations system, making it so much more difficult to establish a permanent, egalitarian incomes policy, which may be the Labour answer to the problems of a mixed economy.

During the past 32 years the strains imposed upon Britain's trade unions have grown more, not less, intense. Like so many other institutions (the city, the civil service, big business) they have been slow to modernise or even accept the necessity of change. In their muddled way they have tried to hold on to familiar ways of doing things and stoutly resisted outside attempts at reform.

The rhetoric of 'free' collective bargaining still dominates the TUC. Union leaders often seem to be the last champions of *laissez-faire* capitalism. But the survival of the fittest is a peculiar dogma for unions to embrace. Those who can see beyond the size of the next wage claim realise the inherent foolishness of such a sectionalist attitude, while those, like the miners, electrical power engineers and electricians, who have muscle can get what they want and the rest of society must suffer from the cruel, arbitrary rules of the market place. Jack Jones told his executive in the spring of 1977 about the pitfalls of voluntarism. As he argued, 'voluntary bargaining does not mean doing the hell what we like'. Unfettered free negotiations over pay have rarely occurred in the years since the war and when they have they did little to help the low-paid and those too weak to be organised in unions. Supply and demand rather than union power has usually decided the issue. Belonging to a union means average pay settlements rather than large awards or very small ones.

As W. G. Runciman discovered in his book *Relative Deprivation and Social Justice*, most British workers share surprisingly small terms of reference when they compare their wage levels with each other. Calls for making the 'rich squeal' seldom manage to achieve any enthusiastic response from rank-and-file trade unionists. Union pressure for egalitarianism is much weaker than many politicians and union bosses realise. As W. W. Daniels found in his 1976 PEP survey, 'It is people's position relative to others in the same social class that influences their evaluation of their own circumstances rather than their position compared to that of people in other classes'; and he concluded that 'disputes over issues of pay relativities spring more from the system of collective bargaining of which they are part than from any spontaneous or deep felt sense of injustice on the part of the workers they represent in the disputes'.

Our conclusion is unclear. We suffer from a fragmented, decentralised system of collective bargaining with a multiplicity of unions. No coherent philosophy binds them together. The Socialist ethic, however vague in conception, still claims the loyalty of most union bosses. The social contract is the latest expression of their alliance with Labour, the party they formed and nurture. But the rank and file, whether they are white-collar or manual workers, seldom share even a rough sense of social justice. To them, market forces are dominant. British workers are not a revolutionary, class-conscious proletariat. Sectionalism and division are still major obstacles to trade union unity. Over the past decade two opposing trends have accentuated the dilemmas for British trade unionism. Pressure for union influence through power over decision-making has grown more intense and successful. The TUC is a mighty power in the land, which no government can ignore. On the other hand, bargaining has grown more fragmented and *ad hoc* and the gulf between full-time officialdom with its formal rubric and the lay part-time members, who pay the dues and carry out much of the unrewarding work that makes unions work, has grown steadily wider. At times of crisis such as July 1975 union leaders can achieve a remarkable degree of consent from those they claim to represent, but so far this has only been for limited periods of time (1948 – 51, 1964 – 7, 1975 – 7). Nothing permanent has yet been achieved which will bind leaders and members together in a common cause.

But Britain is not a collectivist society. The cause of freedom is deeply rooted in all classes. Parliamentary democracy and the mixed economy have many vocal champions in the trade union movement. And despite the serious deterioration in our economic performance since the early sixties, faith in those institutions has not been diminished. The impressive spread of trade unionism since 1969 should not lead the enemies of the unions to assume that Britain is well down the road to a class tyranny. Unions remain flimsy bodies, unsure of their strength and very much on the defensive. The legal gains of 1974 – 6 and the growth of union influence over many

QUANGO organisations promise to give the unions a more constructive outlook, even if most of the members will play only a limited part in their activities and expect them to concentrate their primary effort on materialistic goals. Our unions are prisoners of their own history, so when they change they do so only with reluctance and under pressure. It will take more bitter experience before we can expect British trade unionism to became a progressive force. The hard fact remains—we simply cannot do without the unions. They have become unfortunate necessities.

6 Nationalisation and Public Ownership

David Steel

Few issues in post-war British politics have generated as much heat as nationalisation. Its explosive potential was revealed again during 1976. It might be expected that the decision to nationalise two industries, aerospace and shipbuilding, both of which had in recent years been intimately involved with government, would have provoked little opposition. In fact, however, the passage of the legislation was contested with a ferocity not seen for many years.

To understand why passions flowed so strongly, and the peculiarly bitter political debate on this subject, it is necessary to appreciate the vital role of nationalisation and free enterprise in the bloodstream of British party politics. Since its inception, the Labour Party has accorded nationalisation a high place among its idols and any attempt to downgrade its importance has been strongly resisted within the party. For their part, the Conservatives have seen themselves as the champions of free enterprise and a vast amount of money and energy has been devoted to the protection of private industry and the denigration of publicly-owned undertakings.

However, examination of the record of both parties and of the course of British politics since 1945 reveals that both nationalisation and free enterprise have served more as symbols than as actual goals. First, it is apparent that during the last thirty years there has only been a comparatively small transfer of private assets into public ownership. Moreover, most of it occurred in the first six years of this period. Otherwise the Labour Party has not given nationalisation priority in its election manifestos, still less in its legislative programmes. At the same time, the Conservatives have accepted, however reluctantly, the bulk of Labour nationalisation and have even been forced by the pressure of events to add to the public sector of industry themselves. In other respects also the parties have not differed as much in relation to industry as their rhetoric might suggest. Both have recognised a need to extend government regulation of and intervention in private industry. Equally there has been a striking consensus of opinion on the organisation of the nationalised industries and their relationship with government. The Labour Party adopted an organisational form for the nationalised industries, the public corporation, which had been pioneered by the Conservatives and, although both parties have criticised the manner and the extent of government intervention, neither has been able to resist the temptation to use the industries as tools of economic management.

It is clear therefore that a marked discrepancy exists between rhetoric and reality. An analysis of party speeches would suggest that the ownership of industry had not only been one of the major issues of post-war politics but also that it had been one of the most divisive issues between the parties. Their records in office, however, provide a rather different picture in which continuity and consensus tend to overshadow the genuine disagreements that certainly have existed. This chapter will attempt to explain how it is that issues which have played such a major part in partisan controversy can be approached so pragmatically and flexibly by the parties in office. To do this satisfactorily, however, it is first necessary to pay some attention to defining the terms nationalisation and public ownership.

Strictly defined, nationalisation is a process in which private assets or shares are transferred into national ownership. Such a transfer can occur in any field of activity and can be effected in many different ways. Thus it is as correct to talk of the nationalisation of the hospitals in 1948 as it is to refer to the nationalisation of industry. In this chapter, however, attention will be confined to the industrial sphere. But it will not look only at the nature and importance of this process in post-war British politics. It will also attempt to assess the impact of the public sector of industry on British politics. This sector is much wider than is commonly thought and is surprisingly difficult to delimit satisfactorily. The most important part of it comprises the nationalised industries but this itself is not an unambiguous term. Certain industries invariably appear in any list but it is first necessary to realise that many of them are not in fact the end-product of nationalisation. For instance, the postal service and the atomic energy industry have never been privately owned. However, there are also a number of industries included on some lists but not on others. To overcome this problem a particular organisational form, the public corporation, has often been used as the criterion for inclusion but this is not satisfactory for a number of reasons. Not only is there little agreement as to the essential characteristics of a public corporation; it also overlooks the fact that some industrial and commercial activities are the responsibility of government departments and local authorities and that increasingly public ownership is occurring through other organisational forms such as wholly-owned and mixed-enterprise limited liability companies.

These questions of definition have not been raised merely to confuse the reader. Rather they provide the basic framework for this chapter. First, the extent of nationalisation in its strict sense will be discussed and an explanation sought of its role in British politics. Secondly, the manner in which the affairs of the public sector of industry, defined in this chapter as all industrial and commercial undertakings in public ownership except for those owned by local authorities and those run directly by central departments (see Table 6.2, p.   ), have impinged upon British politics will be examined.[1] Finally a number of recent trends will be identified which have served to reduce the importance of public ownership, at least in its traditional forms, in comparison with other means of state intervention and participation in industry.

Nationalisation 1945-76

The Labour Party entered office in 1945 committed to the enactment of a major programme of nationalisation. Its plans had been given prominence in its election manifesto, *Let Us Face the Future*, and included public ownership of coal, gas, electricity, a large part of inland transport and the iron and steel industry. During the next six years these commitments were implemented, thus achieving the most substantial transfer in industrial ownership that has occurred in British history. By 1951 many of the most important sectors of the economy were in public ownership and the size of the public sector had been increased by some two million employees (see Table 6.1). Nevertheless it is important not to exaggerate the extent of the transfer that took place. Various undertakings, such as the British Overseas Airways Corporation and the London Passenger Transport Board, were publicly owned before the war and substantial parts of the electricity and gas industries had been in municipal ownership. Moreover, the significance of nationalisation in terms of its effect upon the independence of the industries was moderated by the extensive control that had existed beforehand in almost every case.

Thus by 1951 the Labour Party had put into effect its main commitments in respect of nationalisation. In both the 1950 and 1951 elections, however, nationalisation was a major issue. In 1950, although the legislation had been enacted, the nationalisation of the iron and steel industry had not actually taken place and there was also controversy about the Labour Party's intentions in other sectors of industry. Its manifesto only contained two firm commitments, beet sugar manufacture and sugar refining and the cement industry, but the Conservatives made much of the Government's stated intention of reviewing other industries as candidates for public ownership. The outcome of the election was the return of the Labour Government but with a much reduced majority. Nevertheless it was sufficient for the nationalisation of iron and steel to be effected. The Iron and Steel Corporation, however, never grew out of early infancy. Immediately after the Conservative election victory in October 1951, a direction was issued to the Corporation prohibiting further changes in the

Table 6.1   Nationalisation 1945–51

Sector	Bodies created/reconstituted	Vesting date	Numbers employed in 1951
Finance	Bank of England	1946	6,700
Energy	National Coal Board	1947	765,000
	British Electricity Authority	1948	178,900
	North of Scotland Hydro-Electric Board	1948[1]	
	Gas Council	1949	143,500
	Area Gas Boards (12)	1949	
Industry	Iron and Steel Corporation	1951	292,000
Transport	British Transport Commission	1948	888,000
	British Overseas Airways Corporation	1946[2]	
	British European Airways	1946	23,300
	British South American Airways	1946	
Telecommunications	Cable and Wireless Ltd	1947	9,500
			2,306,900

[1] The North of Scotland Hydro-Electric Board had been created in 1943 and its constitution was only slightly modified in 1948.
[2] BOAC had nominally been in existence since 1939.

industry's financial and management structure and the Iron and Steel Act
was repealed in 1953. However, the Conservatives' programme of
denationalisation was modest, the only other instance being the road
haulage industry. Nor was either of these programmes entirely successful.
One major iron and steel company, Richard Thomas and Baldwins Ltd,
and a number of smaller enterprises remained in public ownership as no
private purchaser could be found. Difficulties were also encountered in
disposing of much of British Road Services, particularly those parts which
made up the trunk service, and under pressure from the users of this service
the Government was persuaded to allow the British Transport Commission to retain most of its long-distance fleet.

During the next twenty years British governments engaged in little
nationalisation or denationalisation. For the rest of their long tenure of
office up to 1964, the Conservatives took no steps to return any of the major
nationalised industries to private ownership. However, the powers of some
of the existing corporations to acquire additional undertakings were
curtailed. This policy was reversed after the return of a Labour
Government in October 1964 and led for example to a significant
extension of public ownership in the bus industry. However, in general, the
Labour Government did not accord a high priority to nationalisation. The
only pledges contained in its 1964 manifesto were the renationalisation of
iron and steel and the reorganisation of the water supply industry under
full public ownership. The former was initially frustrated by the
Government's small majority but was duly implemented in 1967 after its
parliamentary position had been strengthened by the 1966 election. This
was the single piece of traditional nationalisation during almost six years of
Labour government. Water supply, a large part of which was already
publicly owned, was not nationalised and although a bill was introduced to
nationalise those ports not already owned by the British Transport Docks
Board its enactment was frustrated by the dissolution of Parliament in May
1970.

Significant changes did however take place in the boundary between
public and private ownership. This period saw a very major extension in
state intervention in private industry and this included the acquisition of
equity holdings in private undertakings. In 1966 an Industrial Re-
organisation Corporation (IRC) was established to promote the re-
structuring of British industry in the interests of industrial efficiency. One
means of doing this was through the acquisition of equity shares and by
1971 the IRC held shares in eleven companies. Nevertheless its sharehold-
ing was relatively modest, especially when viewed in the light of the other
forms of assistance the IRC provided for private industry.[2] Under the
terms of the Industrial Expansion Act of 1968 the Government was also
empowered to give financial support to firms in a variety of ways including
the subscription of share capital. Without further recourse to Parliament it
could acquire even a majority holding in a company and these powers

were therefore vigorously attacked by the Conservatives as 'backdoor nationalisation'. In practice, however, few opportunities were found to make use of this part of the Act, the only major example being the Government's stake in International Computers (Holdings) Ltd. Similarly, although the Government provided substantial assistance to the shipbuilding industry under the terms of the Shipbuilding Industry Act of 1967, it only acquired shares in two cases.

During the 1960s, therefore, there was a marked expansion of state involvement in industry, if not in the size of the nationalised sector, and in reaction to this Conservative attitudes tended to harden. In the 1970 election they committed themselves to a policy of 'disengagement', designed to reduce the role of the state and to encourage efficiency. This covered a wide range of government activities but as far as industry was concerned three specific proposals were made. First, there was to be no further nationalisation, either of the traditional or the new 'backdoor' kind. Secondly, any part of a nationalised industry which was regarded as peripheral to its main functions was to be sold. Thirdly, private capital was to be introduced into the financing of the major nationalised industries in order to promote greater managerial efficiency. For two years after achieving office these policies were pursued vigorously although in overall terms the results achieved were only marginal. The IRC was wound up in 1971 and the Industrial Expansion Act repealed; the Carlisle and Scottish state-owned public houses and the two state-owned travel agents, Thomas Cook & Son and Lunn-Poly, were sold; and certain of the British Steel Corporation's brick-making works were sold. None of these examples of 'privatisation', however, could be said to lie in the mainstream of public enterprise. Nor was much progress made towards the introduction of private capital. Some of the British Steel Corporation's and the National Coal Board's ancillary interests were organised into separate limited liability companies, initially wholly owned by the parent board but designed so as to facilitate the infusion of private funds. The other major industry in which this policy was seriously mooted was gas but the Gas Act of 1972 did not include any measures in this direction.

Thus between 1970 and 1972 some minor changes occurred in the boundary between the public and private sectors. Practical considerations, however, limited the Government's ability to implement its more radical plans. In a dramatic reversal of policy the Government took the aero-engine division of Rolls-Royce into public ownership in 1971 so as to avert its collapse. By 1972, under the pressure of a deteriorating economic situation, a different approach to industry was apparent and led to the enactment of a new Industry Act which, although not providing for the acquisition of equity holdings, resumed and even extended the powers of intervention which had existed before 1970. Similar pressures were also working within the Labour Party to revive the question of nationalisation. During its period in opposition between 1970 and 1974, the party became committed not only to nationalisation, in the traditional manner, of the shipbuilding and aerospace industries, the ports and a substantial part of North Sea oil but also to the creation of a National Enterprise Board to resume and develop the work of the IRC. Concerned that the level of investment in private industry had not generally been responsive to the incentives and exhortations provided by government in the 1960s, it was argued that the National Enterprise Board should acquire holdings in leading firms throughout industry and it was suggested that early in its life a controlling interest should be taken in 25 of the country's largest manufacturing firms.

On achieving effective power in October 1974, many of these Labour plans were put into practice. During 1975 and 1976 the British National Oil Corporation and the National Enterprise Board (NEB) were set up and, but for the intervention of the House of Lords, British Shipbuilders and British Aerospace would also have been established. The NEB's powers of acquisition were, however, more circumscribed than the earlier plans had envisaged, so that its role is more akin to that of the IRC. In any case, its activities initially were dominated by the necessity of mounting a rescue operation for the vast British Leyland car undertaking. In 1975, following the recommendations of a report prepared by the chairman of NEB, Lord Ryder, British Leyland was nationalised and its shares transferred to the Board.

This brief survey of the process of nationalisation and denationalisation during the last thirty years gives rise to a number of general observations. First, it is striking how small the transfer of ownership from private to public hands has been during this period. Very different conclusions, however, would be drawn from an analysis of the content of political speeches and campaigns. To understand how such a relatively minor issue has continued to occupy such a major role in the rhetoric of British politics, it is necessary to examine the anatomy of the two political parties that have shared office since 1945 and the pressures that have been exerted upon post-war British governments.

Between 1945 and 1951 the Attlee Government implemented the programme of nationalisation which had been contained in the Labour Party's original 1918 Constitution. As a result, a debate began during the latter part of this period on the role of nationalisation in the party's future plans. This debate has simmered ever since and has occasionally boiled over into heated and bitter argument. On one side have been those who maintain a strong commitment to nationalisation as an essential means towards the achievement of a socialist society. They have argued that as long as economic wealth and power lies in the hands of a small minority the causes of inequality in society cannot be eliminated and, although they have disagreed both on the extent and the speed of the programme, they have advocated the extension of nationalisation to encompass successful as well as unsuccessful sectors of British industry. Against them, however, have been those members of the Labour Party who have adopted a more pragmatic approach to this question. They have accepted the need for nationalisation in certain circumstances but have refused to give it priority among the party's objectives and have argued that there are other more effective means of promoting social justice.

This latter group's arguments have been underpinned by two persuasive facts of British political life: first, the electoral unpopularity of national-isation and, secondly, the dismal record of the existing nationalised industries. On both counts a case can be made for claiming that public opinion is ill-founded. Many of the financial difficulties of the existing industries can be attributed to underlying problems which are unrelated to questions of ownership and many positive claims can be made in support of public enterprise both in this country and overseas. Nevertheless public attitudes on this question are widespread and extremely deep-rooted and no government can afford to ignore them. To support this contention it is only necessary to point to the numerous surveys which have indicated that generally nationalisation is harmful to the Labour Party in electoral terms. For instance, a survey of attitudes during the February 1974 election revealed that over 60 per cent of the electorate were opposed to further nationalisation and less than 10 per cent favoured significantly more nationalisation.[3]

As a result of this public pressure, the Labour Party's election manifestos since 1950 have contained only limited proposals for further national-isation. On the other hand, nationalisation has not disappeared from its plans, still less has it been relegated in the minds of many party activists. In the constituencies and at party headquarters the commitment to this means of progress towards socialism is very deep-rooted, in many cases being greater than the desire to win office. Thus, when in the wake of the party's third successive election defeat in 1959 Hugh Gaitskell proposed that Clause IV of the 1918 Constitution, which commits it 'to secure for the workers by hand or by brain the full fruits of their industry . . . upon the basis of the common ownership of the means of production', should be amended, he was greeted with a storm of protest not only from those traditionally regarded as being on the left wing but also from many throughout the party and the trade union movement, and the proposal had quickly to be abandoned. On the other hand, as has been seen, this defeat did not mean that specific nationalisation proposals increased in prominence, even in the plans of the extra-parliamentary party, or that the behaviour of the next Labour Government was significantly affected. Rather it is illustrative of the complex nature of the coalition of interests that makes up the Labour Party and of the role of certain symbols in maintaining its unity.

An important factor in understanding the Labour Party's attitude on this question during the 1960s was the accession of Harold Wilson to the leadership in 1963. During the next few years he succeeded in turning the debate on industry both within and outside the party away from the question of ownership by presenting a new alternative of co-operation and partnership between government and private industry. However, the advocates of nationalisation were only temporarily quietened. The success of the new approach was only limited and Britain's worsening economic plight brought the arguments in favour of public ownership once more to the fore. In the early 1970s the Labour Party adopted a policy statement calling for further nationalisation, adding to their traditional arguments the claim that private industry had failed to meet the challenge the Government had provided and that only public participation and control could promote the essential regeneration of British industry.

That the Labour Party has not been committed to a major extension of public ownership has not prevented the Conservatives from exploiting this issue to its advantage. Knowing that Labour's parliamentary leaders were on difficult ground, every demand for further nationalisation, irrespective of its origin, has been given prominence by Conservative spokesmen and most of the financial problems of the nationalised industries have been attributed to the fact of ownership almost regardless of any mitigating factors. At the same time, many Conservative supporters have given free enterprise the worship their counterparts have accorded to national-isation. A defence of the virtues of private enterprise can be guaranteed to receive enthusiastic acclaim at Conservative Party gatherings and within the party there exist powerful groups to promote this interest against state intervention and interference. In its campaigns the party has also received substantial support from industrial organisations such as Aims of Industry (now Aims for Freedom and Enterprise), which have been vigorous in disseminating anti-nationalisation propaganda.

However, as has been shown, Conservative Governments have not in practice engaged in much denationalisation and they have also been responsible for major extensions in state intervention in private industry. In part this merely reflects a reluctant acceptance of the *status quo* because of the practical difficulties of unscrambling what Labour Governments have nationalised. They have also realised that many of the services provided by the nationalised industries could not be provided, at least on the same scale, by the private sector. Thus, there was little opposition to the nationalisation of coal or the railways and in present circumstances there are few Conservatives who believe that there is any practicable alternative to public ownership of most of the nationalised industries. Moreover, Conservative Governments, faced with the formidable problems of managing a mixed economy, have found the nationalised industries a useful weapon of intervention which any Chancellor of the Exchequer would be loth to lose.

None of these factors, however, explain Conservative action to extend state intervention in private industry or the occasional additions they have made to the public sector. To understand this it is necessary to examine the pressures which have been perceived by successive British governments since 1945. During this period governments have repeatedly felt compelled to intervene in industry in order to attempt to offset adverse economic trends. In particular they have felt obliged to act when unemployment has reached certain levels. On the basis of by-elections and opinion polls, governments have been aware of the consequences of a high rate of unemployment and, irrespective of its other effects, have almost invariably acted after the level has exceeded the maximum regarded as tolerable.[4] Conservative Governments have also been worried by the effect of bankruptcies on the reputation of private enterprise. More than anything else, it was these factors which produced the about-turn in the industrial policies of the Heath Government in 1971–2. Earlier it had made a determined effort to break away from the interventionist practices of its predecessors but, faced with unemployment of almost one million and the likelihood of dramatic bankruptcies, it not only saved Rolls-Royce but also enacted legislation which extended the powers of the government to assist private industry.

The other striking feature of post-war nationalisation has been the remarkable consensus of opinion as to how it should be effected. First, with only a few exceptions, nationalisation in Britain has been undertaken on an industry-wide basis and has led to the establishment by Act of Parliament of a state monopoly or near-monopoly. Only recently has there even been serious discussion about the nationalisation of particular firms within an industry, let alone any action in this direction. Thus the proposal to nationalise a number of firms in a wide range of industries, advocated recently by the Labour Party, has received particularly vehement opposition. In part this resistance can be explained by the fact that many of the listed companies are successful: for obvious reasons proposals to nationalise successful undertakings have always encountered stronger opposition. Within the Labour Party also there has been resistance from those who have seen nationalisation as an all-or-nothing process. This long-standing view in the party is based not only in ideological arguments about the purposes of nationalisation but also in the belief that decisions in respect of any one industry can only be taken satisfactorily from some central point. Such a view must appear strange to many European social democratic parties who are long accustomed to competition between publicly and privately owned companies.

This view and the extreme caution with which a Labour Government has treated the proposal to nationalise a number of leading firms also reflects widely-held attitudes towards the nature of government intervention. British practice generally looks unfavourably upon government discrimination between firms or individuals. Thus, in the provision of assistance to industry, governments have been reluctant to choose between firms, preferring instead to offer assistance to all firms falling within a particular category. Much of its aid has therefore been given to firms which did not have the ability or the inclination to make good use of it. In contrast other European governments, notably the French, have had no scruples about identifying firms with potential and then backing them to the hilt. In relation to nationalisation these attitudes in Britain have been bolstered by practical difficulties, such as the necessity of following the parliamentary procedure for hybrid bills, which would be encountered if firms engaged in the same line of business were treated differently.[5] There is some evidence that the climate of opinion on these matters is gradually changing and governments in the last decade have certainly intervened more selectively, but discriminatory action still gives rise to widespread concern.

Partly as a consequence of this approach to the question of its scope there has also been continuity in the methods of nationalisation. What is particularly striking is the consensus of opinion on the form of organisation to be adopted for the nationalised industries. During the 1920s there was some debate as to the relative merits of government departments, local authorities and public corporations and there were also some who advocated various forms of workers' control. However, under the influence of figures such as Herbert Morrison, the Labour Party soon became committed to the public corporation as the vehicle of nationalisation. It was designed to insulate the management of public industry from the full force of parliamentary and Treasury control and to permit the recruitment of staff who were experienced in industrial and commercial management. It was thus seen as providing 'a combination of public ownership, public accountability, and business management for public ends'. This form of organisation was pioneered by a Conservative Government in establishing the Central Electricity Board and the BBC but it was the London Passenger Transport Board, devised by the minority Labour Government although brought into operation by its successor, which served as the model for later governments.

The post-1945 public corporations differed in a number of respects from their inter-war predecessors, notably in the powers given to the minister to intervene in their affairs, but the basic features were retained. Moreover this model has been adhered to with a remarkable consistency. Virtually all nationalisation has resulted in the creation of a public corporation to run the industry and the composition and powers of the corporations have been very similar. Indeed much of the wording of the Iron and Steel Act of 1967 is the same as that of the 1949 Act and the British Steel Corporation is in most important respects a carbon copy of the Iron and Steel Corporation. Until the establishment of the National Enterprise Board the main deviations from this pattern were either peripheral or the result of special circumstances. Thus, in the field of transport, a holding company was established in 1963 to have oversight over nationalised interests in road transport and certain other transport activities. Until 1973 when it was dissolved, the Transport Holding Company not only managed those interests it inherited, which continued to be run as separate companies, but also made significant extensions to its holdings notably in the bus industry. Other exceptions, of which the most important is Rolls-Royce, which retained its company structure, were the result of the special circumstances which had led to nationalisation. However, if it survives a change of government, NEB is of much greater significance. Not only is it an important new style of organisation itself, paving the way for new relationships between government and publicly-owned industry, but it also opens up new possibilities in the field of mixed enterprise. This again is a field in which Britain has surprisingly little experience in comparison with most of her neighbours. For most of the post-war period the only major example of such an enterprise was British Petroleum, in which the government acquired a 51 per cent holding in 1914 because of the strategic importance of oil.[6] Nor does BP provide a model for predicting how NEB will deal with those companies in which it has an interest, as it has been a firm policy of successive governments that they would not interefere in the company's commercial affairs and that they would only exercise the right of veto in relation to certain specific matters of general policy. In practice this right of veto has never been used and the Government's nominees on the company's board have not attempted to exercise any special influence. The other main examples of mixed enterprise are in shipbuilding, aerospace and computers, where the Government acquired holdings in the latter part of the 1960s but none of them really provides evidence which is of general application.

That the public corporation has been so dominant in British national-isation is a remarkable tribute to the foresight of its pioneers. Its persistence is perhaps surprising in view of the poor record of the nationalised industries and the dissatisfaction felt by both governments and boards about many of its features. On the other hand, as long as governments see the nationalisation of entire industries as their objective, there is really no alternative vehicle open to them. It would simply not be practicable in our present system of government for ministerial departments to assume responsibility for the nationalised industries nor, for both practical and political reasons, is municipal operation a feasible or desirable option. Moreover, there remains very little interest in any more radical forms of organisation, such as workers' control. Thus any discussion of the impact of the nationalised industries on British politics is inevitably dominated by consideration of the strengths and weaknesses of public corporations.

The Politics of the Nationalised Industries

By any standard the public sector of industry is of vital importance in the British economy. Overlooking municipal enterprise and those industrial and commercial activities undertaken by central departments, the scale of public enterprise is such that it has a profound effect upon the rest of the economy. As Table 6.2 indicates, it employs 8.3 per cent of the country's workforce and is responsible for 19.5 per cent of fixed investment. But it is not just its size which makes it important. It is also its strategic role, providing many of the basic requirements of the rest of industry and many of the services which are most vital to the community. It is not surprising therefore that the affairs of the nationalised industries have constantly been at the centre of political debate and action. In part, of course, this has been a reflection of the controversy surrounding their ownership and the

TABLE 6.2 The Public Sector of Industry in 1976

1 NATIONALISED INDUSTRIES

Sector	Boards	Employees[1]	Capital Expenditure (£m)
Finance	Bank of England	7,000	—
Energy	British Gas Corporation	103,000	310
	British National Oil Corporation[2]	–	–
	Electricity Boards in England and Wales[3]	166,800	640
	National Coal Board	285,300	211
	North of Scotland Hydro-Electric Board	3,800	70
	South of Scotland Electricity Board	13,900	45
	UK Atomic Energy Authority	13,300	19
Transport	British Airports Authority	5,100	42
	British Airways Board	58,200	128
	British Railways Board	251,600	111
	British Transport Docks Board	11,400	10
	British Waterways Board	3,200	2
	National Bus Company	70,500	24
	National Freight Corporation	44,600	16
	Scottish Transport Group	16,000	7
Communications	Cable and Wireless Ltd	9,500	27
	Post Office Corporation	420,700	963
Industry	British Steel Corporation	210,200	530
		1,694,100	3,155

[1] Figures relate to 1975 or the financial year 1975–76 depending on the practice of individual boards.
[2] BNOC was set up in January 1976. During 1976 its staff grew to nearly 400.
[3] Electricity Council, Central Electricity Generating Board and 12 Area Boards.

TABLE 6.2 *(Continued)*

2 LIMITED COMPANIES IN WHICH THE STATE HAS HOLDINGS

The state has holdings in over 30 companies which together employ about 375,000 people. Most of these companies are either subsidiaries of the National Enterprise Board or are destined for transfer to British Shipbuilders.[1] The following list includes only the largest companies.

National Enterprise Board holdings (14)	*Employees*	*% held by state*
National Enterprise Board	42	—
British Leyland Ltd	164,400	95
Ferranti Ltd	16,300	50
Rolls-Royce (1971) Ltd	60,000	100
Herbert Ltd	6,900	100
Brown Boveri Kent Ltd	6,150	18
International Computer (Holdings) Ltd	28,100	24
Destined for transfer to British Shipbuilders (5)		
Cammell Laird Shipbuilders	5,400	50
Govan Shipbuilders	6,300	100
Sunderland Shipbuilders	4,600	100
Others		
British Nuclear Fuels Ltd (Atomic Energy Authority)	9,300	100
British Petroleum Co. Ltd (Treasury and Bank of England)	24,900	68[2]
Mersey Docks and Harbour Co. Ltd (Dept. of Environment)	9,400	21
British Sugar Corporation (Dept. of Industry)	5,500	11
Harland & Wolff Ltd (Northern Ireland Office)	9,700	100
SB (Realisations) Ltd[3] (Dept. of Industry)	6,000	100

[1] In Scotland and Wales development agencies, established in 1975, have similar powers to those of the National Enterprise Board. Details of their holdings are not yet available.

[2] In December 1976 it was announced that the combined state holding would be reduced to 51 per cent. Only those employed by BP in UK have been included.

[3] SB (Realisations) Ltd has a 69.5 per cent interest in Short Brothers & Harland Ltd.

opponents of nationalisation have given as much publicity as possible to the problems many of the industries have encountered. For a variety of reasons, many of which have nothing to do with questions of ownership and control, the financial performance of most of the industries has been poor and this has placed them on the defensive in the face of a generally unsympathetic public. In this chapter it is not possible to probe into these public attitudes more deeply or to discuss the problems of individual industries. A number of general issues, however, have arisen which have contributed to the problems of the industries and have given rise to political controversy during the last thirty years.

First, serious problems have arisen because of the failure to define clearly the industries' aims. One cause of this has been the conflicting reasons advanced in favour of nationalisation. For instance in many industries the trade unions saw public ownership as a means of improving their standard of living and of protecting their jobs. Others, however, regarded it as a move towards change and rationalisation in which reductions in the workforce would be necessary. But it is also a consequence of the absence of clear direction on the part of the government as to the objectives of the industries. Most seriously, governments have been reluctant to face up to the crucial question of deciding whether the nationalised industries should be commercial enterprises or social services. No single answer can be given to this question which would apply to all the industries, but it is extremely important that those working in any particular industry should know what criteria they are to apply in taking decisions and that those outside the industry should know what standards should be used in judging its results. For instance, if the railways are to be regarded as a social service the performance of British Rail needs to be assessed in terms of the adequacy of the services it provides, tempered of course by some criterion of efficiency. On the other hand, if the railways are expected to be financially successful then the main test of the Board's efficiency must be its profitability, qualified by any non-commercial responsibilities that have been laid upon it. Failure to choose between these alternatives has produced a very unsatisfactory state of affairs. British Rail's managers do not know the basis on which they are expected to take decisions and they feel disillusioned because the public criticise them both for the inadequacies of the service they provide and for their dismal financial results.

Their life, however, is further complicated by the fact that governments have also seen another use for the nationalised industries. In the debate about nationalisation it was argued that public ownership would facilitate economic planning and management. Successive governments have used the nationalised industries in this way but they have failed to think through the consequences of such action both for the industries' profitability and for their ability to provide a public service. Again, therefore, this has had serious consequences for morale in the industry and upon public attitudes.

Surprisingly little attention was given to these matters during the main period of nationalisation immediately after the war. Many seemed to believe that most of the problems of the industries would disappear once they had been taken into public ownership. For instance, it was thought that it would be possible largely to sustain the existing network of railway services as a result of ceasing to pay investors a return on their capital and out of the gains from the rationalisation that would come from the elimination of wasteful competition between the railway companies. Add to this the widespread optimism that existed at the time of nationalisation and it is possible to appreciate how many people both in government and in the industries believed that they were entering a new world. The harsh realities of the post-war British economy did not, however, take long to dampen this optimism. Most of the formidable problems of the industries. remained in as acute a form as they had previously and their solution had now to be faced against the background of a very difficult economic situation and new government responsibilities for economic management.

In so far as any thought was given to the objectives of the nationalised industries at this time, it was concerned with the distribution of responsibility between ministers and the boards they appointed to run the industries. It was argued that ministers should lay down the policy of the industries, leaving it to the boards to put this policy into effect. In doing this, it was expected that the boards would be able both to meet their financial targets of breaking even and promote the public interest. Looking at the powers conferred upon ministers and boards, there is some doubt how far the statutes did in fact provide for such a division of responsibility. In any case, it is clear that ministers failed to provide any firm guidance on most of the major questions concerning the operation of the industries. For instance, the financial requirement was that they should break even financially taking one year with another but no guidance was given as to the precise meaning of this very general phrase. Nor were they given any clear instructions as to the pricing policy they should adopt or the criteria by which investment decisions should be taken. Many of these matters may appear rather technical but they are of crucial importance to those who have to take decisions within an industry. Without this guidance managers soon give an impression of floundering and the public quickly becomes disillusioned as it has no standards by which to assess their success or failure. Moreover, as has been seen, these public attitudes have had a major influence upon the debate about further nationalisation.

Within a very short time, most of the industries which were nationalised in the 1945–50 period began to experience financial difficulties and there was widespread disillusionment about their performance. Board members felt frustrated at the lack of guidance given to them and at the frequent ministerial intervention in matters they considered to be their responsibility; employees found their new employers much the same as their predecessors; and consumers found little difference in either the quality or range of goods and services provided and no improvement in their price. In reaction to this the Conservatives proposed a number of changes in the structure of the industries, designed to reduce the extent of centralisation and to introduce some element of competition. To some extent these policies were put into practice after 1951, for instance in the coal and transport industries, but their effect was only marginal. The financial performance of the industries continued to deteriorate and more radical solutions, such as drastic reductions in services and complete re-organisation, were widely canvassed. For instance, in 1956 a very important report on the electricity supply industry, prepared by a committee under the chairmanship of Sir Edwin Herbert, proposed the break-up of the unified structure that had existed since nationalisation and this was implemented the following year.[7] Similarly a confidential review of the transport industry led in January 1963 to the dissolution of the British Transport Commission, its functions being shared out among five separate boards, and the new chairman of the railway board, Dr Richard Beeching, set about the task of restoring commercial success by proposing the closure of a substantial part of the railway network.

Only in the 1960s did governments begin to take action to resolve the conflicting demands made of the nationalised industries. This problem was one of the questions considered by the Herbert Committee and it had proposed a radical solution. Its advice, however, was not accepted by the Government. Instead it published in 1961 a White Paper which set out to clarify the existing situation in relation to the financial and economic objectives of the industries.[8] For instance, some guidance was given as to the interpretation of their statutory financial obligation. This attempt to codify existing practice failed to deal adequately with the problems. To ease the financial difficulties of the industries radical action of some kind was needed and, as far as their public reputation was concerned, no amount of tinkering was going to produce change.

A more radical approach was advanced in 1967.[9] The boards were given firm guidance on the pricing policy and the investment criteria they should adopt. In addition, taking up the arguments of the Herbert Committee and the Select Committee on Nationalised Industries, the Government took a tentative step towards altering the terms of reference under which the boards operated. For the first time it was conceded that in certain circumstances the industries should be compensated for non-commercial activities they undertook at the Government's behest or at least that these activities should be taken into account when fixing the industries' financial targets. In return it was announced that more stringent tests of commercial efficiency would be applied.

These recommendations have proved difficult to put into practice and have been criticised both on economic grounds and by those who believe that a division of responsibility based upon a distinction between social and commercial obligations is as impractical as the one it was intended to replace. However, in a number of areas they have led to important changes. Thus, under the Transport Act of 1968 and the Railways Act of 1974, decisions about uneconomic passenger lines and services are taken by the Government and local authorities and compensation is paid to offset the losses they incur by running such services. Similarly, in the 1970s all the nationalised industries have been compensated for the losses which arose from the Government's decision to restrain their prices as part of its counter-inflation policy. Nevertheless, the new approach has never been applied across the board and the fundamental problem outlined at the beginning of this section cannot be said to be much nearer resolution. This is illustrated each time the report and accounts of any of the nationalised industries are published. Ought they to show a profit or should their performance be judged by other criteria? As long as this question is fudged, the present unsatisfactory position will continue. Ministers will continue to resent the independence of the industries and the political unpopularity they incur from having to defend decisions which they did not take and often had little opportunity to influence; managers will continue to feel frustrated when they are criticised by the public for not doing things which ministers have prevented them from doing and to resent the unsympathetic climate in which they have to work; employees will feel they work for undertakings which have failed to provide them with better standards of living and a guarantee of future employment; and consumers, who had hoped for a new deal, will continually feel exasperated by rising prices and contracting services.

One feature of the debate on this issue has been the general absence of partisan controversy. In the adversary environment of British politics, the decisions of successive governments have almost invariably been attacked by their opponents but in general the political parties have not taken up distinctive positions on this question and the changes in official policy have not arisen from changes in government. Indeed, the behaviour of successive governments, both in terms of style and substance, has been strikingly similar. On the one hand, ministers have preferred to intervene informally and have not limited their involvement to those matters specified in the nationalisation statutes. This situation has made comprehensive analysis of their position very difficult. Examination of the exercise of statutory powers by ministers would give a totally misleading picture of their role. For instance, it would be wrong to infer from the fact that the power of general direction on matters affecting the national interest, about which there was heated debate at the time of nationalisation, has only been used on three occasions that ministerial intervention on such matters has been infrequent. On the other hand, many commentators, in recognising the frequency of informal pressures and the wide range of issues on which they have been applied, have tended to underestimate the large areas of decision-making in which the boards have been free to act independently. An important examination of this relationship was undertaken in 1967–8 by the Select Committee on Nationalised Industries.[10] Although few of its recommendations have been adopted, its report not only provides a balanced picture of the situation but also reveals very clearly the views of both ministers and boards as to their respective roles. In particular, it brings out the relatively minor importance attached in British government to the statutory framework and the clear recognition on both sides of the political nature of their relationship.

One of the trends which emerges very clearly from the Select Committee's report is the widening in the scope and increase in the intensity of government intervention on such matters as prices, wages and investment. As has been mentioned, one of the claims made for nationalisation was that it would facilitate the government's management of the economy but, apart from certain powers over investment and borrowing, the statutes did not explicitly provide for detailed government intervention in these fields. In practice, however, such intervention has been frequent and has grown markedly in intensity in the 1960s and 1970s. Immediately after the war, the entire economy was of course subject to extensive control. However, these controls were generally applied more harshly in relation to the newly created nationalised industries. Their investment was under the direct control of their sponsoring ministers, although their treatment varied widely according to the importance the government attached to them. In the case of wages and prices, informal pressure for restraint was applied from about 1947 onwards. This had two consequences. First, it started the slide in the industries' finances as prices failed to keep pace with rising costs; and secondly it produced a sense of grievance on the part of employees as they saw many of their counterparts in the private sector being treated more generously.

During the 1950s almost all the direct controls on private industry were lifted and the Government attempted to influence its behaviour by general fiscal and monetary measures and by exhortation and persuasion. On a number of occasions, however, the nationalised industries were treated more harshly. For instance, 1956 the chairmen of the industries were 'requested' by the Prime Minister to set an example in price restraint and their investment plans were drastically curtailed. This treatment continued into the 1960s with sudden changes being made in the investment plans of nationalised industries on a number of occasions and after 1965 it was significantly extended. As part of the Labour Government's prices and incomes policy all proposed price increases in the nationalised industries were referred to the National Board for Prices and Incomes and the boards of the industries were very unhappy about the way in which these were handled, particularly in comparison with equivalent proposals of private industry. Discriminatory action, however, became even more apparent after 1970. Initially, the Conservative Government which came into office in 1970 eschewed a formal incomes policy but determined to use the nationalised industries and the rest of the public sector as an example to the rest of industry. Pressure was applied on them not to concede wage increases above the Government's norm and this led to a number of serious disputes such as in the electricity supply industry in 1970 and the Post Office in 1971. Wage restraint continued after 1972 under the terms of the Government's general counter-inflation policy but the nationalised industries were also singled out to give a lead in price restraint. The consequences of this policy in a time of very rapid inflation were so serious that it became necessary for the Government to pay them compensation, and in November 1974 the Chancellor of the Exchequer recognised that this policy could no longer be maintained and announced that the industries' prices would be permitted to rise to their proper level.

The use that successive governments have made of the nationalised industries in this way illustrates very clearly the dilemma of their situation. Given their weak financial position and, in most cases, their dependence upon government assistance, the industries have not been in a position to resist the pressure that has been applied upon them. In any case, the political realities of British government do not make it possible for any appointed board to resist ministerial wishes, at least for long.[11] But artificially low prices and frequent interruptions in investment have only added to their financial weakness and ensured that next time round they are even more susceptible to government pressure. This has added greatly to the frustration felt by those entrusted with responsibility for running the industries. Not only have they been uncertain what the government and the general public expected of them. They have also found their plans repeatedly being disrupted for reasons which had little or nothing to do with their own position. As a result the relationship between ministers and boards has long been unhappy and the embittered comments of the most recent casualties, Sir Monty Finniston and Sir Richard Marsh, past chairmen of the British Steel Corporation and British Rail respectively, are only the latest in a long history of dissatisfaction.

Controversy has surrounded not only this aspect of the nationalised industries. Despite the continuity in the basic organisational framework of the industries, dissatisfaction has been expressed about most of its features. Most important perhaps has been the concern about the extent of public accountability. The relationship between ministers and boards has already been examined from the point of view of the boards. But ministers have also felt restricted in their ability to influence those decisions on which they feel their voice should be heard. Parliament has also felt that the nationalised industries were outside its effective control. Initially it was unable to deal with the industries directly and could only obtain information through the mouth of the sponsoring minister who frequently found himself in the difficult position of acting both as spokesman and as critic. Since 1956 this situation has been ameliorated by the establishment of the Select Committee on Nationalised Industries, to which a number of references have already been made. It has produced many valuable reports and has generally been welcomed not only by MPs but also by the boards of the industries, who have appreciated the opportunity of justifying their decisions and discussing their problems before a well-informed body. Nevertheless there remains a widespread feeling that public industries are not as accountable to the public as they ought to be. Moreover, the consumers of their goods and services feel particularly dissatisfied with the machinery that exists for their voice to be heard. The nationalisation statutes established bodies known as consultative or consumer councils which were designed not only to act as a channel for complaints but also to serve as informed bodies in which managers could discuss the affairs of their industry. These bodies, however, have been regarded as very ineffective; most consumers do not know of their existence and those who are aware of them doubt their impartiality and effectiveness.

All these anxieties need to be set against a background of a further problem: the scale of all the major nationalised industries. Almost without exception, they are very large national organisations. This has led to charges that they are inflexible and bureaucratic and to a feeling on the part of consumers and employees that their views are never heard. On the other hand technical problems make some degree of centralisation inevitable. This dissatisfaction has given rise to frequent reorganisations which have had a very disruptive effect on the operation of the industries. Moreover, even in those industries in which some decentralisation has been introduced most of the criticisms continue. Any survey of public attitudes towards the electricity and gas industries, both of which of course have a particularly direct impact on the public, reveals the depth of hostility and resentment felt towards undertakings which are regarded as inefficient, inflexible and unsympathetic.

Throughout this chapter reference has been made to public attitudes towards nationalisation and the nationalised industries. This is not to say that these attitudes are all well founded. In fact, there are many positive claims that can be made for the industries. Recent surveys have shown them in a favourable light on such matters as improvements in productivity and the industries have many notable achievements to their credit.[12] Moreover, in their defence, it can be stated both that the record of private industry is not invariably better and that many of the essential goods and services provided by all the nationalised industries would not be available either at the same price or on the same scale if they were the responsibility of the private sector. Nevertheless, the general hostility of the public has served not only to keep the nationalised industries at the centre of political controversy but also has had a major effect on the debate about future nationalisation. As long as there is so much uncertainty as to the purposes of nationalisation and dissatisfaction with the form it has taken, it is unlikely either that the existing industries will be able radically to improve their performance or that new candidates for nationalisation will be assessed on their merits.

Given this situation, it is not surprising that there is a lack of enthusiasm for further nationalisation of a traditional kind. What pressure there is for extensions in public ownership is therefore increasingly being channelled into new forms. Thus, although the post-1974 Labour Government has engaged in some traditional nationalisation, the creation of NEB is potentially much more important. As yet British experience of this type of public ownership is extremely limited and a whole host of new questions need to be considered. How will the triangular relationship between ministers, holding company and individual company work? What will the role of state-nominated directors be on the boards of partly-owned companies? Indeed, what sort of person will be sought to perform this role? All these questions urgently need to be answered before further progress is made in these new directions but at present there is little sign certainly within the political parties but also among industrial commentators that they are recognised, let alone discussed.

In any case, a strong case can be made for arguing that ownership is a factor of declining importance. Such a claim, of course, would be denied by those at both extremes of British politics. But, for the overwhelming majority of British politicians the aims of industrial policy are similar: the achievement of greater efficiency and the promotion of some degree of social responsibility. In pursuing these objectives there are many in both political parties who argue that nationalisation, far from solving anything, tends to create further, often more intractable, problems. For instance, it was not only Conservative politicians who expressed alarm at the claim of the National Union of Railwaymen in 1974 that the financial position of British Rail was of no relevance in assessing their pay demand as it was the national exchequer which in effect would provide the money. Moreover, there are many who claim that changes in the performance and behaviour of industry can more easily be effected in other ways, notably by state intervention and participation in private industry. In the 1960s an elaborate and extensive system was built up for public regulation of industry and for the provision of financial and other assistance. It must be admitted that the success of this approach has not been unqualified. Most of the basic problems of British industry remain unresolved and there is some evidence to suggest that many of the regulations have been evaded and that much of the assistance has not achieved the purposes for which it was intended.[13] As has been seen, the failure of exhortation and inducement to promote industrial investment was one of the factors behind the renewed enthusiasm for nationalisation in the Labour Party in the 1970s and accounts for the specific proposals that have been made to acquire a state interest in any company which receives financial assistance.

The National Enterprise Board is unlikely to survive a change of government and a new Conservative administration can be expected to dismantle some of the machinery and procedures that the Labour Government has established in the industrial sphere. However, it is most unlikely that the interventionism of the 1960s and early 1970s will be reversed entirely. Private industry has by now grown accustomed to extensive state involvement and, despite some of their public pronouncements, there are few industrialists who appear keen to eschew state assistance and to live with the consequences of their mistakes and misfortunes. Similarly employees and consumers look to the government for protection on a very wide range of issues. All these attitudes strike a responsive chord among most politicians and officials, few of whom care to admit that the world is beyond their control and to ignore cries for help.

Moreover, the severity of the current crisis makes it all the more likely that these attitudes will persist.

Thus, in some form or other, it is likely that current trends in government-industry relations will be maintained. What is alarming is that political debate on this question is generally so far removed from reality. For many British politicians the symbols of nationalisation and free enterprise remain as vivid today as they were thirty years ago and they can be relied upon to set the adrenalin flowing among the party faithful. In contrast there are only a few politicians who seem to have awoken to the reality of the interpenetration of government and industry. This raises all sorts of vitally important political and administrative questions which urgently need to be faced and which will necessitate choices between fundamentally different alternatives. A new industrial order has arrived or at least is on the threshold of arriving but only a few seem to have realised it. The serious consequences of this shortsightedness are too obvious for them to need to be stressed.

NOTES

1. Important municipal undertakings, notably the transport services run by local authorities in London and most of the major conurbations, are thus excluded. The water supply industry is also omitted from this chapter.

2. By 1971, IRC had been involved in 90 projects and had invested a total of £122m of which £87m comprised loans, £22m loans convertible into equity and £13m equity.

3. See J. Alt *et al.*, 'Partisanship and Policy Choice: Issue Preferences in the British Electorate, February 1974', *British Journal of Political Science*, 6:3, p. 281. Nine per cent favoured a lot more nationalisation, 16 per cent a little more, 41 per cent no more and 21 per cent the return of some nationalised industries to private ownership.

4. The level of tolerance has, however, changed over time. For instance, until 1975 it was considered that no government would allow unemployment to exceed one million.

5. Hybridity was one of the snags encountered by the Government in attempting to nationalise the shipbuilding industry in 1976. Its bill included only certain ship-repairing firms and it was therefore claimed in both Houses of Parliament that it should have been subject to the lengthy and expensive procedure for considering hybrid bills. This claim was overcome in the Commons by the use of the Government's majority but it caused more trouble in the Lords.

6. The original 51 per cent interest fell to 48.6 per cent in 1966 when more shares were issued. In 1975 however it rose to 68 per cent when, to ease the financial problems of Burmah Oil, the Bank of England took over its stake in BP. In December 1976 the Chancellor of the Exchequer announced that the state holding would be reduced to 51 per cent.

7. Cmd 9672, 1956, *Report of the Committee of Inquiry into the Electricity Supply Industry.*

8. Cmd 1337, 1961, *The Financial and Economic Obligations of the Nationalised Industries.*

9. Cmd 3437, 1976, *Nationalised Industries: A Review of Economic and Financial Objectives.*

10. HC 371, 1967–8, *Ministerial Control of the Nationalised Industries.*

11. In the last resort a minister has the power to dismiss the board of a public corporation.

12. See for instance, R. Pryke, *Public Enterprise in Practice* (MacGibbon & Kee, 1971).

13. For instance in 1969–70 the Public Accounts Committee discovered that investment grants had been paid to four British firms in respect of ships which were being built abroad.

7 The Challengers to the Two-Party System

Chris Cook

In the General Election of 1951, the Conservative and Labour parties accounted for 96.8 per cent of all votes cast in Great Britain. By 1964, this percentage had fallen to 87.5 per cent. By the General Election of October 1974 it had fallen again to account for only 75.1 per cent of votes cast. In only two decades, a dramatic decline in support for the two major parties had occurred. Whereas in 1951, only one person in thirty supported one of the minor parties, by October 1974 this had risen to one in four.

What reasons lie behind this major shift in public support? Which parties have benefitted from this revolt against the established two-party hegemony? And how near is Britain to the break-up of the established two-party system?

The most obvious beneficiaries have been the Liberals, the Scottish Nationalists and, to a lesser degree, the Welsh Nationalist Party, Plaid Cymru. Except for the peculiar sectarian example of Ulster, the extremist parties, (whether of the Left or Right) have had no part in this challenge to the two main parties. Even the National Front, at its most successful, has never been remotely near winning a parliamentary by-election or even a G.L.C. seat.

The Liberal and Nationalist challenge, however, did not begin to emerge in the decade after 1945. The years from 1945 to 1956 marked a high point of the two-party hegemony. No Liberal secured a parliamentary by-election victory between 1929 and 1958. In 1950, in the most disastrous election the Liberals had ever fought, 319 Liberal candidates lost their deposit. From 1951 to 1958, there were times when it seemed the last remnants of the Liberal Party might finally disappear. During the same period, the old Liberal National Party, the heirs of the Simonite Liberals of the 1930s, virtually lost their separate identity as a result of the Woolton – Teviot pact of 1947. This effectively merged the parties at constituency level.

Nor had the Nationalists yet emerged from the political fringe. No

Nationalist was returned at a by-election or general election in the twenty years after 1945. The first post-war Nationalist break-through came in Wales (in Carmarthen) in July 1966; the Scottish National Party swiftly followed this at Hamilton in November 1967.

In fact, the first successful challenge by a minor party was the Liberal victory at Torrington in March 1958. Although Torrington was only of limited significance, this first Liberal revival is worthy of detailed analysis. It came in 1957 in the wake of the Suez crisis when, in a variety of by-elections, the Liberals began to achieve some impressive results, taking over 20 per cent of the vote at Edinburgh South (20 May 1957) and over 36 per cent in Dorset North (27 June). Further impressive results followed at Gloucester and Ipswich.

The Liberals began 1958 in even happier fashion with a remarkable by-election result at Rochdale. For the by-election, in a seat which had seen a straight fight in 1955, the Liberals chose Ludovic Kennedy, a well-known television personality, as their candidate. His spirited and energetic campaign produced a Conservative humiliation and a near-triumph for the Liberals. The Liberals finished in second place, only 4,500 votes short of victory, with 35.5 per cent of the poll.

Two weeks later the Liberals achieved the by-election breakthrough that had eluded them for a generation, when they won Torrington from the Conservatives. Mark Bonham-Carter's triumph was not quite the dawn of the new era that many Liberals imagined. The seat had been held by George Lambert, sitting as a Conservative and National Liberal. No independent Liberal had fought in 1955, and clearly much of the traditional Liberal vote in this constituency had either abstained (turnout rose by 11.4 per cent to 80.6 per cent in the by-election) or found a temporary home in the Conservative ranks. As it was, the Liberals gained Torrington by the narrow margin of 658 votes in a seat with a recent Liberal tradition.

Torrington failed to inspire any similar Liberal breakthrough, although the party polled some impressive performances. With the exception of Rochdale, all these good Liberal performances had been concentrated in rural Tory backwaters (such as Dorset North, Argyll and Galloway) or in middle-class seaside constituences with a generous sprinkling of poujadist landladies (Southend West, Weston-super-Mare). In the 1959 General Election, it was in these two types of constituency that Liberals polled best.

The October 1959 election saw a modest but important improvement in the Liberal position. Although the party returned only six members, failing to hold Torrington or regain Carmarthen (lost to Labour in the 1957 by-election), the Liberals had polled 1,640,761 votes, over twice their percentage share in 1955. Only 56 of the 215 candidates had forfeited their deposits, whilst the average vote in contested seats rose from 15.1 per cent in 1955 to 16.9 per cent in 1959.

However, there were many unhappy features about the Liberal results.

Although Jeremy Thorpe gained the rural Devon North constituency, there had been no other breakthrough. Indeed, the party fared worst where its electoral prospects were strongest. The Liberal vote fell in eight of the thirteen seats in which the party had received over 30 per cent of the votes in 1955.

The explanation was easy to see: although Torrington had given the party a much-needed boost, its organisation had fallen too far for the party to revive overnight. The significance of the Torrington revival was to prepare the ground for the far more impressive revival that was to follow after 1959.

The first real indication—in parliamentary terms—of the Liberal revival came with the by-election in April 1961 at Paisley. In a Labour stronghold, a spirited campaign by John Bannerman brought the Liberals within 2,000 votes of victory. In the space of the next ten months, the Liberals managed to secure second place in eight by-elections in constituencies in which the party had been third in 1959. Similarly, in the municipal elections, the party improved its base in May 1960 (electing 130 Liberals) and in May 1961 (returning 196 Liberals). By the autumn of 1961, the increase in Liberal support had gathered momentum. The climax of the Liberal revival came in March 1962. On 14 March, a Liberal candidate came within 973 votes of victory in the rock-solid Conservative seaside resort of Blackpool North. The following day, when polling took place in Orpington, a middle-class Kent commuter suburb, a Conservative majority of 14,760 was overturned into a Liberal majority of 7,855. The Conservative share of the poll had fallen by 22 per cent to give Eric Lubbock a resounding victory. Orpington had proved to be the most sensational by-election since East Fulham in October 1933.

For the Liberals, after a generation in the wilderness, the promised land seemed at last to have arrived. Indeed, for a fleeting moment, the *Daily Mail* National Opinion Poll (published on 28 March 1962) showed the Liberals to be the most popular party in the country (the figures were: Liberals 30 per cent, Labour 29.2 per cent, Conservatives 29.2 per cent). Meanwhile, on the same day as Orpington, the Liberals forced the Conservatives into third place at Middlesbrough East. Other by-elections, though not repeating the Orpington victory, indicated the force behind the Liberal revival. The party took 27 per cent of the poll at Stockton-on-Tees (April 1962), 25 per cent in Derby North (also in April), whilst in the Montgomeryshire by-election following the death of Clement Davies this Liberal stronghold was easily retained—the only example in post-war history of a Liberal seat being passed on to another Liberal. In West Derbyshire, the party missed victory by a mere 1,220 votes, whilst on 12 July in North-East Leicester there was an excellent Liberal vote.

In addition to these by-elections, the most impressive evidence of the Liberal advance was to be seen in the May 1962 municipal elections. In such safe home counties territory as Aldershot, Finchley, Kingston and

Maidenhead, the Conservatives lost every seat they were defending. In a variety of seaside and spa towns (such as Southend, Blackpool and Harrogate) the Liberals made equally impressive gains.

After autumn 1962, however, the Liberal tide began to recede. During 1963, no further by-election victories were secured; the party's rating in the opinion polls slipped.

The continued polarisation towards the two main parties could be seen in both by-elections and in the opinion polls. By June 1964, support for the Liberals in the National Opinion Poll had slumped to a mere 9 per cent. It was against this background that the Liberals entered the October 1964 election. The results confirmed that the Liberals had failed to break the two-party system, for although the party polled over 3 million votes, it returned only nine Liberal MPs. For all their efforts the Liberals had gained only four seats, all in the celtic fringe: Bodmin in Cornwall, and Inverness, Caithness and Sutherland, and Ross and Cromarty in Scotland. They lost Bolton West and Huddersfield West, where Conservatives fielded candidates for the first time since 1950. The Liberal revival had clearly failed and confirmation of this fact could be seen in the 1966 election.

This election was, for the Liberals, the sequel to its failure to break through in 1964. In the tightrope parliamentary situation between the general elections of 1964 and 1966 very few things went right for the Liberals. Almost the only exception was the victory of David Steel in the Roxburgh by-election, but this was a victory of only local significance.

With few exceptions, the by-elections were registering a loss of Liberal support that was mirrored in the morale of the party. This was to be seen in the nominations for the 1966 election. The party fielded 311 candidates, 54 fewer than in 1964. With a reduced field of candidates, the Liberal vote went on to fall by more than 750,000, (to 2,327,533). Ironically the party had emerged with its representation increased to twelve, the result of Liberals 'squeezing' third-party candidates in such seats as Cheadle and Colne Valley.

The election, even though it had produced the largest Liberal contingent for over twenty years, also clearly marked the end of the road for 'Orpington-style' Liberalism. Whichever way the position of the party was reviewed, the underlying fact was that the hopes of the Orpington era had been finally shattered.

In the period from the 1966 General Election until the Rochdale by-election of October 1972, the electoral fortunes of the Liberals were at a low ebb. Although both Conservatives and Nationalists benefitted from Labour's shattering loss of popular support after 1966, the Liberals stayed in the doldrums. Wallace Lawler's personal triumph on the Liberal ticket in Birmingham Ladywood (in June 1969) was an isolated example of grassroots community politics. It in no way reflected rising Liberal support—and in the 1970 election the Liberals managed only 2,117,638 votes and a mere six seats. The last symbols of Orpington were lost, and Orpington itself fell to the Conservatives.

Yet the 1970 election, or rather the growing unpopularity of the Heath Government after 1971, marked the start of the most pronounced challenge made against the two-party system. The Liberal revival of 1972–3 was all the more remarkable in that so little had gone right for the Liberals after 1970. Both the by-elections and municipal elections were disasters. It was not until the luck of a by-election in Rochdale, one of the very few constituencies in the country where Liberals were the main challengers to Labour, that the Liberals had their first opportunity. Cyril Smith won a decisive (if no doubt partly personal) victory, taking the seat with a 5,093 majority on 26 October 1972.

Critics of the Liberal revival could dismiss Rochdale relatively easily, but the sensational result in the Sutton and Cheam by-election of 7 December 1972 could not be ignored. In a rock-solid true blue Conservative commuter suburb, an able and youthful Liberal candidate swept to a landslide victory, overturning a Conservative majority of 7,417 on a greater turnover of votes than even Orpington had witnessed.

After Sutton, the Liberal bandwagon began to roll, accompanied by a strong Nationalist showing and a sensational personal challenge to the two-party system by Dick Taverne at Lincoln (see pp. 155–6). The Liberal electoral record was unlike anything the party had achieved for a generation. Indeed, its nearest parallel was Lloyd George's last revival in 1927–8—another example of a Liberal revival under a *Conservative* government.

After Sutton, the Liberals achieved a remarkably high vote in Chester-le-Street (38.6 per cent), a Durham Labour stronghold in an area where Liberalism had been dead for a generation, and in the Exchange division of Manchester. Here, the Liberals took 36 per cent of the vote; the Conservatives suffering the humiliation of a lost deposit.

The 1973 round of local elections provided the Liberals with equally sensational results. In addition to a striking breakthrough in Liverpool, the party not only swept to outright control in Eastbourne but became the largest party in five other authorities. In a further 20 councils Liberals succeeded in becoming either the main opposition group or the second largest party, while in hitherto barren areas, Liberals established a council toehold.

In parliamentary by-elections, the Liberal upsurge reached its climax on 26 July 1973, when polling took place in two of the safest Conservative strongholds in the country – Ripon and the Isle of Ely. At Ripon David Austick, the Liberal candidate, fought a community politics campaign centred on suburban Lower Wharfedale. He achieved a remarkable victory, taking the seat with 43 per cent of the vote and a 946 majority. Meanwhile, an equally sensational victory was achieved by Clement Freud in the Isle of Ely. Freud won by 1,470 votes, taking 38.3 per cent of the poll. It was the first occasion in living memory that the Liberals had won two by-elections on the same day. A final by-election victory was achieved by the Liberals in November, when Alan Beith narrowly won the Berwick-on-Tweed constituency that had once returned Beveridge to Westminster. With this background of by-election triumphs, striking successes in local government elections and a revitalised radical policy, Liberals were understandably buoyant. As the winter of 1973 approached, Liberal support in the opinion polls was now at a high level and gathering increasing momentum.

It was against this background that a general election was called for 28 February. The calling of an election provided the Liberals with an unrivalled opportunity. Never before had they faced an election when riding so high in the opinion polls. Never had the opportunity to transform a by-election revival into a general election breakthrough seemed so possible. And not since 1929 had the Liberals been strong enough to field over 500 candidates. The most crucial Liberal assult on the two-party system was about to take place.

It was the system, not the Liberals, who came out as the victors. Having entered the contest with their highest hopes for a generation, the Liberals came out of the battle with a staggering 6 million votes, but a mere fourteen seats. Their only gains were Cardiganshire and Colne Valley (from Labour), Bodmin and the Isle of Wight from the Conservatives and the new suburban seat of Hazel Grove, won by the former Liberal MP for Cheadle, Michael Winstanley. Perhaps the greatest individual triumph was the victory of Stephen Ross in the Isle of Wight, where he increased the Liberal share of the poll from 22.2 per cent to 50.2 per cent. The Liberal leaders also achieved outstanding personal results. But there had been no real breakthrough. Indeed, in many respects, the seats won such as Colne Valley and Hazel Grove were really repeat performances of 1964 and 1966.

As with the 1964 election a decade earlier, the outcome of the election could hardly have been more difficult for the Liberals. Thorpe faced a delicate task. With a minority Labour Government, and with a General Election widely forecast for the autumn, it was essential to keep the Liberal Party in the public view. Although Liberal support in the opinion polls held relatively steady during 1974, the absence of by-elections prevented the Liberals from achieving any renewed momentum, even though the defection in July of a sitting Labour MP, Christopher Mayhew, was given maximum publicity.

The October 1974 election, at least for the Liberals, bore very close parallels with the 1966 election. The party was in retreat from its high-water mark. Although the Liberals entered the October election with their largest-ever field of candidates and with high hopes that the 6 million votes secured in February would prove a spring-board for parliamentary success, they came out of the battle with fewer votes, a reduction in seats and with morale having suffered a severe setback.

The Liberals managed only a solitary gain (Truro) in October 1974, while two seats (Hazel Grove and Bodmin) were lost to the Conservatives. None of the hoped-for Liberal gains, such as Bath, Newbury or Hereford, materialised.

Meanwhile, the total Liberal vote had fallen from the 6,063,470 (19.3 per cent) cast in February to 5,346,800 (18.3 per cent) in October. This decrease tended to disguise the fact that with 102 more candidates than in February, in 93 per cent of constituencies contested by Liberals on both occasions, the Liberal share of the vote declined.

From whichever angle the results were analysed, the Liberal revival was over. The disastrous Liberal by-election record after October 1974 (the party lost its deposit in almost all of the by-elections which occurred) and the personal crisis of Jeremy Thorpe's leadership only served to deliver this message even more strongly. When David Steel established himself as Liberal leader at the Llandudno Conference in September 1976, the party he led seemed as far away as ever from breaking the two-party system. Ironically, only six months later, in March 1977, the Liberals were to come closer to the corridors of power than for a generation.

The occasion was the disappearance of the Labour Government's tiny overall majority in the House of Commons. Weakened by the defection of two MPs to the breakaway Scottish Labour Party, and weakened also by by-election losses in such 'safe' seats as Workington and Walsall North, the Labour Government were faced in March 1977 with a possible defeat on a Conservative vote of 'no confidence'. With the Nationalists stating that they would vote against Labour, Callaghan made the only move left to him: an 'understanding' with the Liberal Party.

But if this deal gave Liberals more influence than for many years at Westminster, in the country it did nothing to restore a disastrous slump in Liberal fortunes. In the first nationwide test of Liberal support (the May 1977 local elections) the Liberals fared disastrously. Thus in Greater Manchester the party lost all twelve seats it was defending. In Greater London, the only Liberal-held seats (at Sutton and Richmond) were both lost. In no less than 32 GLC contests, the party finished in a humiliating fourth position behind the National Front. In the whole Home Counties area of Buckinghamshire, the GLC, Hertfordshire, Kent, Surrey and Sussex, the Liberals could win only four seats. Even worse, local bases of Liberal strength crumbled. In all, these elections removed nearly two out of every three Liberal councillors. The next Liberal revival seemed as far away as ever.

Why then had the Liberal revivals at Orpington or after Sutton, Ripon and the Isle of Ely come to grief?

The Liberal revivals were a response to particular combinations of political circumstance. In 1962–3, the Liberal revival was the product of a double opportunity. First, there was the opportunity provided by the fratricidal warfare which engulfed Labour after its third successive

General Election defeat. Secondly, the Liberals were able to exploit the economic difficulties in which the Conservatives increasingly found themselves after 1961. To this extent, the Liberal revival owed little or nothing to its own strength – even though the party proclaimed a series of attractive policies and possessed in Jo Grimond a vigorous and popular leader. Essentially, the Liberal revival was dependent on the weakness – temporary as it proved – of its Conservative and Labour opponents. The same basic equation was present in 1973, but Labour's revival, and the closed ranks of the Conservatives, hindered the Liberals. But this was only part of the explanation of the Liberal failure.

The party faced other fundamental handicaps: it had no large source of income (it had no real backing from industry; none from the trade unions); it lacked the numbers of agents needed to turn winnable seats into strongholds. The party also lacked a secure outlet in the media (there were many Liberal journalists, but no mass Liberal daily papers).

Despite these pressures against a small party, nonetheless, in 1964, 3 million people voted Liberal. In 1974, over 6 million voted Liberal. Why was so massive a tally of votes not translated into seats at Westminster? The explanation lies not merely in the nature of the British electoral system but also in the spread and composition of the Liberal vote. At the heart of the Liberal failure was the fact that at each revival Liberals simply could not concentrate their vote. In 1964, the Liberals took over 25 per cent of the poll in a variety of Home Counties seats. Similarly, in the North-West, the party polled well in such Manchester commuter suburbs as Cheadle (which recorded the highest Liberal vote in the country). But the party could not get to the 35–40 per cent level needed to be first past the post (except in the special case of the Scottish Highlands, where three seats were gained). Secondly, the best Liberal results were limited to particular types of safe Conservative seats, mostly middle-class suburbs and rural back-waters. Here, with very little Labour vote, Liberals needed over 40 per cent of the vote to unseat sitting Conservatives. Exactly the same phenomenon was to occur in the 1973–4 Liberal revival. Thus, even at the peak of the Liberal revival in February 1974, in no area of the country did the Liberals achieve the 35–40 per cent of the vote needed for breakthrough. In the party's best area, Devon and Cornwall, the percentage achieved was 34.4 per cent. Nowhere else was it above 30 per cent. In the other areas in which high hopes were entertained, the party fell just short. Thus the suburban south-east was 27.5 per cent, the East Anglian area around the Isle of Ely 24.9 per cent. By October 1974, except for Devon, Cornwall and the rest of the south-west, there was not a single area in which Liberals achieved over one in four of the votes cast.

A second failure revolved round the fact that the areas of Liberal success at municipal level were no pointer to success in parliamentary elections. Thus in February 1974, in Liverpool, the magic of 'Jones the Vote' worked so ineffectually that they were nowhere near success in Edge Hill and not even second in Trevor Jones's own constituency of Toxteth. In areas outside Liverpool where Liberals had built up a local power base, such as Nelson and Colne or Richmond, local government success again failed to transform itself into seats at Westminster.

A third factor explaining the Liberal failure was the almost complete absence of 'tactical voting', whereby supporters of a party in a hopeless position would vote Liberal to unseat the sitting Conservative or Labour member. In 1964, this had been noticeable even in the Orpington area. In not a single constituency adjacent to Orpington had Liberals achieved even second place. It was the October 1974 election, however, which was most cruelly disappointing, for there had been much talk of tactical voting. In such seats as Bath, Chippenham, Hereford, Newbury, South Bedfordshire and Leominster, Liberals had entertained high hopes that the Labour vote would go over to the Liberals. In one or two seats (such as Truro) a very limited amount of tactical voting occurred (and in Colne Valley and Cardiganshire Tories seem to have voted Liberal to keep Labour out) but such examples were rare in the extreme. It is a significant comment on Labour's ability to retain its vote even in the most hopeless agricultural or middle-class constituency that the party lost only twenty-eight deposits in February 1974 and thirteen in October.

Equally important in explaining the Liberal failure was the party's inability (both in 1962–3 and in 1973–4) to make any real inroads into the Labour working-class vote. Thus in 1962, the Liberals polled well in the Tory suburbs of London, but the Labour areas were virtually unaffected. In such boroughs as Mitcham, Watford or Acton, there was no Liberal breakthrough. In the industrial areas of England—in the north-east, the West Midlands and the north-west, the story was repeated. The same phenomenon was to be seen a decade later. At the height of Liberal popularity in 1973, Liberals made virtually no inroads into Labour territory. In the elections to the G.L.C. and the new metropolitan and county councils, Liberals won only 178 of the 2,514 seats at stake. Even these 178 seats were heavily concentrated. Liberals won only six seats out of 308 in the Labour-dominated metropolitan areas of South Yorkshire, Tyne and Wear and the West Midlands. Outside Merseyside (where Liberals picked up 19 of 99 seats at stake), the Liberals polled well, albeit unevenly, in Greater Manchester (13 out of 106) and West Yorkshire (11 out of 88). Even these figures disguised the extent to which many industrial towns, especially in South Yorkshire and the West Midlands, were still utterly barren Liberal territory.

These electoral shortcomings, added to the policy dilemma of a Liberal party simultaneously trying to attract disgruntled Tories from the Right and Radicals from the Left, and added also to the political structure of an established two-party system, help explain the Liberal failure.

They also serve to point the contrast with the other challengers to the two-party system—the Nationalists. And here, it is the Scottish National

Party which has achieved most success.

Originally formed in April 1928 as the National Party of Scotland, the party was renamed the Scottish National Party on being joined by the Scottish Party in April 1934. The early electoral history of the party hardly augured well. The five candidates fielded in 1931 polled only 20,954 votes. In 1935, eight candidates managed 29,517 votes, with three deposits saved and creditable results in the Western Isles (28.1 per cent), Inverness (16.1 per cent) and the Combined Scottish Universities (14.2 per cent). During the electoral truce of 1939 to 1945, SNP candidates were nonetheless brought forward, achieving remarkably high polls in Argyll (April 1940) and Kirkcaldy Burghs (February 1944). In April 1945, the SNP achieved its first electoral victory when Dr R. D. McIntyre won the Motherwell by-election.

However, when normal party politics resumed in the 1945 General Election, the SNP was reduced to relative insignificance. The eight candidates fielded polled only 30,595 votes, a mere 1.2 per cent of votes cast in Scotland. McIntyre was out at Motherwell. Only in Kirkcaldy Burghs, besides Motherwell, could the party save its deposit. The party's peformance at subsequent General Elections followed this pattern:

The Scottish National Party Vote 1945–1959

Election	Candidates	MPs elected	Forfeited deposits	Total votes	% of Scottish total
1945	8	0	6	30,595	1.2
1950	3	0	3	9,708	0.4
1951	2	0	1	7,299	0.3
1955	2	0	1	12,112	0.5
1959	5	0	3	21,738	0.8

In each General Election from 1950 to 1959, the SNP had polled less than 1 per cent of the votes cast in Scotland. From 1945 to 1959, the SNP contested only five by-elections, on no occasion managing to save its deposit.

After 1959, however, the Scottish political climate began to change. The first opportunity for the SNP arose during 1961, when a combination of mounting unemployment in Scotland, an unpopular and out-of-touch Scottish Conservative Party and divisions within the Labour ranks resulted in a creditable SNP performance in the by-election in Glasgow Bridgeton in November 1961. The Nationalists polled over 3,500 votes, 18.7 per cent of the total poll, and finished only 400 votes behind the Tory in this Labour stronghold.

A further opportunity for the Nationalists came in a by-election in West Lothian in June 1962—three months after Orpington, at a time when Conservatism in Scotland was hitting rock bottom. Several factors played into the Nationalist hands. The threat to the local oil-shale industry was a theme which the Nationalist candidate, William Wolfe, had campaigned on for some time. Labour gave the issue one line in their election address. Furthermore, the Conservative Government announced the withdrawal of tax relief on home-produced shale oil during the campaign. These factors (plus a Liberal standard-bearer in a constituency last fought in 1924) produced a startling result. Although Labour retained the seat with a 11,000 majority, the Conservative candidate's percentage of the poll fell from 39.7 per cent to 11.4 per cent, the Nationalist took nearly 10,000 votes, 25 per cent of the poll, and a comfortable second place. Significantly the Liberals, in this seat clearly the weaker protest Party, lost their deposit.

Despite this Nationalist upsurge, the remaining by-elections of the 1959–64 period were disappointing. In the four by-elections contested by the SNP between November 1962 and the October 1964 General Election, the party failed to save its deposit, averaging only 8.9 per cent in these contests.

However, for the General Election, encouraged by the support received in by-elections, the Nationalists fought on a wider front than hitherto—fielding fifteen candidates. Although the party averaged only 10.9 per cent of the vote in the seats contested, in certain areas the Nationalists made definite progress. In West Lothian – the great SNP hope – a concentrated effort and a spirited campaign produced a Nationalist vote of 15,000 and more than 30 per cent of the total vote. There was also a perceptible advance into such Labour-held seats as West Dunbartonshire (12.0 per cent) and Stirlingshire East and Clackmannan (12.2 per cent).

The 1964 results, even if encouraging in a few areas, gave no indication of the definite advance that was to come two years later. The General Election of 31 March 1966 produced the first signs of a distinct Nationalist upsurge. The SNP fought twenty-three of the seventy-one Scottish seats, polling an average of 14.5 per cent in the seats contested. Compared to 1964, the SNP had increased its vote from 64,044 (2.4 per cent) to 128,474 (5.0 per cent). In addition, the SNP managed to save thirteen deposits, although not a single deposit was saved in the four largest towns of Glasgow, Edinburgh, Dundee and Aberdeen. The most noticeable feature of the Nationalist progress was the increased support received in the industrial Labour-held seats of central Scotland. The Nationalists were clearly making most headway in Labour strongholds. In 1966, the SNP contested none of the Highland crofting seats and few rural seats. In other areas where Liberals were strong (as in Roxburgh, Selkirk and Peebles), the SNP made no progress. So far, at the time of writing (Autumn 1977) the SNP has yet to win a Parliamentary seat from a sitting Liberal.

The results of the 1966 election gave the SNP a new impetus and sense of purpose. By 1969, the SNP could claim 486 branches. The result of all this was displayed when a by-election occurred in the Pollok division of

Glasgow on 9 March 1967. The omens did not appear favourable for the Nationalists. The party had not fought the seat before, whilst the constituency was also highly marginal. The result, however, was a sensation. Although the Conservatives took the seat from Labour (with 36.9 per cent, to Labour's 31.2 per cent) the SNP had come within 3,500 votes of victory with over 28 per cent of the vote. It was a tonic whose effect was felt throughout Scotland and whose impact on the burgh elections was immediate and dramatic. The SNP with 159 candidates for the 1967 local elections (compared to only 58 the previous year) polled 144,000 votes, over 15 per cent of the votes cast. This was a dramatic improvement on the 34,000 votes achieved the previous year.

Between the burgh elections of 1967 and those of 1968 there occurred the Hamilton by-election of 2 November 1967. In the second safest Labour seat in Scotland (the Party obtained 71.2 per cent of the votes cast in 1966), Mrs. Winifred Ewing was able to wrest the seat for the SNP. The result was: SNP, 18,397 (46.0 per cent); Labour 16,598 (41.5 per cent); Conservative 4,986 (12.5 per cent). Even though the result was very similar to the heavy anti-Labour swings in by-elections in England, in Scotland the result caused a sensation. Membership of the SNP rocketed upwards and by 1968 the party claimed 125,000 members. In the burgh elections the party went on to sweep the board in many large towns.

No further parliamentary by-elections occurred until the Glasgow Gorbals vacancy in October 1969 and South Ayrshire in March 1970. Neither was the kind of seat in which the Nationalists particularly expected to do well. The SNP polled 25 per cent of the vote in the Gorbals and only 20 per cent in South Ayrshire. This clear decline in Nationalist support (reflected also in the opinion polls) was similarly demonstrated in the 1970 burgh elections. The SNP vote in the burgh elections fell from a peak of 343,000 (30.1 per cent) in 1968 to 221,500 (22.0 per cent) in 1969 and a mere 131,300 (12.6 per cent) in 1970. The net result was rather similar to the Liberal approach to the 1964 election. The party had clearly passed its peak, while the morale of its rivals was improving.

The results of the 1970 election were mixed for the Nationalists. Although, with 65 candidates, the party polled over 300,000 votes (11.4 per cent of the total Scottish poll), no fewer than 43 of its candidates lost their deposit. In the seats fought on both occasions, the average SNP vote slipped from 14.5 per cent to 12.2 per cent. Hamilton was lost, but the one bright beacon for the SNP was the victory secured in the Western Isles – the first occasion in the party's history when it had won a seat at a General Election. As with the Liberals, in the immediate aftermath of the 1970 election, little went right for the SNP. In the burgh elections of 1971, the sweeping gains of three years earlier were obliterated. In Glasgow, every sitting SNP councillor went down to defeat. The climate changed, however, with a large Nationalist vote in the Stirling and Falkirk by-election of 16 September 1971. In a safe Labour seat, a strong Nationalist challenge secured 34.6 per cent of the vote. This was followed, in March 1973, by a remarkable campaign in Dundee East in which the Nationalist challenge brought the party to within 1,141 votes of victory. It was a particularly significant by-election, for oil had been at the forefront of the Nationalist campaign. The Nationalist bandwagon received its final spurt with the capture of the Govan division of Glasgow in November 1973. Like the Liberals, the SNP thus went into the February 1974 General Election riding higher than they had ever been before. Unlike the Liberals, the SNP came out with a dramatic increase in its parliamentary representation.

The party had entered the election defending two seats (Western Isles and Glasgow Govan). Although Govan was lost to Labour, the SNP returned seven members to Parliament, a major success for a party that had never won a single seat in a General Election until 1970.

These SNP gains were mainly at the expense of the Tories, who went down to defeat in Argyll, Moray and Nairn, Banff, and Aberdeenshire East, while Labour lost Clackmannan and East Stirlingshire and also Dundee East. Several of the SNP victories were little short of spectacular. In the Conservative stronghold of Moray and Nairn, Gordon Campbell, the Secretary of State for Scotland, was unseated by Winifred Ewing, who transformed a Tory majority of 6,109 into an SNP one of 1,817, a swing of more than 13 per cent.

Equally satisfactory to the Nationalists was the victory of Gordon Wilson, director of the party's oil campaign, in Dundee East with a 2,966 majority. Perhaps the most remarkable of all the SNP triumphs was George Reid's victory in Clackmannan and East Stirlingshire, overturning a previous Labour majority of more than 10,000. Less happily for the SNP, they failed to win back Hamilton or to make any advance in West Lothian. Nor did their candidates make any real impression in Glasgow or Edinburgh. Apart from these relative setbacks, however, the SNP had every reason for satisfaction. Compared to 11.4 per cent of the Scottish vote in 1970, they obtained 21.9 per cent on this occasion. Only six deposits were lost (compared with 43 in 1970). With its best results in exactly those areas most affected by the impact of the North Sea oil boom, the February 1974 election provided the SNP with a potential springboard for a further major electoral advance. The local elections of May 1974 provided just that springboard.

Although Labour easily dominated the cities, and did especially well in Strathclyde, the SNP achieved some important successes. At Cumbernauld the SNP secured an overall majority. In East Kilbride they finished as the largest single party, whilst they took second place in 30 of the 72 Glasgow seats at stake averaging 25–30 per cent of votes cast. The confidence of the SNP was growing almost daily. An Opinion Research Centre poll published by the *Scotsman* in May showed the SNP's general election vote had more than held up. The poll gave the SNP 24 per cent of the Scottish vote, compared with an actual 22 per cent in the general election, whilst another poll at the same time actually put the party up to 30 per cent, only 6 per cent behind Labour and with the Conservatives trailing in third place.

The SNP thus approached the October 1974 election in a mood of optimism. In the event, although not making quite the massive break-through that they had hoped for, the SNP achieved a major advance. Their tally of seats increased from seven to eleven, all four gains coming in Conservative-held rural territory. The seats captured were Galloway, Perth and East Perthshire, East Dunbartonshire and Angus South.

These SNP victories have now changed the face of Scottish politics: in the last decade, a transformation has occurred:

Parliamentary Representation in Scotland: 1964–74

		Cons	Lab	Lib	SNP	Total
	1964	24	43	4	–	71
	1966	20	46	5	–	71
	1970	23	44	3	1	71
(Feb)	1974	21	40	3	7	71
(Oct)	1974	16	41	3	11	71

In terms of votes cast, the change has been even more dramatic:

Votes cast for SNP.: 1964–1974

		Vote	% in Scotland
	1964	64,044	2.4
	1966	128,474	5.0
	1970	306,802	11.4
(Feb)	1974	632,032	21.9
(Oct)	1974	839,628	30.4

From 1964 to February 1974, the SNP had, on average, doubled its vote at each general election. From fifteen candidates, no MPs and 2.4 per cent of the vote in 1964, the party had grown to a point where, by October 1974, it had candidates in every Scottish constituency, won eleven seats and polled over 30 per cent of the total vote, making it the second party in Scotland. Indeed, by October, in parts of rural Scotland the SNP (with 34.6 per cent of votes cast) had emerged as the largest single party. It was similarly poised to become the largest party in East Central Scotland and Strathclyde.

The possibilities for a further SNP advance are certainly strong. In October 1974, the SNP achieved 42 second-places, compared to 17 in February. No fewer than 35 of these were in Labour-held seats, five in Conservative and two in Liberal. On a 10 per cent swing to the SNP from

Labour, 23 seats would fall. A simultaneous swing of 5 per cent from Labour and Conservative to SNP would give the Nationalists 26 seats. A simultaneous 10 per cent swing would give them 39 seats, well over half of all the seats in Scotland.

Since October 1974, all parliamentary by-elections (at least up to summer 1977) occurred in England. The only test of public opinion north of the Tweed was thus opinion polls and the local elections of May 1977. The varying support for the SNP in the opinion polls is set out in the table below.

SNP support since October 1974 *

	Oct 1974 %	Feb 1975 %	Apr 1975 %	Sept 1975 %	March 1976 %	Feb 1977 %	April 1977 %
SNP	30.4	29	27	24	33	31	36
Con	24.7	28	31	32	28	32	27
Lab	36.3	40	37	38	24	29	27
Lib	8.3	3	5	5	6	5	5
SLP	—	—	—	—	8	3	3

* Source: System Three Scotland opinion polls.

These figures show an SNP decline until late autumn 1975, followed by a rapid rise after the Government's devolution White Paper and the formation of the breakaway Scottish Labour Party (SLP). It was the district elections of May 1977 which thus provided the first hard evidence of Nationalist support.

Although the SNP seized 107 seats, their overall success was less than expected. Their best results were in the new towns and in parts of Glasgow (where the SNP gained 15 seats). The Nationalists won control of four councils (Falkirk, Cumbernauld, East Kilbride and Clydebank). Elsewhere, however, in such places as Dunfermline and Aberdeen, SNP successes were very patchy. In all, something like an 8 per cent swing from Labour to the SNP since October 1974 had occurred. This, coupled with a strong Conservative advance in some areas, was enough to destroy Labour's once vice-like grip over central industrial Scotland.

What will happen to the SNP in the coming months is clearly unpredictable. But even if the SNP advances no further, and if the nationalist tide in Scotland is stemmed by devolution, the success achieved in the past decade deserves close analysis.

Why have the Nationalists succeeded while the Liberals have failed? Essentially, the breakthrough achieved so far by the SNP has been the result of a combination of four factors: the inadequacy and sterility of the Labour Party in Scotland; the lack of any alternative to Labour because of the weakness of Conservatism in Scotland (although since October 1974 there has been some evidence of a revival in Scottish Conservatism); the latent resentment in Scotland of economic neglect and a remote Whitehall administration; and, perhaps most potent of all, the transformation which oil has brought about to the Scottish economy and the political aspirations of its people. Labour's weakness in Scotland has perhaps not been fully appreciated in accounting for the rise of the SNP.

The accusation of Jim Sillars, the leader of the breakaway Scottish Labour Party, that Labour was demoralised and had lost any sense of purpose, is fair comment. Labour's Scottish membership was one such weakness. Although its *nominal* membership in 1976 was 74,000, Transport House itself estimated its real membership at 'possibly 25,000'. The 70,000 SNP members are thus double or even treble Labour's active membership. The Labour recruiting campaign launched in 1976 was aimed to remedy this defect, particularly among the under-45 age group.

Labour's organisational weakness was equally severe in terms of full-time agents. Outside its Glasgow head office, Labour had only five agents in the whole of Scotland. Labour admitted that its 400 branch organisations (compared to the 475 of the SNP) were 'relatively inactive'. By and large, their councillors and activists were older men. The party was an ageing party. And, inevitably, in areas which had seen one-party rule for many years, there were instances of corruption by Labour councillors. An embarrassingly high number of municipal by-elections after October 1974 were due to vacancies from this score.

The opportunity provided by Labour's weakness, the political 'capital' to be gained from 'Scotland's oil' and the economic recession have all helped the SNP. But it is the SNP itself which has transformed an opportune climate into political success by attracting support from so many sections of society. Here lies another factor to explain why the SNP has succeeded where Liberals have failed. It seems clear (from surveys carried out by Systems Three, the Dundee-based opinion poll organisation), that the SNP's strongest support comes from the 18–34-year-old skilled workers, especially in the new towns. The 1977 district elections in such new towns as Cumbernauld and East Kilbride were added evidence of this fact. But the SNP has attracted support from across the whole social and economic spectrum. It is this which explains why the SNP has been able to overcome the electoral system and break through (even though on average it needed 71,853 votes in October 1974 to elect an SNP MP, compared to 35,950 votes for Labour and 37,778 for a Conservative). It should also be stressed, however, that the SNP has often found the going hardest where its opponents have been very firmly anti-devolutionist. Two such examples are the Labour MP Tam Dalyell in West Lothian and the Tory MP 'Teddy' Taylor in Glasgow Cathcart. In neither seat has the SNP progressed recently.

It is an interesting analysis to compare the fortunes of the SNP and the other Nationalist Party, Plaid Cymru, in Wales. Like the SNP, the Plaid got off to a poor start in its very early years.

From its foundation in August 1925 until the Carmarthen by-election of 14 July 1966, the Plaid had never won a parliamentary election. Its record at General Elections between 1945 and 1966 had been uninspiring.

The Plaid Cymru Vote

Election	Candidates	MPs elected	Forfeited deposits	Total votes	% of Welsh total
1945	7	0	6	16,017	1.2
1950	7	0	6	17,580	1.2
1951	4	0	4	10,920	0.7
1955	11	0	7	45,119	3.1
1959	20	0	14	77,571	5.2
1964	23	0	21	69,507	4.8
1966	20	0	18	61,071	4.3

In the 1964 General Election, when its 23 candidates had polled 69,507 votes, the Plaid had saved its deposit in only two constituencies (Caernarvon 21.4 per cent and Merioneth 16.8 per cent). In only four other constituencies (Carmarthen, Cardiganshire, Caerphilly and West Rhondda) had it secured over 10 per cent of votes cast. These results laid emphasis to the fact that its strength rested very much in rural Welsh-speaking North Wales, with a small protest vote in some of the South Wales valleys. Very much the same pattern was to be seen in the 1966 election. With 20 candidates, its total poll had slipped to 61,071 votes. The party marginally improved its vote in Caernarvon (21.7 per cent and increased its performance quite strongly in Carmarthen (to 16.1 per cent). But these were the only two deposits saved. Once again only four other candidates managed to secure 10 per cent (Merthyr Tydfil; Llanelli; Caerphilly and Merionethshire).

There was little in either the 1964 or 1966 results to suggest that the Plaid was poised for a breakthrough. Nor, indeed, had it previously ever polled particularly well in a by-election (in by-elections in Wales between 1950 and 1966, it had saved its deposit only once, at Aberdare in 1954).

The by-election of July 1966, in the sprawling rural Carmarthen constituency, set Welsh Nationalism alight. The Plaid's candidate was Gwynfor Evans, president of the party since 1945 and easily its most commanding figure. In the 1966 election he had achieved the Plaid's second-best result in Wales – but he was still in third place, over 14,000 votes behind Lady Megan Lloyd George who had held the seat for Labour. Indeed, even though Carmarthen had always possessed a highly individual political history, most pundits thought that the Liberals (who had held the seat until 1957) might be the most likely party to take the seat. In the event, aided by such local factors as the closure of the

Carmarthen – Aberystwyth railway line, Evans swept to an historic victory. For the first time in history, the Plaid had returned a representative to Westminster.

No further by-elections occurred in Wales until March 1967, when Labour was faced with a vacancy in West Rhondda – one of the most working-class, declining communities in all Wales, with an unemployment level twice that of the average for Britain as a whole. In the wake of the party's triumph at Carmarthen, Rhondda West was a situation ideally suited for the Nationalists. With a Labour-controlled council for many decades, the Plaid could lay the blame for the decline of the Rhondda very much at Labour's door.

The Nationalist challenge failed; but they had cut the Labour majority in one of the most cast-iron of all Labour seats to a desperately marginal 2,306 (9.1 per cent). The increase in the Nationalist vote was far greater even than in Carmarthen. In some ways, it was an even more significant result. Carmarthen could be, and indeed had been dismissed as rural, isolated, untypical. Rhondda was a bedrock of the Labour movement; the Nationalists' base had been feeble compared with Carmarthen. And yet they had very nearly captured Rhondda West too.

Labour's stronghold in Wales was to suffer one more challenge before the next election. This time the constituency was Caerphilly, another old mining stronghold. Once again, Labour was faced with waging an essentially defensive campaign. And again, the Nationalists came within an ace of taking the seat from Labour. It seemed that no Labour seat could be counted as secure in the face of this Nationalist challenge.

With this background of successes, the Plaid went on to fight the 1970 General Election on a broad front—with thirty-six candidates. Although none was elected, the party polled 175,000 votes. Significantly, its best performance was in the traditional rural Welsh-speaking part of North Wales. The Plaid finished within range of victory in Caernarvon and Merioneth in addition to polling strongly in Carmarthen (although Gwynfor Evans lost the seat), Cardigan and Anglesey. In the valleys, the Plaid took over 10,000 votes in Aberdare and Caerphilly, proving that there was clearly still a reservoir of protest votes to be polled.

Meanwhile the success of the Plaid between 1966 and 1970 changed the character of the Party. The hard core of the Plaid was joined by a new influx of working-class supporters—men uncertain of their future in the declining heavy industries of the South. This influx created its own problems. For example, the language issue has been of little interest to the newcomers from the South. Their aims (symbolised by Party Vice-President Phil Williams) were much more an economic nationalism.

From 1970 to February 1974, under the Conservative Government of Edward Heath, the Nationalists were presented with virtually no by-election openings in Wales. The only exception, once again in a traditional Labour South Wales valley stronghold was the Merthyr by-election of 13

April 1972)—the seat that the veteran S. O. Davies had won as an 'Independent Labour' in the 1970 General Election. Although the Plaid again ran Labour very close, it failed to seize the seat. It was against this background—and with the Liberals and Scottish Nationalists riding high—that the Plaid entered the 1974 election.

In the February 1974 election, the Nationalists in Wales fared very differently to their colleagues north of the Border. Plaid Cymru's share of the vote in Wales dropped from 11.5 per cent in 1970 to 10.7 per cent, even though it had once again contested all Welsh seats. But to compensate for this, the party gained its first-ever seats in a General Election, taking Caernarvon and Merioneth from Labour, and missing Camarthen by a mere three votes.

In contrast to this success in the rural areas, Plaid Cymru did not do so well in solid Labour districts in South Wales. In Aberdare, one of the South Wales seats where it seemed to have a good chance, the party hardly increased its 1970 vote. Partly, perhaps, the Liberal revival in Wales (the Liberals fielded 31 candidates and their vote rose from 6.8 per cent in 1970 to 16.3 per cent in 1974) may have held back the Nationalists. For whatever reasons, Welsh Nationalism was achieving nothing like the erosion of the two-party system being witnessed in Scotland.

Very much the same pattern was repeated in October. Unlike the Nationalists in Scotland, Plaid Cymru had a very mixed outcome in Wales. Although the party captured Carmarthenshire – which it had missed so narrowly in February—thereby increasing its parliamentary representation to three, it came nowhere near to victory in any other seat. Its total share of the Welsh vote was 10.8 per cent, virtually unchanged from the 10.7 per cent achieved in February and still below the 11.5 per cent secured in June 1970. Meanwhile, Labour, with 49.5 per cent of the total vote, still dominated Welsh politics. No amount of disappointment in the total vote achieved by the Plaid could disguise the tonic achieved by the triumphant return of Gwynfor Evans for Carmarthenshire.

Since October 1974, there have been no parliamentary by-elections to test the Plaid's strength. In local elections in 1976 and 1977 however, the Plaid could claim some success. In 1976, it registered a net gain of 63 seats, but many of these were in rural areas where political labels were being introduced for the first time. Plaid Cymru lost ground in the council where it had been strongest, Cynon Valley (roughly the Aberdare constituency), and in the Welsh capital city no Plaid candidate was remotely close to winning—even in the ward which went Welsh Nationalist in 1969. The absence of any general tide in their favour makes their good result in Rhymney Valley (the Caerphilly constituency) and their victory in Merthyr Tydfil quite outstanding (Plaid had 21 councillors to Labour's 8). The 1977 elections likewise saw some minor successes but no major breakthrough. But local elections are not General Elections. So far, the

Plaid has not been able to rival the SNP in parliamentary victories.

Why, then, should this be so? First, its real strength is concentrated in rural Welsh-speaking Wales (all three of the Plaid seats rest in this category). Secondly, so far it seems its isolated successes in the valleys have been protest votes which have melted away. The Plaid has yet to build on its valley by-election or municipal successes at a general election. With the exception of Carmarthen (which, as already discussed, is a sprawling rural constituency), the Plaid has rapidly declined after by-election polls.

Date of by-election	% PC	Constituency	1970	Feb 1974	Oct 1974
9 Mar. 1967	39.9	Rhondda West	14.0	12.9	8.3
18 July 1968	40.4	Caerphilly	28.5	27.6	24.5
13 Apr. 1972	37.0	Merthyr Tydfil	(—)	22.9	14.8

Between the respective by-election and the General Election of October 1974, the Plaid vote has declined 31.6 per cent in the Rhondda, 22.2 per cent in Merthyr and 15.9 per cent in Caerphilly.

Partly, also, the Plaid's lack of success can be explained by the continued strength of Liberalism in Wales. Wales boasts (in Montgomeryshire) the only constituency to have returned a Liberal at every election this century. Liberalism has tenaciously survived elsewhere in Wales. Thus Liberals polled relatively well in Wales even in October 1974; their total vote declined only by 0.2 per cent compared to February. In many ways, the Plaid and the Liberals are fighting for the same radical heritage. It is no coincidence that all the seats held by the Plaid were Liberal in 1945. There is little doubt, however, that there is a very large reservoir of protest votes to be tapped in South Wales. This was well demonstrated in the 1976 local elections when resentment at Labour control produced shock results. Not only did Conservatives capture Cardiff and Newport, but the Ratepayers swept to power in Swansea, a city which had been in Labour control for 40 years and which stayed faithful even in the 1968 election massacres.

But the Plaid has a mammoth task to translate protest votes into parliamentary victory. In the South Wales valleys, as the table below shows, even in the six seats where the Plaid came second to Labour, their chances of future victory seem remote. In each seat, Labour's majority had increased since the February election.

Labour-held seats in which Plaid Cymru came second in October 1974

Constituency	Labour majority	Labour % majority
Caerphilly	13,709	32.1
Aberdare	16,064	42.0
Neath	17,723	43.5
Merthyr	16,805	55.8
Abertillery	18,355	66.8
Rhondda	34,481	68.8

These figures serve to emphasise that, at least in the present climate, a major Nationalist tide in Wales is not likely.

Between them, the Liberals and Nationalists have launched a succession of challenges to the two-party system. In Scotland, and to a lesser degree in Wales, the two-party system has been partly destroyed. But England seems as far away as ever to returning a major parliamentary third-party contingent. The growing demand for electoral reform and proportional representation (itself ironically partly a reaction to SNP success in Scotland) may in the longer term produce some form of realignment. In the short term, Liberals are fighting for their existence as a major party.

Ironically England, which has lent most support to Liberal challenges to the 'system', has given no encouragement to the parties along the political fringe. At no time have extremist candidates of the Right or Left achieved any substantial success.

The electoral history of the Communist Party since 1945 has been one of almost total disaster. In 1945 the Communists, benefitting from the shift to the Left in the country as well as the popularity of Russia as our war-time ally, achieved a poll of over 100,000. Two MPs were elected, in Mile End and West Fife. Since 1945, they have never elected an MP; in the last two decades they have not been remotely near to electing anyone. In 1950, even with a massive 100 candidates, only three saved their deposit. Since then, the party has been an electoral irrelevance.

The Communist Vote: 1951 – 1974

Election	Candidates	MPs elected	Forfeited deposits	Total votes	% of U.K. total
1951	10	—	10	21,640	0.1
1955	17	—	15	33,144	0.1
1959	18	—	17	30,896	0.1
1964	36	—	36	46,442	0.2
1966	57	—	57	62,092	0.2
1970	58	—	58	37,970	0.1
1974 (Feb)	44	—	43	32,741	0.1
1974 (Oct)	29	—	29	17,426	0.1

Even in the general election of February 1974, when support for third-party candidates was at its highest, the Communists fared disastrously. Only one candidate (Jimmy Reid, a very prominent local shop steward at Upper Clyde) saved his deposit.

Having done badly in February, October proved even worse. Only in Dunbartonshire Central (where Jimmy Reid was the standard bearer) could the party poll even moderately respectably (with 8.7 per cent of the vote, down from 14.4 per cent in February). Not a single Communist candidate saved his deposit, and none except Jimmy Reid even managed 3 per cent of the vote. It was, perhaps, some small comfort for the Communist Party that the other left-wing candidates suffered equally severely. Thus the Workers Revolutionary Party (WRP), with 10 candidates in the field in October 1974, fared disastrously. No candidate obtained more than the 572 votes (1.5 per cent of the vote) polled by Vanessa Redgrave in Newham N.E.

If the WRP performance was abysmal, the five candidates fielded by the Marxist Leninists fared even worse. Only one candidate secured more than 1 per cent of the vote whilst the other four candidates fell back from their vote in February.

Since 1945, a rapidly changing succession of extremist right-wing parties have at various times fought at General Elections and by-elections. The Union Movement, formed by Oswald Mosley in February 1948 and renamed the Action Party in January 1973, fought eight contests between 1959 and 1972. Its best result was the 8.1 per cent secured by Oswald Mosley himself, fighting North Kensington in 1959. The only other occasion it has secured over 5 per cent of the vote was in November 1961, in a by-election in the Moss Side seat in Manchester, a constituency with a strong immigrant vote. In the 1966 election, the four Union Movement candidates secured an average 3.7 per cent, with Mosley obtaining 4.6 per cent of the vote in Shoreditch and Finsbury.

Of the older right-wing movements, the League of Empire Loyalists (formed by A. K. Chesterton in April 1954) never secured above 4 per cent of the poll in the four parliamentary contests which it fought before it merged with the National Front. The British Empire Party, formed by P. J. Ridout in 1951, fought only one contest—taking 3.4 per cent of the vote in Ogmore in 1951.

Of the parties securing support on a strongly anti-immigrant ticket, Colin Jordan's British Movement secured 3 per cent in a by-election at Birmingham Ladywood in June 1969. The British National Party (formed in February 1960) had rather more success, taking 9.1 per cent of the vote in Southall in 1964. In 1966, its three contested seats were Deptford (7.1 per cent), Smethwick (1.5 per cent) and Southall (7.4 per cent)—all areas of high immigrant concentration.

In special circumstances, the National Democratic Party took 21 per cent of the vote opposing the Speaker at Southampton Itchen, and Edward Martell's National Fellowship took 19 per cent opposing Tony Benn in Bristol S.E in August 1963 (in a straight fight). Otherwise, the Right had been impotent in electoral battles. A new dimension was introduced, however, in March 1967 with the birth of the National Front.

The National Front was formed by John Tyndall in March 1967 as an amalgamation of five small extreme right-wing groups – the League of Empire Loyalists, the British National Party, the Greater British Movement, the Racial Preservation Society and the English National Party. Its first entry into electoral politics was in a by-election in Acton in March

1968. Its candidate, Andrew Fontaine, a Norfolk landowner, secured only 5.6 per cent of the vote. No other by-election was fought before the General Election of June 1970. For the General Election, the Front fielded ten candidates, polling 11,349 votes. Its best two results, where it obtained over 5 per cent of the poll, were Islington North (5.6 per cent) and Deptford (5.5 per cent).

Between 1970 and February 1974, the Front fought five by-elections. It secured two extremely creditable votes in these five contests – 8.2 per cent at Uxbridge in December 1972 and no less than 16 per cent at West Bromwich in May 1973. Encouraged, no doubt, by these results, the Front fielded 54 candidates in February 1974. It secured 76,429 votes, an average of 1,423 per candidate compared to 1,135 in 1970. In seven constituencies, all with heavy immigrant concentrations, it secured over 5 per cent of the poll. Between the General Elections of February and October 1974, only one by-election vacancy occurred – in Newham South. The Front had secured 6.9 per cent of the vote here in February; in the May by-election, its vote increased to 11.5 per cent (securing second place for the Front).

In the October 1974 general election, although the Front fielded 90 candidates, and polled 114,954 votes these figures were in fact a step back from February for, in addition to polling *fewer* average votes than in February, all 90 candidates lost their deposit and none secured over 10 per cent of the poll (the Front's best result was in Hackney South and Shoreditch, where, fighting the seat for the first time, it secured 9.4 per cent).

Of the 23 seats in which the National Front captured over 4 per cent of the poll, the best results were obtained in London, especially in the East End and in the Tottenham and Wood Green areas. Despite the relatively poor results obtained, the Front had still polled over 114,000 votes, a greater total than the Communist Party has ever polled in a General Election.

Since the General Election of October 1974, the impact of the National Front on British politics has begun to increase. It has fed on growing unemployment in areas of immigrant concentration.

The Front has polled well in a variety of by-elections in Labour areas in such seats as Walsall and Stechford, but its most impressive results have been in municipal polls. In local council elections in May 1976, 176 National Front candidates contested 34 wards and collected 49,767 votes. In 21 wards the National Front pushed Liberal candidates into fourth place. In Blackburn, the breakaway National Party led by John Kingsley Read won two council seats, while the Front's most dramatic result was in Leicester, where it secured nearly 20 per cent of all votes cast in the city and was within 100 votes of victory in several city-centre wards with a large immigrant population. Much publicity was again attracted by the Front in the 1977 local elections. In the G.L.C. elections, fighting 91 of the 92 wards, the Front obtained 119,000 votes, (5.3 per cent of the total) and pushed the Liberals into fourth place in 32 seats. But nowhere could the Front manage second place. Its best results – in Bethnal Green and Bow (19.2 per cent) and Hackney South and Shoreditch (19.0 per cent) – reflected its appeal in the East End. Outside London, the Front's showing was patchy. It slipped back in Leicester, while all but four of its eighteen candidates were bottom of the poll in Bradford. In the West Midlands it managed an average 9 per cent of the vote in Warley, West Bromwich and Wolverhampton.

Though the National Front has polled better than any extremist party since Mosley's Blackshirts fought local elections in London's East End in the 1930s, and although in July 1976 the Front declared its intention to field 318 candidates at the next General Election, it remains as far from challenging the two-party system as ever.

The difficulties experienced in breaking the two-party domination have been felt equally severely by would-be rebels from within a party attempting to retain their seat at a General Election or by-election against official party candidates. Isolated examples of this occurred in the early 1950s and in 1970 S. O. Davies proved at Merthyr that a successful rebellion is possible. Most such Labour rebels, however, have met with failure.

One such example was the case of Desmond Donnelly, a right-wing backbench Labour MP who had been vociferously opposed to steel nationalisation. He had been elected Labour MP for Pembrokeshire in 1950. He resigned the Labour whip in January 1968 and in March 1968 he was expelled from the Labour Party. A month later the Pembrokeshire Constituency Labour Party was disaffiliated. He remained an Independent Labour MP until he founded the Democratic Party in May 1969. The Democratic Party fought two by-elections prior to the 1970 General Election (at Newcastle-under-Lyne in October 1969 and at Louth two months later) polling 3.6 per cent and 4.5 per cent respectively. In the 1970 election, the Democratic Party fielded five candidates, Desmond Donnelly himself fighting a losing battle to retain Pembrokeshire (he came third, with 21.5 per cent of the poll). The Conservatives took the seat. The four other Democratic candidates polled abysmally. In April 1971 Donnelly joined the Conservatives, and the Democratic Party appears to have disbanded.

The most famous example of a Labour rebel in recent times has been the case of Dick Taverne in Lincoln. The background to Taverne's conflict with the Lincoln Labour Party was long and complicated. It came to a head when he resigned his seat as Labour MP on 6 October 1972. In one of the most famous by-election campaigns in British history, and with powerful support from both the press and well-known individuals, Taverne won the by-election of 1 March 1973 as a 'Democratic Labour' candidate with a massive 13,000 majority. Coming at a time when Liberals and Nationalists were also hammering the established parties, Taverne's triumph seemed yet further evidence of the erosion of the two-party system. But like the Liberal triumph, it was short-lived lived. Although Dick Taverne narrowly retained the seat in February 1974 he was defeated in October by 985 votes (even though on both occasions Liberals had not contested the seat). Taverne's 'Campaign for Social Democracy' itself was an electoral disaster. The four candidates other than Taverne in the February election polled an average 1.5 per cent. None fought in October.

The other Labour rebels of October 1974 also went down to defeat. At Blyth, Eddie Milne lost by a mere 78 votes after a determined Labour assult on the seat. In the Sheffield Brightside constituency, where Eddie Griffiths had been ousted by his local party, Joan Maynard retained the seat comfortably for Labour, although Griffiths polled 10,182 votes (27.9 per cent of the vote).

Over the coming months, there may be other Labour rebels, but history is not on their side. For the record of the electorate since 1945 (at least in England) is clear. However unpopular the two major parties may be, in the long term it is they who have survived and their challengers who have been defeated.

8 Devolution and Regionalism

Alan Butt Philip

Britain is once more a disunited kingdom. The unity of the British state is, for the first time in fifty years, under direct attack from within. There is in fact a constitutional crisis. The pressing problems arising from the growth of nationalism in Scotland, Wales and Northern Ireland, and from the less marked rise in regional consciousness in England, have not been helped by confusion over terminology. Devolution is for many a word devoid of clear meaning, a non-word; for that very reason it has a special political usefulness. In this chapter, 'devolution' will refer to the transfer of power from central government to a subordinate tier of government. Devolution in current British politics is largely a response to nationalism, but in this contemporary debate 'nationalism' does not usually carry with it aggressive or fascist connotations. 'Nationalism' will refer to the active solidarity of a group of human beings who share a common culture or history and a sense of nationhood, and who seek to give these a political reality, for example, through self-government. 'Regionalism' also necessitates the solidarity of a group of people, but their bond need only be geographical contiguity and an active desire for political recognition, helped perhaps by a quasi-cultural affinity.

Historical Development

The significance and suitability of devolution within the United Kingdom can only be understood if the various nationalisms within Britain are recognised as nationalisms with a real historical basis. The nineteenth century saw the development in Europe of nationalist ideologies and political movements for self-determination typified by the revolutions of 1848. But the twentieth century has witnessed the greatest development of nationalism, epitomised in Europe by the German problem and the Treaty of Versailles which divided up the Austrian and Ottoman empires in 1919;

and elsewhere in the world by the collapse of the colonial empires and more recently by the Bangladesh war. In Victorian Britain the furthest parts of the kingdom were becoming fully assimilated into a modern integrated state for the first time; in this process mass migrations and the vast improvement in rail, sea and press communications all played a major part. Yet even at this stage there appeared the paradox of the growing strength of autonomist movements just at the time when the world was becoming a smaller place—the movement for home rule in Ireland which led to the first break-up of the United Kingdom. Until the 1920s the Liberal Party was the principal vehicle of the new nationalisms and advocate of home rule. Gladstone's firm stand in the mid-1880s provoked Chamberlain's Liberal Unionist breakaway; the young Lloyd George led the unsuccessful Cymru Fydd (Young Wales) movement in the 1890s calling for a Welsh Parliament; Asquith, then Prime Minister, pledged the Liberals to 'home rule all round' for Ireland, Scotland and Wales in 1912. Before the First World War these ideas also formed part of the received wisdom of the burgeoning Labour movement, notably under Keir Hardie's influence.

The urgency of the Irish crisis and the onset of world war, however, transformed Britain's political climate and pushed the Scottish and Welsh claims into the background. Lloyd George as British war leader became the new Welsh St David; Scottish and Welsh national consciousness became subsumed in Britain's Imperial role. The playing of the Orange card in Ulster and the Irish revolt from 1916 started the process which led to the creation of the Irish Free State in 1922. With Ireland out of the way the demands for home rule elsewhere no longer seemed pressing, particularly after a Speaker's conference on devolution in 1920 foundered in disagreement. Following the Irish example, however, nationalist parties were formed in Wales in 1925 and in Scotland in 1928; but their contribution to the politics of the period was very limited and their influence largely confined to sections of the intelligentsia. Unemployment, depression and the slump were to dominate the thinking of the Scots and the Welsh in the 1930s; their language was the language of socialism or communism, not nationalism.

The nationalist influence emerged strengthened from the Second World War despite the stand of conscientious objection made by many individual nationalists and severe restrictions on their political organisations. In particular, the Scottish Nationalists—who had polled sizeable votes in elections in the early thirties—gained their first MP in Dr Robert McIntyre when he snatched victory in the 1945 Motherwell by-election, largely as a result of the wartime electoral truce between the major parties. This victory was not sustained in the general election which soon followed; the Scottish National Party polled on average 10 per cent in Scotland and Plaid Cymru in Wales 8 per cent of the votes cast in the seats they contested. The new Labour Government headed by Clement Attlee was not willing to meet even the modest demands of some of its own supporters in the Commons for the appointment of a Secretary of State for Wales to complement the Scottish Secretary and the Scottish Office which had been set up in 1885 under Gladstone's third administration. Aneurin Bevan, Labour's leading Welsh politician, spoke for very many socialists when he argued that it was impossible to isolate the important problems of Wales (or Scotland) from those of Britain as a whole and that such problems required common treatment.

The notion of a beneficent centrally planned economy and the virtues of a fully integrated uniform British state were strongly held. Nationalism was also associated at this time in a European context with pre-war fascism. The very success of the Labour Party in British electoral terms, and the critical importance of its support in Scotland and Wales to that success, also made devolution less attractive on the Left. Political considerations thus coincided with the common presumption of the English majority that Scotland and Wales were not separate nations but indeed were part of England, as opposed to Britain. Yet at the same time as Labour was backpedalling during the late forties on the devolution issue, Plaid Cymru, the Welsh Nationalist Party, under its new leader Gwynfor Evans, was enjoying a spell of electoral strength reflected in healthy votes obtained in the Aberdare and Ogmore by-elections in 1946. Early in 1947 the beginnings of the Scottish Covenant movement in support of a Scottish Parliament took shape in the form of a Scottish National Assembly made up of representatives of much of Scottish life and of most political persuasions. This was inspired by Dr John McCormick, a Liberal and ex-SNP politician, and led to the drawing up late in 1949 of the Scottish Covenant which was ultimately signed by two million Scots. As a demonstration of popular support for a Scottish Parliament it was a brilliant device, but for practical political purposes it was a disaster. The challenge of the Covenant to the existing (Labour) Government made Labour more hostile to devolution, and the signatures to the Covenant were not backed up by votes at elections. The new Conservative government set up a Royal Commission on Scottish Affairs in 1952 which recommended minor administrative changes. A similar campaign in Wales in favour of a Parliament for Wales ran for five years. The Welsh petition carried 250,000 signatures but this did not save a bill to set up a Welsh Parliament from being voted down by 48 to 14 in the House of Commons in March 1955. This unfortunate result left Labour and Liberal devolutionists less keen to pursue the cause of home rule in Wales.

Yet it was from the Welsh corner that the debate over administrative devolution re-emerged in 1957. The Advisory Council for Wales recommended to the Government that a Secretary of State for Wales with Cabinet status be appointed to match the Scottish Secretary of State. Although the Conservative Government lacked interest in the proposal, the opposition took up the issue strongly. The Labour Party examined the plan and committed itself to create a Secretary of State for Wales and a Welsh Office on return to power. The prevailing sentiment seemed to be that the Scottish Secretary was certainly helpful to Scottish interests, and no harm was likely to come about if a similar arrangement was made for Wales. James Griffiths, the Welsh deputy leader of the Labour Party, pressed the matter and influential Welsh colleagues such as Aneurin Bevan and James Callaghan did not resist. Labour's decision reflected a rising interest from all the three major parties in articulating specific Scottish and Welsh concerns, issuing separate Scottish and Welsh political programmes and using the Welsh language much more in their literature. The competition for votes found its counterpart in competing pledges to extend administrative devolution and to attend to special Celtic cultural concerns.

The prosperity of the 'never-had-it-so-good' period in the late 1950s and early 1960s did not stem the slow development of nationalist and regionalist attitudes. Indeed the very unevenness of the distribution of that prosperity highlighted the structural economic problems of the heavy industrial and the remote rural regions. At the same time the growth of regional commercial television from the mid-fifties and the competing development of the BBC's radio and television services and of the regional press served to strengthen and to articulate Scottish, Welsh and regional consciousness and nationalist-regionalist demands. This was backed up by such omens as the rising activity of the nationalist parties at elections, spearheaded by Plaid Cymru in Wales, and the political swing (to Labour) in Scotland in the 1959 general election which was the opposite of that in the rest of Britain. From 1961 the rise of the Scottish National Party became clearly discernible from the results of by-elections, especially the strong challenge at West Lothian in 1962 the year that marked the Liberal revival in other parts of Britain. Ironically at this moment the Welsh nationalists were at one of their lowest points as a result of bomb explosions attributed to nationalist splinter groups (attacking pipelines and dams) and of the direct action tactics adopted by the Welsh Language Society formed in 1962. In Scotland too new nationalist groupings such as Wendy Wood's Scottish Patriots and Roland Muirhead's Scottish National Congress reflected a mood of frustration among nationalists at the relative failure of pursuing a strategy of victory through the ballot-box; there was a strong desire to try other methods, both bridge-building and boat-burning in character. Viewed in this light the upsurge of nationalist electoral fortunes in the mid-sixties came none too soon; techniques of violence or direct action lost their glamour and savour when success could be had much less dangerously at the polls. Nevertheless it was a sign of the times that the removal of the Stone of Scone from underneath the Coronation throne in Westminster Abbey in 1950 (the most intriguing piece of nationalist freelancing since 1945) found as its counterpart before the investiture in Caernarfon Castle in 1969 of Prince Charles as Prince of

Wales an unsuccessful bomb attempt in Abergele which killed its two participants.

The contours of the entire British political system were visibly changing from 1961 onwards. The certainty of economic success waned; the first attempts at incomes policy and regional policy were made; the instruments of planning were sharpened. Old faces left the political stage, such as Eden, Macmillan, Gaitskell and Bevan, to be replaced by new leaders—Edward Heath, Reginald Maudling, Harold Wilson and George Brown. The Liberals revived their electoral fortunes, followed by the Nationalists; confidence in the constitution and the workings of parliament declined sharply. At the 1964 election, the Labour Party squeaked into government with a majority of five seats; in the Scottish Highlands the Liberals captured every seat from Muckle Flugga to Ballachulish, while elsewhere Scotland followed the swing to Labour. One of the first results of the change in political complexion of the government was the appointment of James Griffiths as Secretary of State for Wales with Cabinet rank and with a new Welsh Office to support him. Another consequence was the formation in 1965 of the Highlands and Islands Development Board with a brief to develop both the economic and community life of the region. Finally an institutional framework was given to regional policy-making through the setting up in 1965 of eight regional planning councils in England with regional planning boards composed of civil servants working for the councils but under the overall supervision of the new Department of Economic Affairs. This marked a new stress on the economic problems of the regions, which had only begun to be fully recognised in the early 1960s with the introduction of new financial incentives for industrial development in regions with high unemployment and with the appointment of Lord Hailsham, a member of the Cabinet, as Minister for the North-East of England. This attention to the problems of the poorer regions was intensified by a scheme for regionally-discriminated investment grants towards the purchase of plant and machinery for manufacturing industry and the physical control of all but the smallest industrial developments by imposing a mandatory requirement for an industrial development certificate issued by the Board of Trade. The acceptance of these new economic aids to the regions was based on the belief that regional unemployment was primarily the result of the decline of traditional industries and that the remoter regions were the casualties of the 'stop-go' approach to the Treasury's management of demand. The onset and the strengthening of regional economic policy in England had no political counterpart, although governments of whatever party were anxious to minimise loss of voter support. The same could not be said of the position in Scotland and Wales where from 1966 the nationalist parties staged their first prominent revival.

The nationalist trail was blazed by Plaid Cymru at the Carmarthen by-election in July 1966, which took place as a result of the death of Lady

Megan Lloyd George who held the seat for Labour. Although there were local factors at work, the decisive victory of Gwynfor Evans, the Plaid's leader and candidate, was clearly an event of national significance in Wales and gave tremendous encouragement to Scottish and Welsh nationalist opinion. The first Plaid Cymru MP was joined in the House of Commons by a Scottish Nationalist, Mrs Winifred Ewing, after the sensational Hamilton by-election in November 1967. A string of by-elections between 1966 and 1969 and evidence from local council elections all pointed to a striking upsurge in nationalist electoral support, although the desire for independence for Scotland and Wales (according to opinion surveys) was not shared by all nationalist voters and by only 10 to 20 per cent of the Scottish and Welsh public. The nationalist challenge made a serious impact on the politicians at Westminster; the Scottish and Welsh Offices were given increased powers and in 1967 a Welsh Language Act was passed which gave equal validity to the use of Welsh and English in Wales. Yet neither the Conservative nor Labour parties were inspired to react directly to the constitutional issues raised by the Nationalists. The Labour Government decided to postpone that set of problems by appointing, late in 1968, a Royal Commission on the Constitution chaired by the independent economist, Lord Crowther (who was succeeded on his death by Lord Kilbrandon, a Scottish judge). The Kilbrandon Commission did not report back until 1973, so great was the complexity of its task and so considerable its divisions. In the meantime, a Royal Commission on Local Government Reform in England chaired by Lord Redcliffe-Maud, an academic and former diplomat, and a parallel commission in Scotland under Lord Wheatley, a leading Scottish lawyer, had both put forward their proposals for reforming the structure of local government in 1969, although their schemes differed from each other. These reports were followed by legislation in 1972 – 3 which enacted some of their ideas and which greatly reduced the number of local councils. But whereas the Scottish reforms included a regional tier of government between the Scottish Office and the district councils, the Conservatives preferred to retain counties as the top tier of local government in England. They ignored Maud's recommendations for the formation of twelve indirectly-elected regional councils to play a co-ordinating role between the different branches of national and local administrations.

The year 1969 saw a diminution of Nationalist pressure as Britain's economic difficulties lightened after devaluation. Wales celebrated the Investiture of Prince Charles as Prince of Wales, a nationalist occasion which served too to strengthen the union with England. The crisis in Northern Ireland came to the centre of the stage when British troops were sent in to keep the peace in August 1969. The illusion of the success of devolution on the Stormont model was shattered by the physical reaction of supporters of the Catholic minority to decades of denial of civil rights and religious discrimination by the Protestant Unionist majority.

In the 1970 General Election, the existence of the Kilbrandon Commission allowed Labour and Conservative politicians to plead to the electors the need for leaving their options open on home rule and related issues. The Liberals, now fully committed to a federal solution to Britain's constitutional problems, suffered a setback and while Nationalists in both Scotland and Wales fought on a much broader front and made notable electoral progress the promise of the period 1966–8 was not fulfilled. Both Gwynfor Evans and Winifred Ewing lost their seats, but the Scottish Nationalists were represented in the new Parliament by the new MP for the Western Isles, Donald Stewart, provost of Stornoway. It was a feature of this election that the Nationalists, alone of the main parties outside Northern Ireland, had offered opposition to the principle of Britain's joining the European Economic Community. They feared an even greater drain of capital and labour towards the prosperous English regions and abroad, and they were critical of the likely impact of the EEC's agricultural and fisheries policies on the poorer farming and fishing communities. However, the meagre election results for the Nationalists encouraged Conservative and Labour leaders to ignore their challenges and claims for the next three years.

The surprise Conservative victory in the 1970 election brought to the office of Prime Minister Edward Heath, a passionate supporter of Britain's membership of the European Community who had played a leading role in the abortive negotiations in 1962–3. The Heath Government succeeded in its European objective but foundered badly on the domestic front, both in the spheres of relations with the trade unions and the accelerating inflation. Yet at the same time, the Labour Party was in disarray after its election defeat, divided both about EEC membership and the broad sweep of economic and industrial policy. The scene was set for a substantial revival of Liberal fortunes from 1972 (including five by-election gains in thirteen months) and for a parallel resurgence of SNP support north of the Cheviots. The significant by-election votes recorded by Nationalists at Stirling and Falkirk (1971), Merthyr Tydfil (1972) and Dundee East (1972) gave the lie to the claim that Nationalists would only do well in elections while Labour was in power. Finally, in November 1973 the SNP candidate at the Glasgow Govan by-election, Mrs Margo Macdonald, snatched victory from Labour in a previously safe inner city seat. A great lift to Scottish morale and to SNP voting support had undoubtedly been given by the discovery and development of oil in the North Sea, mostly off Scotland's coast. The idea that the Scottish economy could be self-supporting no longer seemed fanciful. Much to their regret the Welsh could not find oil or any similar natural resource to boost their wealth and confidence, other than an abundance of water.

At the close of October 1973, the Kilbrandon Commission had revived the constitutional questions raised by home rulers with the publication of its report which advocated (by a majority vote) legislative devolution for Scotland, some form of administrative devolution for Wales, and the creation of separate Scottish and Welsh directly-elected assemblies using a proportional electoral system. Henceforth the Scottish and Welsh cases were clearly distinguished from that of Northern Ireland, where direct rule was imposed in 1974. The sudden decision of the Heath Government to call a general election in February 1974, when faced with a miners' strike and a rapid rise in oil and commodity prices, ensured that a key question in the Scottish and Welsh election campaigns was home rule and devolution; the Nationalists were riding high and in Scotland were seen as a direct challenge to Conservatives, Labour and the Liberals. Thus a rather separate election campaign was fought in Scotland, largely on the devolution issue, for the first time in decades. The massive swing to the Nationalists in Scotland (where the SNP took seven seats) and the success of Plaid Cymru in winning two seats in Wales despite a reduced total vote demonstrated that the political configuration in these two countries had been radically and permanently altered. The overall result for the United Kingdom produced no majority for any single party, and ensured that the Nationalists in the House of Commons enjoyed substantial leverage. The threat of further SNP inroads, and at Labour's expense, was also a potent spur to action and prompted the Labour Party centrally to force its Scottish section to reverse their dogged opposition to devolution. The Secretary of State for Scotland, Mr William Ross, changed from a stern and unbending opponent into a conscientious supporter of an elected Scottish assembly: the Welsh Labour Party, which had supported since 1966 the idea of an elected Welsh Council, had no problem in this respect. The Nationalist advance had diverged markedly as between Scotland and Wales since 1970, and this trend was confirmed at the second 1974 general election held in October. Labour's rapid conversion to Scottish devolution lacked credibility, and Tory distaste for the whole idea greatly assisted a wholesale desertion to the Scottish National Party, which had acquired considerable momentum since the February election. The Conservatives sank to third position in Scotland behind the SNP in terms of votes, although winning sixteen seats to the SNP's eleven: Labour seemed to gain sufficient numbers of votes from Conservatives and Liberals to offset its losses to the Nationalists. The SNP gained a further four seats, all from the Conservatives, and finished second in 35 seats behind Labour, in five behind the Conservatives and in two behind the Liberals; in sixteen of these 42 seats the SNP lost by a small enough margin for each seat to be gained on a direct 5 per cent swing from the winner to the SNP candidate. Plaid Cymru in Wales did not achieve any real advance in voter support but Gwynfor Evans did succeed in winning back Carmarthen to bring the number of Plaid MPs up to three—the language question and the lack of oil complicating the Welsh dimension. Given the continued strength of Nationalist voting in Scotland and Wales and the pledges given by Labour during the October election campaign, the re-elected Labour Government, with its slender majority of three in the Commons, was politically obliged to bring forward legislation to set up Scottish and Welsh elected assemblies. The bill was produced only at the end of 1976, after much deliberation in the Cabinet and its specially established constitution unit. A corresponding scheme for a measure of regional government in England failed to win the Government's support and a White Paper published at the close of 1976 rejected the idea of any English regional assemblies. This registered Whitehall's lack of certainty and of enthusiasm for so novel a concept as regionalism. In truth, the whole notion of constitutional and governmental reform was subjected to jaundiced criticism from the many who disapproved of the recent local government reforms in England, Scotland and Wales. These critics feared that plans for devolved assemblies and a new tier of government would simply repeat the mistakes of the previous reforms and add markedly to the cost, remoteness and duplication of the functions of government. Ironically, at the same time as Parliament was preparing to spend the first half of 1977 considering the devolution proposals (and little else besides the Budget) the economic indicators were showing a marked evening-out of the variations in unemployment between the different parts of Britain, although the overall level of unemployment remained high at around 6 per cent of the workforce. Regional policy itself was being called into question and the only direct regional employment subsidy was withdrawn early in 1977. Such trends reflected the changing economic condition of Britain and the scarcity of government funds rather than the much-heralded English backlash against the process of devolution. While the prospect of further special treatment for Scotland and Wales, in terms both of finance and of governmental arrangements, provoked opposition and fear among many English people towards devolution, some English representative bodies, particularly in the North of England, were preparing the ground for demanding some devolution and special treatment to meet their own regional interests.

A Review of the Issues

The periodic demands for home rule and the most recent rise of nationalism on the periphery of the United Kingdom have frequently been dismissed by English observers in the past as impractical, not economically viable and thus not to be taken seriously. The fact that leading politicians and many others in the 1970s are taking such demands for home rule seriously is a reflection of the political 'clout' devolutionists and Nationalists now exert. Critics of those who wish to concede some autonomy to Scotland and Wales rest their case on two main arguments; first, that the large jump in the Nationalist vote is but a reflection of a quarter of a century of unsuccessful government in the UK as a whole; and secondly, that the attempt to meet the Nationalists half-way by supporting devolution, but not independence, for Scotland and Wales is no more likely to succeed than the policy of appeasement of Hitler's ambitions in the 1930s. The first argument nevertheless implies that Scotland and Wales have sufficiently separate national identities to react very differently from England in terms of voting behaviour (why is there no equivalent English Nationalist party?). As to the other argument, there is a qualitative distinction to be made between 'appeasement' and 'compromise'. The propensity to compromise may have saved Britain from revolution and still forms the secure basis on which was built British parliamentary democracy and an industrial society. Federal systems of government elsewhere in the world, such as those of Switzerland, West Germany, Canada, Australia and the United States of America, do not suggest that subsections of conglomerate states must necessarily break away from a large and single all-embracing unit of government. There are a few examples, however, where unitary states have had to be broken up under pressure of separatists within; hence the creation by the leading European powers of Belgium in 1830 at the expense of the Netherlands, the voluntary dissolution of the Union of Norway and Sweden in 1905, the birth of the Irish Free State in 1922 and the violent and bloody breakaway of Bangladesh from the rest of Pakistan in 1971. The unanswered question thus remains whether the Nationalist upsurge is the product of misgovernment common to the whole of Britain or whether it reflects faults that are endemic either in the British system of government or in the union of different peoples within the UK. Undoubtedly, the failure of successive governments to realise the ambitions and expectations of their supporters has aggravated their difficulties in retaining the support of Scottish and Welsh opinion and has accelerated the nationalist challenge. Yet there is plenty of evidence that the growth of nationalism and of national consciousness in Scotland and Wales owes its origins also to more historical and long-term influences. The nationalist challenge to the United Kingdom is the result of both a 'push' and a 'pull' effect upon Scottish and Welsh opinion.

Amongst the influences pushing opinion away from adherence to the current constitutional arrangements in Britain can be counted the relatively depressing economic record of London governments since 1945, the increasing accretion of power to Westminster and Whitehall, and the end of the British Empire, which has left a domestic political vacuum concerning Britain's role in world affairs, intensified by Britain's relative economic decline. The economic record of the UK since 1945 can be summarised as a succession of economic crises which have jeopardised investment and economic growth and have seriously weakened the value of sterling as an international currency. Britain has achieved the lowest rate of economic growth and the lowest rate of investment in Western Europe since 1945, and has been more prone than most to suffer the ravages of inflation and continuing and damaging breakdowns of

TABLE 8.1   Unemployment in Great Britain, Scotland and Wales 1955 – 77
(percentage rates for June)

	Great Britain	Scotland	Wales
1955	1.0	2.2	1.6
1965	1.2	2.6	2.2
1968	2.2	3.6	3.6
1970	2.4	3.9	3.4
1973	2.4	4.3	3.3
1977	5.6	7.7	7.4

Sources: *Ministry of Labour Gazette* and *Department of Employment Gazette*.

industrial relations in major industries, notably coal and motor vehicles. The peripheral regions until the 1970s have usually been the last to benefit from such increases in wealth as have occurred and unemployment has stayed higher than the average as the accompanying table illustrates (See Table 8.1). The increasing power of central government has taken place not only through the nationalisation of large industries such as coal, railways, gas, electricity, airways and steel but also by the expansion of government activity in agriculture, roads, housing, health and social services, education, employment and social security, price and wage levels, industrial development and environmental questions. An index of this expansion can be found in the rising share of the gross domestic product which is accounted for by government expenditure (less than 40 per cent in the 1950s; 52 per cent in 1975/6). Much of this activity has in fact been administered by local councils who in 1976 relied for two-thirds of their income on central government grants, and whose freedom of action was correspondingly diminished despite an increase in the services provided. An alternative index of this increased central government intervention is the volume of legislation passed by the Houses of Parliament. In the period 1906 – 13 the number of statute book pages per session of Parliament averaged 355; in the 1945 – 6 session this total was 995 and in the 1975 – 6 session it was about 3000 pages, to which a further estimated 10,000 pages of delegated legislation must be added. Despite minority appeals for a decentralisation of power, if only to lighten the legislative and adminis-trative loads in Westminster and Whitehall, central government has retained its old-established powers as well as acquiring new ones; it has presided over a similar centralising trend in the nationalised industries. In 1976 it was still not possible for a local council to erect a traffic light or a pedestrian crossing or approve a shop sign in a conservation area without the consent of central government. The growth of central government, however, is not unique to Britain, nor is the sense of powerlessness, verging on apathy, of the-individual in the face of an expanding, insensitive and largely unaccountable bureaucracy with which such growth is synonymous. Big government is only a major manifestation of a common international trend towards larger units in the quest for more efficient use of economic resources. Common metropolitan values and standards are replacing local and national cultural differences, just as the supermarket and the hypermarket are eliminating large numbers of smaller shops. But these actions on an international plane have produced local reactions, as evidenced by the frequent diminution of social control and the rising strength and stridency of autonomist groups throughout the Western world: Canada has its Québequois, France its Bretons, Occitans, Corsicans and Lorraines, Spain its Basques and Catalans, Italy its Tirolese and Sardinians, Belgium its Flemings and Walloons, Britain its Scots, Welsh, Irish and other communities. In parts of the United Kingdom, the advantages of the political and economic unity of the United Kingdom are open to question. Domestic uniformity of economic decisions and of most, but not all, political decisions can be blamed for some of the special problems of Scotland and Wales, with their high concentrations of poverty, unemployment and declining industries. Dissatisfaction is expressed not only by rejecting the leaders, the promises and the results of ruling political parties but also in condemning the system of government itself. There is no proof that a separate Scottish or Welsh parliament would have served their peoples better or worse than Westminster; but given the dissatisfaction with London government, many are prepared to take the risk of opting for separate parliaments for Scotland and Wales. The union of Scotland and Wales with England ties the management of these countries' economies together in every detail and is not considered by many Scots and Welsh to be worth the supposed political gains which arise from belonging to a larger world power. Britain's power has in any case receded dramatically since 1945 as the British Empire has been dismantled and British economic strength and influence has dwindled. The sense of political and economic alienation at Britain's periphery has probably been compounded by the significant failure of central government to undertake successfully radical political and governmental reforms. Local government reform took twenty-five years to achieve and is now commonly judged to have failed (even the reform of London's government in 1963 was hardly a success, to judge by various political demands for the abolition of the Greater London Council). At the centre itself, ministries and super-ministries have been reshuffled without great effect; no agreement can be found on a reform of the largely hereditary House of Lords; the burgeoning of Select Committees of the House of Commons threatens to bury MPs in detail without any accompanying increase in their powers; and the unchanged Commons procedure discourages the debate of urgent issues, denies minorities a voice and seems incapable of allowing thorough discussion of the business of the European Community. The one successful reform has been the formation of the Welsh Office in Cardiff in 1964. If the past failures of modest attempts at governmental reform have made politicians and the public disinclined to undertake further radical changes to the political structure of Britain, the clear political demands of Scotland for more autonomy (and the more muted demands in Wales) have forced the issue, and account for tensions among both Labour and Conservative MPs at Westminster, and the incomprehension of much of the English public that so much political time has been given to bringing about a devolution of power.

TABLE 8.2   Attitudes towards devolution policy in 1970

Policy preferred	England (mean of 10 Regions)	Scotland	Wales
	%	%	%
Leave things much as they are	38	25	42
Some devolution	23	26	21
Extensive or complete devolution	37	47	36

Source: Kilbrandon Commission on the Constitution, Research Paper No. 7.

Nevertheless attitudes in Scotland and Wales have hardened over time in favour of greater political recognition of their special needs and traditions, and public opinion polls seem to indicate that there is a solid current of opinion in favour of devolution (see Table 8.2). This has come about not simply as a result of the 'push' factors already discussed but also as a result of a strong and increasing sense of national consciousness and identification in Scotland and Wales which, although prospering on a mood of rejection of the English connection, has nevertheless a solid and irrefutable historical basis. The Scottish nation has had for most of its life a separate political identity: the union of the English and Scottish crowns in 1603 was only consolidated in the Act of Union of 1707 which brought together the two parliaments and administrations. Even after this date, Scotland retained a separate established church and a separate legal system. A Scottish Secretary of State was first appointed in 1885 and the embryo of a separate Scottish administration was set up in 1939 at St Andrew's House in Edinburgh. The Welsh case is perhaps less clear since the unity of Wales (with or without Monmouthshire) was never clearly established even in medieval times nor by the Act of Union imposed by Henry VIII in 1536. The subsequent development of communications on an east-west rather than a north-south axis served to reinforce the English connection at the expense of Welsh unity. Indeed, Wales has never enjoyed so strong a sense of its own political identity as it has since 1964 when the Welsh Office and the post of Secretary of State for Wales were established, and when Monmouthshire was simultaneously included in Wales. Nevertheless, that separate political identity is now a fact, and had already been recognised by occasional separate legislation for Wales, starting with the Welsh Sunday Closing Act of 1881, and by the creation of separate administrations earlier this century to govern Welsh education and agriculture. It should also be recognised that the strong Welsh identification with the nonconformist churches (and consequent rejection of anglicanism) and the survival and influence of the very distinct Welsh language, now spoken by only one in five of the population as against one in two at the turn of the century, are cogent illustrations of Welsh isolation from the main English cultural tradition. The recent electoral behaviour of both Scotland and Wales, from the Crofters' movement of the 1880s, the rejection of Unionist (Conservative) men and measures, and the recent rise of nationalist parties serves only to confirm the separate national identities of Scotland and Wales.

Cultural nationalism is one of the main operating factors in this process. There has been a resurgence this century of distinctively Scottish and Welsh literary writing, criticism and interest; even the Gaelic language, spoken by less than 2 per cent of Scotland's population (and then mainly in the Western Highlands and Islands) is enjoying a renewal of interest and a revival of confidence. The Welsh language is battling with some success for more status and more government support in Wales. In several important ways its position has been improved, whether by the growth of the Welsh League of Youth (Urdd Gobaith Cymru) since 1922, the slow and often reluctant development of bilingual education in the state schools, or by the activities of the Welsh Language Society whose foundation in 1962 was inspired by Saunders Lewis, one of Wales's foremost intellectuals and writers this century. Parliamentary recognition of Welsh cultural requirements may have been cursory but led to the passage of the 1959 Eisteddfod Act, allowing local councils to use rate revenue to support the National Eisteddfod, and the Welsh Language Act 1967, allowing the Welsh language equal validity, but not as of right, in official business. As a result of the special linguistic problems of Wales, the expansion of local television and radio programmes by the BBC, heralded by the Pilkington Report of 1962, came first to Wales and only later to Scotland. This development was partly a reaction to the arrival of commercial television in the 1950s which was based on regional networks (ultimately three for Scotland and one for Wales). More recently, television reception and radio coverage have been substantially increased; local radio stations have been set up, amongst which Radio Clyde has enjoyed a huge success, and traditional radio services specially for Scottish listeners have been extended to over 40 hours a week on the air (44 hours a week in Wales, a majority of which is in Welsh). The strengthening of broadcasting services special to Scotland and

Wales has had a profound effect not only in the channelling and dissemination of news, comment and features of particular Scottish or Welsh interest. The new media have also stimulated an enormous amount of new work of a creative character, thus enlivening the local artistic communities, and have succeeded in proving to the public that Scottish and Welsh standards can be as good as London's. In contrast, the somewhat parochial news and current affairs programmes, which often exclude parallel London-originated material, may have limited the horizons of part of their audiences in a manner favourable to nationalist thinking. The daily press in Scotland remains largely independent of London newspapers and has certainly sharpened its local perspectives since the 1950s. The Welsh press has equally raised the amount and quality of its Welsh reporting but its influence continues to be restricted because of the much larger circulation of the London press in Wales. The cumulative effect of cultural revival, and expanded local radio and television services has been a marked increase in the sense of national identity and consciousness to be found in both Scotland and Wales.

Even those who will not accept the strong claims of Scotland and Wales to separate nationhood must now reckon with a straightforward political demand for more self-government in Scotland and Wales, which is evident not only from the vast rise in the Nationalist vote and the presence of fourteen Nationalist MPs in the House of Commons but also from the clear support now given to devolution by other political parties in Scotland and Wales. For some, such as the Liberals, this is a matter of long-standing conviction, for others, as is the case with Labour in Scotland, a recognition of political necessity in the face of a pressing electoral challenge. The question was changed by the result of the 1974 general election from whether there should be any devolution of power to what form of devolution should be conceded to Scotland and Wales. The balance of public opinion in both countries appeared to be strongly against national independence but equally in favour of a measure of devolution. This consensus corresponds to the essential quality of loyalty to Scotland (or Wales) *and* to Britain which has long been present in Britain's Celtic dependencies. Yet the links between Scotland and the UK seemed in the nineteen-seventies to be becoming more fragile the longer the settlement of this constitutional crisis was delayed.

Commitment to the principle of devolution does not provide a fixed formula for the allocation of functions and powers between different levels of government. Much of the anguish experienced by the British government since 1974 over the devolution issue can be traced to the problems of trying to find a devolution formula which would reconcile political demands for decentralisation with Whitehall's desire to maintain centralised control for the management of the economy and uniformity of administrative policy. The constitutional choices in this respect lie between a system of devolution, federalism and independence. Federalism requires a written constitution which provides for a strict division of functions between different governments, with certain powers such as those of taxation running concurrently. Usually each tier of government is solely responsible for specified functions, with conflicts over where power lies being settled by judicial process (e.g. by the Supreme Court of the United States). The adoption of a federal system in Britain, as advocated by the Liberals, would bring in its wake a whole series of radical political and administrative reforms.

Independence would vest supreme political power in the authorities at Edinburgh and Cardiff, and any decision by those authorities to pool sovereignty with other countries, for example concerning economic affairs, either with the rest of Britain or with the European Community, would be completely at the discretion of the Scottish and Welsh parliaments. Common market arrangements within Britain or a shared monarchy, such as Nationalists in Scotland and Wales advocate, would not alter the existence of independence and the location of supreme power in Cardiff or in Edinburgh. By contrast, any scheme for the devolution of power must by definition retain supreme power in the hands of a higher authority. Thus, under current proposals, Westminster and especially the Secretaries of State for Scotland and Wales would have the power of veto over many decisions taken by the devolved assemblies in Cardiff and Edinburgh; for some matters the power of veto would be relinquished, again at Westminster's discretion. Devolved assemblies are, and always will be, ultimately subordinate, as the suppression by Westminster of the fifty-year-old Northern Irish parliament in 1972 demonstrated.

It is often objected that any process which divides up further political authority in the world flies in the face of the fact of and need for more internationalised authority at the expense of the nation-state. Is it compatible for Britain to opt for supranationalism by becoming a member of the European Community and at the same time to divide up its residual powers among new subordinate organisms of government? The answer to such objections can only be that as a result of both the phenomena of supranationalism and decentralisation we are experiencing a re-distribution of powers and functions away from the nation-state in favour of a more appropriate level of authority. This recognises that we live in an age both of growing international interdependence and of oversized central governments. Given this perspective the 'incompatibles' of devolution and supranationalism become part of the same process, accepting that the accumulation of powers in the hands of nation-states may no longer be the most suitable arrangement for meeting the interests of their peoples. Yet extreme claims made by some nationalist protagonists about the merits of independence have more and more to be tempered by the recognition that Western countries are highly dependent on selling finished goods and services to each other and on imports of food, energy and raw materials. All but the largest and most self-sufficient states have less and less room for national manoeuvre and national sovereignty has been devalued accordingly. Thus the problems posed by trying to devolve power to Scotland and Wales provoke the unease of Westminster and Whitehall because they are part of a wider challenge to the authority of national governments. Already the development of a common agricultural policy for the European Community has removed most detailed powers to determine prices and production to Brussels – and slowly attempts are being made in other sectors, such as commercial policy and energy, to adopt the same approach. This leaves open the question of what powers should remain at Westminster and which should be vested in the authorities at Cardiff and Edinburgh.

At present, most domestic government functions are already administered by the Scottish and Welsh Offices with the principal exceptions of industrial affairs, economic affairs, employment and social security. Foreign affairs and defence are clear fields of policy for retention by Westminster, although there is argument about the representation of regional and devolved interests at European Community level. Curiously, the Home Office functions—such as running the prison service, the police and the nationality laws—have attracted less attention from devolutionists. Some functions will continue to be split between Westminster and the new elected assemblies including agriculture (because of its European dimension) and education, where the University lobby has succeeded in keeping itself free of provincial pressures. Yet in a strange way the logic of devolution prevents Whitehall and Westminster from parting with any powers of substance governing what the Scots and Welsh are most concerned about—the renewal of their industry and the provision of employment. Central government will always claim for itself the right to manage the economy and to raise and distribute funds as it thinks fit; these activities are essential to unified economic control. The only industrial matter whose control it is proposed to devolve relates to the activities of the Scottish and Welsh Development Agencies; and on employment matters, responsibility for the Manpower Services Commission's operations on the labour market is to be taken from the London-based Secretary of State for Employment and given to the London-based Secretaries of State for Wales and Scotland. Thus Scottish governmental functions, for example, may end up split three ways between a devolved Edinburgh assembly (and its attendant executive), the Secretary of State for Scotland, and other ministers of the UK Government. Given the overlapping interests of these various bodies and the formidable proposed power of the Secretary of State to veto on UK policy grounds many decisions of the Scottish assembly, a certain amount of confusion of responsibility seems inevitable.

Further complexity will arise if the Labour Government's planned discrimination between Scotland and Wales in regard to the extent of devolution is effected. Scotland would then be given legislative devolution, the power to make laws and implement them, and an elected assembly which would elect a government run on Cabinet lines with a Chief Executive and other ministers with defined responsibilities. Wales, however, may be treated differently, being granted administrative devolution, the right only to decide administrative regulations within the framework of statutes passed by the Westminster parliament; the Welsh elected assembly would be run on a committee system familiar to local government, and without ministers.

Nowhere do the built-in tensions of devolution reveal themselves more clearly than in relation to finance and taxation. Any authority which is wholly or largely dependent for finance on any other authority exercises its powers with at best conditional freedom: the paymaster can usually impose his preferences. Yet when the Labour Government searched for suitable sources of revenue for the proposed Scottish and Welsh assemblies it could only suggest a precept on the rates as an acceptable candidate, the rates being an antiquated and uneven property tax which is perhaps more loathed than any other tax in Britain. Other possibilities, which were rejected, were a precept on income tax or a surcharge on value-added tax. The new assemblies may well find themselves wholly reliant on an annual Treasury block grant for their finance. While this is an administratively simple device it does carry with it certain risks. A block grant system of finance would not encourage the devolved assemblies to accept full responsibility for their own actions, as they could always fall back on blaming their failures on a lack of funds over whose availability they have no final control. In addition, the annual negotiation between the devolved assemblies and the Treasury for the block grant would .egularly highlight this financial dependence and could be made into a platform for escalating Scottish and Welsh demands on the Exchequer if backed by an angry and well-briefed public opinion. The greater the latitude given to a devolved assembly in revenue-raising the less likely is this scenario, but the more economically disunited will be the United Kingdom. This conflict of objective is probably central to Britain's future constitutional development.

Federalism offers a way out of such difficulties by conceding that no one authority should be subordinate to another and by providing that each authority should operate exclusively in defined areas. This approach would require a lengthy constitutional settlement setting out the separate fields of competence and the powers (including those of taxation) attaching to each authority. The rights of the individual might need to be incorporated in a bill of rights applying to all levels of government. A system of legal arbitration would have to be established to adjudicate between competing governmental claims over jurisdiction. A written constitution would include such provisions but might prove inflexible and difficult to amend. Modern examples of federalism in practice point to a *de facto* drift of power away from the smaller units of government up to the federal level, both because federal governments have more resources at their disposal and because of common agreement on the need for concerted action over many spheres of policy which are not formally federal responsibilities. This is not a conclusive argument against federalism and might even suggest to those who seek a less radical formula for the allocation of powers between governments that the independence of action bestowed on non-federal authorities may in some respects be more apparent than real. In the United Kingdom context, however, a further difficulty arises when considering the federal solution since a basic imbalance of population and resources exists between England and the other constituent countries. A federal parliament would be dominated by an English majority representing 80 per cent of the population. Federalism in the UK might thus appear to be an unequal solution leading either to advantageous provisions at federal level to protect Scottish and Welsh interests, or the rendering of an effective whiphand to the English majority, depending upon the balance between and the alignments of the political parties. This problem could be resolved by the reconstitution of the House of Lords as a Senate representing the regions and nations of Britain with the power of veto or delay, or the creation of English regional parliaments parallel to the Scottish and Welsh parliaments; but as yet there is little political demand for such an arrangement.

One difficulty with all proposals for new assemblies or parliaments is that such additions to the political system may only further complicate the business of government and public understanding of its workings. If all present tiers of government remained unscathed after devolution, the Welsh would be faced with six levels of government – from community council, through the district and county councils, up to the Welsh, the UK and ultimately the European Community parliaments: a similar situation would obtain in Scotland. There is an obvious danger that by increasing the number of tiers of government the electors could become more confused about where power and responsibility lie and more apathetic or disillusioned with the political process. This is why some politicians are trying to ensure that after devolution at least one intermediate level of local government disappears, and at that point the Scottish Assembly would have the power to put such a reform into effect. An alternative to this would be to abandon the idea of separate Scottish and Welsh assemblies and to carry out administrative devolution by greatly strengthening the powers of existing local authorities. That option perhaps misses the point behind the nationalist element in the current Scottish and Welsh discontent, but has a certain logic.

Opponents of devolution have made special play of a further problem that arises, the level of representation of Scottish and Welsh opinion in the House of Commons. This has usually been more generous to Scotland and Wales in terms of the number of electors per MP than to England. If the ratio of electors per MP used in England were applied also to Scotland and Wales the number of Scottish MPs would need to be reduced from 71 to 57, and MPs from Wales would number 31 instead of 36. Under present electoral arrangements and conditions such reductions would particularly hurt Labour's fortunes. If devolution is carried out in Scotland and Wales but not in England there is a case for reducing the number of Scottish and Welsh MPs since so many of their interests will be looked after by the new assemblies and not by Westminster. However, Scottish and Welsh MPs will continue to be able to speak and vote on English matters in the House of Commons while English MPs will no longer be able to do the converse: this side-effect could only be avoided by adopting devolution or federalism for the whole of Britain or by reducing the rights of Scottish and Welsh MPs in the House of Commons. The relative under-representation of Northern Ireland at Westminster is also relevant to this argument following the abolition of the devolved Stormont parliament: using English MP/elector ratios there should be sixteen, not twelve, Ulster MPs at Westminster. Thus the devolution debate could undermine the established political balance inside Westminster, let alone the con-stitutional balance between different levels of UK government. Such a balance may well turn on the political complexion of any devolved assemblies and their executives.

The political balance within devolved assemblies will be principally determined by the type of electoral system to be used in choosing representatives to sit in them. The traditional British system of single-member seats where the 'winner takes all' does not make any pretence of securing proportional representation, biases the results in favour of the parties with the largest followings and often allows parties with a minority of the votes to win a majority of seats. While most Conservative and Labour leaders have strongly supported this voting system because of its capacity (albeit reduced recently) to produce one-party majorities, the prospect of a Nationalist party winning a majority in a Scottish elected assembly with less than 40 per cent of the popular vote has made them pause for thought about the choice of electoral system. The winner-takes-all system works most easily when there are only two contestants; in a closely fought Scottish election with four major parties that system is likely to produce results that are at best bizarre and at worst constitutionally disastrous. A Nationalist majority in the Scottish Assembly would certainly be claimed as a mandate for Scottish independence and could easily be used to extract as many political concessions out of Westminster as possible. The House of Commons is unlikely, however, to yield quickly to pressures to minimise such a potential outcome because of the implied challenge that the introduction of proportional representation for one set of elections poses to the systems used for other elections, including that for the Commons itself. Without a proportional system the traditional conduct of politics at Westminster is likely to be repeated in Scottish and Welsh assemblies until such time as one party ceases to have a majority. On this basis, the normal outcome of Welsh assembly elections would be that

Labour would win a substantial and permanent majority of the 80 seats
with the opposition divided and small in numbers. In the long term, this
might open the way for an alternative radical or socialist party to emerge in
Wales (possibly combined with the Nationalists) which might desist from
fighting Westminster elections. As for the Scottish assembly, the future
alignment of Scottish opinion is very uncertain, and it is conceivable that
any one of three parties could win a majority of the 150 seats, especially as
the Assembly representatives are to be elected for multi-member constituencies. If the absence of a majority were, however, to become normal
in this Assembly then a more co-operative style of consensus, if not
coalition politics, might result. Assemblies with one-party majorities
would, of course, speak with a single determined voice, but their mandate
could be questioned both on grounds of lack of voter support and by the
rival elected government at Westminster. Assemblies which sought and
depended on a multi-party consensus might find it harder to reach
agreement amongst themselves but would thereafter have a stronger
negotiating position *vis-à-vis* national government. A worrying feature
about such assemblies, if elected on the traditional British voting system
and perhaps covering England as well as Scotland and Wales, is that a
majority of them would be controlled permanently by the same one party.
The absence of an alternating governing party does create opportunities
for the abuse of political power which have been clearly revealed in recent
corruption trials concerning local government in Northern England and
South Wales.

The relative position of England after a devolutionist settlement for
Scotland and Wales has only recently been considered seriously, largely
because most English commentators began to take an interest in the
devolution debate a decade after it had begun in Scotland and Wales. As a
result of devolution only to Scotland and Wales, the English run the risk of
being denied the sensitive and devolved government they have voted to
their Celtic neighbours. They also may be asked to increase their
contribution to Scottish and Welsh public expenditure following the
annual negotiations with the Treasury to settle the block grant for the
Edinburgh and Cardiff assemblies. An increase in the English contribution
to the Scots and Welsh might be used to maintain British political unity
and to buy off the threat of nationalist agitation each year north and west of
the border. The more disadvantaged parts of England, which are already
denied decentralised administration, development agencies or a Secretary
of State with Cabinet rank, stand to suffer further relative deprivation *vis-
à-vis* other parts of the United Kingdom. Hence the concern about the
results of devolution expressed by representative bodies in Yorkshire,
North East England, Merseyside and the West Country. The choice facing
those English regional interests is either to concentrate on blocking the
existing devolution plans, at the risk of breaking up the United Kingdom,
or to put forward proposals which protect the English from the future

depredations of the Scots and Welsh. The choices available appear to be the following: federalism or devolution all round, with national and regional elected assemblies each having equal powers, including Scotland and Wales: a stronger form of devolution for Scotland (and possibly Wales) and a weaker form for the other regions, each with separate administrations and with all residual powers held at Westminster; an elected English parliament or assembly to correspond to the Scottish and Welsh assemblies, also with a separate administration, and a Secretary of State for Regional Affairs in the Cabinet to speak for English interests; an English Grand Committee to be set up from among the English MPs at Westminster and to exercise functions similar to the Scottish and Welsh assemblies, but without the benefit of a separate administration to implement its decisions; a network of regional advisory councils comprising nominees of local councils and other interests which could draw together a regional view of government policy, exert pressure for action and reform, and co-ordinate the work of local authorities in regard to economic planning, land use, housing and industrial development.

To each of these schemes can be made a whole list of objections such as their administrative confusion and duplication, the problem of the differing political balance between England and other parts of the UK, and the unequal rights that might be bestowed on different Westminster MPs. There are, however, two overwhelming difficulties in the way of encouraging effective political regionalism in England; first, there is no clear sense of regional identity in much of southern England and no agreement anywhere about the desirable number of regions or their boundaries; secondly, there is little political demand for regionalism in England, and this is at present confined to the Liberal Party and a few parts of the Labour Party with a direct interest in local government. The latter problem can of course be changed and may well be if devolution plans are implemented, but the absence of regionalist identities is not going to be changed at the stroke of a legislator's pen. Such identification will need time to develop. Disputes as to whether Plymouth prefers to be ruled from London rather than Bristol are likely to break out in the same way as the Shetland islanders tried to maintain direct links with London rather than Edinburgh during the debate on the Scotland and Wales Bill through the House of Commons in 1977. There are any number of schemes for a pattern of regional authorities in Britain in the range of four to twelve, starting with two schemes in the Redcliffe-Maud report. Yet, without the groundswell of public identification with the regions as units of government or the established links between the administration at regional level and the governed, there are grave dangers that the sudden formation of regional authorities in a political vacuum would only add to the remoteness of government from the people.

In this respect the position of Scotland and Wales is already different. Through the Scottish and Welsh Offices they have their own settled administrations *in situ*; and their special problem is that, owing to the lack of time at Westminster, MPs there have little chance to investigate the multifarious activities of these two departments. That fact provides one of the most cogent arguments for setting up an elected assembly to exercise democratic control over a part of government where little has so far existed.

No survey of the issues raised by devolution can overlook the experience of devolution in Northern Ireland from 1921 to 1972, although this Irish example is clearly a special case because of the sectarian divisions among the people and the peculiarities of Irish history since 1800. In retrospect, the setting up of a separate Northern Irish government in the stately surroundings of Stormont was both a very tangible concession to Loyalist opinion and a device by which governments in London could conveniently keep Northern Ireland out of British politics. Relations between Stormont and Westminster, at least until 1969, were highly ambiguous; for despite its subordinate constitutional status, Stormont was conceded in practice considerable autonomy by London governments. The legislators at Stormont also chose on most occasions not to depart from the law governing the rest of the United Kingdom, despite their political differences with London, except for special categories of policy such as civil liberties and the provision of investment incentives. Nevertheless it should be noted that the Stormont parliament lacked the financial resources to be very independent of London; the 'imperial contribution' which was devised originally as a payment by Northern Ireland to London for imperial expenses (such as defence) became in fact an ever expanding imperial subsidy. Even so, Westminster preferred not to exercise any strict control over Stormont's expenditure. Yet the example of Northern Ireland does still point some lessons about devolution elsewhere. Powers which are legally reserved to London governments in regard to devolved assemblies may deliberately not be used, if only to let sleeping dogs lie. There is a case that civil liberties and human rights should remain protected and legislated for by the superior parliament, because of the risk of causing public disorder. The financial relationship between superior and subordinate parliaments does appear to be crucial to the subordinate parliament's effective dependence or independence of central government.

Conclusion

The issue of devolution to Scotland and Wales has been complicated by deliberate political delays on the part of governments and the largest political parties. Politicians and civil servants in the late sixties preferred not to recognise, or to neutralise, the potential challenge of Celtic nationalism because of the fundamental disturbance to the constitution and to the political balance at Westminster that devolution could entail.

By 1974 the seriousness of the nationalist challenge had intensified to such a degree that speedy reform was required from government ministers at a time when they were completely unprepared for radical changes. Meanwhile, the hold of nationalism on public opinion of all parties and classes had deepened, especially in Scotland. Its challenge had to be answered because of the pivotal position of Nationalist MPs at Westminster and their threat to Labour's political base. Thus a programme for devolution was framed by the Labour Government less out of conviction than from political necessity. The initial delays in taking action ruled out a pre-emptive reform designed to strengthen the union of Britain; instead, a package was devised by the Cabinet, with some difficulty, which sought to minimise the threat of separatism. It is possible that the government delayed too long and the escalation of nationalist political demands in Scotland, having gained momentum from a long-developed economic discontent and political disillusion, can no longer be stopped. The economic prospects for Scotland and Wales in terms of the position of industry and employment suggest no immediate improvement and thus no favourable change in popular expectations of central government. Just as the original design for devolution in Northern Ireland was a hasty response to loyalism, so a similar verdict may await current devolution proposals for Scotland and Wales. The Ulster Loyalists in 1920 mistook the shadow of self-government that they were offered for the substance, as Westminster finally proved with the imposition of direct rule in 1972. There is a corresponding danger now that devolutionists and Nationalists may welcome a system that imposes on Scotland and Wales constitutional and financial dependence on London, without their recognising that it may only be a matter of time before Westminster uses its financial muscle to control policy in Scotland and Wales. Devolution is a political response to nationalism but it does not carry with it any promise that it is the answer to nationalism. However, it may be necessary to take that risk of failure, on purely party political grounds, given the direct electoral menace of the Nationalist parties. Despite all the nationalist rhetoric, the SNP and Plaid Cymru have shown that even in the United Kingdom parliament Scotland and Wales can pack a very powerful punch. It is ironic that the Celtic tail, after decades of submission, has now found a way to wag the English dog, while the English must now learn how in this contest to defend their own interests: regionalism in England has yet to become a politically acceptable solution to this need.

9 The Europeanisation of British Politics

Stanley Henig

1 Introduction

Convention suggests a greater degree of continuity and bi-partisanship in foreign policy than is the case with domestic issues. The extraneous nature of most of the parameters determining foreign policy increases the power and influence of officials who receive and interpret information about the rest of the world. When a new government is returned to office, briefing sessions in the field of foreign policy are much more likely to be directed by officials than by ministers. Only on extremely rare occasions has an incoming government diametrically reversed a part of its predecessor's foreign policy. Despite this, however, there is a long history of dispute within and between political parties over issues of foreign policy. Even if policy evolves slowly, it does change in time and the complexion of the government may make a difference. Developments in the Indian sub-continent would surely have been affected by a Conservative victory in 1945, whilst a Labour Government would surely have reacted differently to the nationalisation of the Suez Canal as would a Conservative to Rhodesia's unilateral declaration of independence. With regard to British policy towards integration in Western Europe it is quite possible to discern a relatively consistent overall trend which is a function of our own economic and political decline and the gradual development of the Communities. However, this cannot conceal considerable differences at various times between the two major parties. Changes in government— 1951, 1964, 1970 and 1974—cannot be overlooked in any analysis of British policy.

Before examining in detail the impact of Europe on British politics and parties, it is worth making a few general points about the development of integration. The modern origins of the drive towards European unification are to be found in the period immediately after the Second World War. The nation-state – recognised for well over a century as Europe's most 'legitimate' form of political expression and Europeans' most 'legitimate' aspiration—was discredited. In its two prime purposes—protection against external assault and internal preservation of stability, law and justice—it had failed. The states of Europe which had so recently dominated the world now seemed threatened by it, particularly by the superpowers whose intervention had been necessary to settle a European conflict. For the economically enfeebled and politically shattered states of Western Europe, the only immediate means of avoiding the fate of their Eastern neighbours—liberated and occupied by the Red Army—seemed to lie in ever greater dependence on the United States. Against this background influential groups in the governments of France, Italy and the Benelux countries saw European unification as a further alternative, a way out of the dilemma, offering back to Europe the chance once again to control its own destiny. In addition, even prior to the establishment of a sovereign Federal Republic in Western Germany there was widespread support in that country for a close-knit European framework as a guarantee of stability. On all sides there was recognition that a concerted effort was needed to solve the German problem and end the long history of conflict between France and Germany. A United Europe seemed to offer the ideal framework.

The successive European Communities—Coal and Steel in 1951, Atomic Energy and Economic in 1957—were established by Belgium, France, Germany, Italy, Luxembourg and the Netherlands as part of a conscious drive to bring about economic and political unification. The structures and functions of the Communities were not seen as goals in themselves, but rather as means to an end: their ultimate guarantee of success and the cement binding the enterprise were the shared belief in unification as a goal of policy firmly based on an enlightened view of national interest. It is hardly necessary to make the point that no British Government has ever taken this view of our national interest or subscribed to that goal of policy: this is why there was no question of our joining the Communities in the 1950s. By the time economic and political pressures forced a British Government to reassess the position and seek membership, growing affluence and a new-found sense of security throughout Western Europe had already led to some dilution of the belief in unification, a process which was to continue. President de Gaulle's imposition of a ten-year delay on British membership coupled with his reassertion of nationalism within the Communities ensured that there was a greater congruence of political views among the nine governments involved after enlargement. Today the cement binding the Communities is that they are an increasingly indispensable contrivance for carrying on the ever-growing volume of traditional inter-state relations within Western Europe. Economic integration has become an almost automatic process with ever-increasing trade, capital and labour movements, economic inter-penetration and tourism. The Communities offer a framework for organisation, mediation and control—a European equivalent of part of government's role in the pluralist society. Meanwhile, the long-term political future of Europe and its own identity in the international environment remain open questions.

Neither the rise nor the subsequent decline of the 'European' idea have owed much to popular involvement. Initially there were attempts to create various mass movements, but these reached an early peak with the creation of the European Movement in the wake of the 1948 Hague Congress and the subsequent establishment of the Council of Europe. The ease with which governments could brush aside weakly articulated manifestations of popular feelings highlights the effectiveness of Jean Monnet's approach, working through opinion formers in politics, civil service and both sides of industry. It was Monnet who successively inspired the Schumann plan and the Coal and Steel Community and then established the Action Committee for a United States of Europe which laid the groundwork for the two later Communities as well as subsequent British adhesion. The political approach of the Action Committee prospered whilst the European Movement and other Federal organisations declined into mere stage armies, but the result has been to remove any real popular element from the integration process. It remains to be seen whether direct elections to the European Parliament can reverse this trend. Within the original six member countries the earlier, if ultimately temporary, rejection of the nation-state and subsequently the acceptance that much economic progress was attributable to the Communities have given a degree of legitimation to the idea of European integration. For the United Kingdom, joining in quite different international circumstances, this has never happened. British membership was brought about through decisions of élites in politics, bureaucracy, business and finance. Ultimately the people were given the opportunity to ratify the decision, but in circumstances which virtually precluded any repudiation.

2 Britain and Europe—post-war history

Before examining in detail the attitudes of British parties towards Europe it is worth giving a brief chronological account of relations with the Communities. Immediately after 1945 British prestige was high throughout Europe—the one nation-state which had been vindicated. Britain's traditional political institutions and democratic practices had emerged apparently unscathed, whilst the country had fought the war throughout without being militarily conquered at any time. If these were reasons why many on the Continent wanted Britain to join in the unification effort, they also explain the hesitant answer. Although Britain had fought in two twentieth-century European wars and now implicitly recognised the Rhine as a security boundary, policy-formers continued to regard her imperial interests and the political and military links with the USA as being of greater importance. There was amazing confidence that the country could retain a great power role, whilst domestic preoccupation with social change and the creation of the welfare state left little time or energy for speculative European adventures. Most regarded the aspirations of the federalists as little more than idealistic nonsense and were unable to visualise a united Europe as a practical proposition. The Labour Government grudgingly agreed to the establishment of the Council of Europe and sent a reasonably high-powered delegation to the early meetings of the Consultative Assembly, but there is little indication that it was taken seriously. For the Conservative Opposition the Assembly was a useful sounding-board and Churchill continued to deliver oratorical masterpieces in favour of European unification, even supporting a European army. The absence of any real party controversy is, though, indicated by events after the change of government in 1951: Britain showed the same lack of interest in the Coal and Steel Community and refused to join the projected European Defence Community (EDC). Throughout the period there was broad consensus in policy-making circles that Britain continued to play a significant role in three worlds—North Atlantic, Imperial/Commonwealth, and European. As the difference in Britain's power compared to pre-war became more apparent, the North Atlantic strand loomed ever larger in Foreign Office thinking. Britain's two major European initiatives which led to the creation of the Organization for European Economic Cooperation (OEEC) and Western European Union (WEU) resulted from American pressures. The second of these was after EDC had collapsed through French fears of German domination. With the USA still anxious for German rearmament in some form, Britain took the lead in finding a new inter-governmental framework. It was to be our last moment in Europe's centre stage for a generation.

The work of Jean Monnet is evidenced in the remarkable speed with which the Six recovered from the EDC fiasco to establish within three years Euratom and the EEC. Economically the latter seemed to pose some threat to Britain's trade and the riposte was a proposal for a Free Trade Area (FTA) covering the whole of Western Europe and including the EEC as a single unit. Without a common external tariff or any joint policies FTA was clearly designed in Britain's own economic interests and there were widespread fears that it might dilute and even destroy the EEC itself, jeopardising the whole future of European integration. The French, with a protectionist tradition, were incensed that Britain might gain the economic benefits of integration without paying the political price. It was de Gaulle who torpedoed further negotiations, but there were few expressions of regret within the Six. Britain's reply was to join with six other non-EEC members to found the European Free Trade Association (EFTA). The notion that in this way economic pressure might be brought to bear on members of the EEC, particularly Germany with her extensive Scandinavian trade, turned out to be over-optimistic. The USA, willing to accept some adverse trade discrimination in the interest of strengthening Europe politically, was hostile to EFTA, whilst the EEC showed no interest in a multilateral accomodation between the two groupings. The prospect of real trade discrimination against British exports as the two groups solidified, coupled with the increasing shift in European power to the Community led to a fresh *volte-face*: in August 1961 the Macmillan Government applied for membership of the Communities.

The first set of negotiations for British membership amounted to little less than an attempt to marry Britain's own world trading system with the nascent Community. Heath, as chief negotiator, went to Brussels with a long list of demands for exemptions, exceptions and changes in EEC practice. The French, by no means enthusiastic for British political rivalry within the Communities, played a waiting, delaying game. By summer 1962 negotiations were not completed, but de Gaulle had solved the Algerian problem, the persistence of which had hitherto limited his capacity for pursuing chosen goals in foreign policy. Following his victory in the French elections in November 1962 de Gaulle was no longer dependent upon the pro-European centre: using as excuse Britain's lack of European vocation, evidenced in the Polaris missile deal with the USA, he vetoed further negotiations and plunged the Communities into a major crisis.

Immediate British reactions were to speak vaguely of the 'friendly five', but close relations between Paris and Bonn precluded any major developments or realignment: entry was not possible. The Labour Government elected in 1964 showed no immediate interest in Europe, seeking initially to boost links with the Commonwealth and the USA. Failing in both and in the wake of economic disappointment and the Rhodesian imbroglio, the Cabinet determined upon a new approach to ascertain if conditions were ripe for a second application. After nearly twenty years of differences between Britain and France over virtually every European question, relations at official level were nearing a nadir. It is extremely doubtful whether the British Government even asked what de Gaulle's terms for entry might be, but in any event no answer was given. Presumably believing that he would outsmart or outlast de Gaulle and anxious in any event to put down a marker for the future, Wilson submitted the second application. This time de Gaulle simply blocked any negotiations, but in 1969 he was replaced as French President by Pompidou, who had a less clear European vision and might be expected to agree a price for British entry. In fact growing German economic dominance of the Communities was gradually weakening France's scope for political leadership and Pompidou was unlikely to find the same room for manoeuvre as his former master. After the Social Democrats became the major party and dominant force in the German government,

Pompidou even began to feel somewhat isolated inside the Communities and the return to office of a Conservative Government in Britain was welcomed in Paris as offering some scope for a European realignment.

In the 1961 – 3 negotiations Britain had sought to solve a whole range of complex and detailed problems as a pre-condition for entry, rather than accept the approach used in constructing the original treaties of making the solutions conditional on, and consequent to, agreement on the major principle—in this case the bringing about of an enlarged Community. By 1970–1 Britain was economically and politically weaker and much more anxious for success in the negotiations. Adoption of the Community method led to a broad, framework agreement which brought about British membership without prior definitive solutions to all of the major, let alone the minor problems. They could be dealt with inside the enlarged Community. Initially a stick with which to beat the Conservative Government, these lacunae were in the end to help Labour find the means of reconciling their opposition to the Community through so-called 'renegotiation'. There is little point in continuing with this chronology. At the very moment when negotiations for entry had at last been successfully concluded, Britain's relations with the Communities came to be intertwined with, and conditioned by, the differing attitudes of the political parties.

3 The European Community and the political parties

Prior to 1960 the 'European' issue had little salience in ideological conflict between the two major political parties, with only a few isolated individuals advocating British participation in the integration process. The Liberals were early advocates of membership of the Communities but were quite unable to stimulate any public debate. The situation was transformed by the Macmillan Government's decision to seek membership. Macmillan himself was influenced by a variety of considerations. As an early member of the Consultative Assembly of the Council of Europe he made speeches with a more fervently European ring than most of his colleagues, even arguing on one occasion: 'We British will certainly be prepared to accept merger of sovereignty in practice if not in principle.' The years of Macmillan's premiership coincided with Britain's final, formal relegation from the league of great powers, with the virtually complete break-up of the Empire and the cooling of relations with the USA after the Suez fiasco. There was growing official pressure, particularly from the Foreign Office, for a change in European policy. Finally, an element of party strategy was involved. After winning three successive general elections, the Conservatives might be running out of ideological steam. In the early 1950s they had 'freed' the economy from Labour's post-war controls and this had been followed by a period of reasonable economic expansion culminating in the 'You've never had it so good' cry which won the 1959 election. Entry into Europe offered a chance for a further policy success and a new rallying cry for the 1960s. In support of this last argument there is some evidence that initially the Labour Opposition sought to be kept in touch with the unfolding negotiations: they were rebuffed.

Whilst views in the Conservative Party did differ, there was no significant group opposed in principle to the government initiative. The most likely source of dissent, the imperialist wing of the party, was for obvious reasons itself in a state of decline. The situation in the Labour Party was quite different, for doctrinal considerations soon came to the fore as pressures grew to formulate a riposte to what was becoming a major item of government policy. Attitudes struck in this initial Labour debate were to have a lasting significance. By 1960 Labour was one of only three Western European Social Democratic parties to have been able to win overall parliamentary majorities, the others being in Norway and Sweden. Between 1945 and 1951 Labour had been able to implement a radical programme. In contrast the Social Democratic parties of the Six were unable to attain political power unaided and they seemed to be making increasing compromises to join coalitions—themselves anathema to Labour. The steady evolution of the German SPD away from its doctrinal base reinforced these fears, whilst the strength of the Communists in France and Italy seemed to guarantee centre-right domination. To many in the Labour Party Socialism in one country looked a viable proposition: a Socialist Europe might be desirable, but it was impossible. Some historians have noted that the Keep Left group, the 1940s precursor of the Tribune group, had once advocated a European third force between the USA and USSR. In truth the left of the Labour party never showed any real interest in Europe as such: their major concern was to change a foreign policy too heavily based, in their view, on the alliance with the USA. Europe was a card to play against this in the 1940s, but once the USA began to give heavy backing to the idea of a united Europe, the left soon lost interest.

Anti-revisionist critiques of social democracy on the Continent have not been confined to the left wing of the Labour Party. Rather they represent a broad gut-reaction which would have made the task of pro-Europeans difficult even if initial espousal of Europe by a Conservative Government had not given the venture a right-wing appearance. Labour's pro-Europeans have come from two chief sources – a number of trade unions, particularly those on the moderate wing of the party, and the professional, intellectual element so heavily represented in parliament. In both cases the clinching argument was economic—the enormous progress made by the Community countries and Britain's failure on her own to engender the economic advance needed for the implementation of socially radical programmes. The group has always had some strength on the party's National Executive Committee (NEC), whilst accounting for about one third of the parliamentary party and an even higher proportion of the Cabinet or Shadow Cabinet: however, it has never been more than a minority in the party as a whole. One of the ironies is that this minority has always contained many of the British politicians who believe in political unification.

As early as 1950 the NEC issued a first major statement on European Unity. Replete with references to international co-operation, the Commonwealth, Sterling Area and even world government, the document categorically rejected a European bloc, economic union and supranationalism. A decade in opposition did nothing to change this instinctive reaction. As leader of the party Gaitskell had never flinched from any argument based on principle and it is improbable that he was motivated by other than his own predilections and assessment of the arguments. Nonetheless, after the violent inter-party disputes in 1960 and 1961 over nationalisation and unilateral disarmament, there must have been some pleasure in the overwhelming, even rapturous, reception given to his speech at the 1962 Brighton conference when Gaitskell called in effect for fidelity to a thousand years of history in rejecting entry into the Community. Gaitskell laid down five conditions for British entry—safeguards for Commonwealth trade; freedom to pursue our own foreign policy; fulfilment of pledges to EFTA; the right to plan our own economy; and guarantees for British agriculture. Confrontation between the parties was postponed by de Gaulle's veto, which also damaged the Conservatives' chances of winning the next election. Gaitskell died about the same time and when Labour returned to office in 1964 they were led by Harold Wilson, whose early objections to the Community had been political and tactical rather than ideological or strategic.

Concentration on the 1961–3 period is justified because it was then that the main arguments of the next decade were conditioned. The Conservatives have never lost their European vocation, although they have also not shown quite the same unity again. The development of some opposition within the party can be attributed to a mixture of causes. During the 1940s and 1950s the Conservatives had maintained a broad unity of purpose – in defeat and victory – under the continued leadership of an older, almost heroic generation. Macmillan's application to the Community could even be seen as a logical development from Churchill's broad pro-Europeanism. The gradual disappearance of that generation coupled with the political dominance of Harold Wilson from his first election victory in 1964 until the mid-seventies fractured the illusion of easy unity characterised in 1962 by Butler, himself no out-and-out European—'For them a thousand years of history; for us the future!'. Most of the opponents have been from the right wing of the party and it is not unfair to describe them as nationalists.

Opposition within the Conservative Party should not be exaggerated, for the large majority have remained instinctively faithful to what has almost become a part of their ideological legacy. Reasons other than a perfectly understandable desire for consistency may be adduced. The virtual disappearance of the British Empire and its replacement by a multiracial Commonwealth of independent countries unwilling to accept British leadership has profoundly affected traditional Conservative views of the world. Suez demonstrated the obsolescence of those views, but it also confirmed many of the worst fears about the USA – her jealousy of Britain's imperial past and willingness to appease, particularly at her allies' expense. British membership of a strong European Community was seen as a means of avoiding over-reliance on the USA. Perhaps above all by the late 1960s the member states of the Communities, particularly France and Germany, came to epitomise what many Conservatives wanted to achieve in Britain – high-growth economies with continuing increases in living standards, opportunities and rewards for enterprise and, generally, political leadership from the centre-right. If many in the Labour Party continued to fear that British social democracy might be diluted in a right-wing European Community, this was echoed by Conservative supporters, especially in the business world: entry into the Community might put Labour and the trade unions in their place.

Labour's dilemma has been more interesting in many ways. A section of the party has always been happier in opposition when it is possible to articulate the purest political philosophy, untrammelled by considerations of office and government. As has been shown, the party's gut-instincts were to oppose British membership, but in office Labour Governments have been confronted by the same objective circumstances as Conservative – enormous national economic problems, the better growth records of the Six and the increasing international power of the Communities. The small band of pro-Europeans was not slow to point out that Britain's poor rate of economic growth consistently hampered the attainment of Socialist goals in domestic politics, that several Community member states had larger public sectors and more advanced social policies and that social democratic parties have been slowly gaining ground. During the Labour Government from 1966 to 1970 there were majorities in the Cabinet and the parliamentary party to support the opening of negotiations, whilst rank-and-file members were held somewhat uneasily at bay. The 1970 election manifesto was the nearest Labour had come as a party to any formal pro-European position, but this gave no more than a commitment to negotiate in order to ascertain terms. Whilst there can be no doubt that in office Labour would have accepted arrangements similar to those actually negotiated, in opposition there was a gradual drift to an anti-Community position. Wilson's tactics during 1971 and 1972 were to stand aside from day-to-day controversy in order to give leadership to the side which emerged as a majority—inevitably those opposed to entry. Finally the decision by the Shadow Cabinet to contemplate a referendum – a course of action rejected out of hand by the Labour

Government—occasioned the resignation of a number of leading pro-Europeans, including Roy Jenkins from the Deputy Leadership. Tactically this was probably a mistake, for the parliamentary party remained fairly evenly split as demonstrated by the fact that in the critical vote on entry into the Community, 69 Labour MPs defied their own Whips to vote with the Government and a further 20 abstained. Thereafter a few Labour MPs, most of whom were not standing at the next election, gave surreptitious help to the Government in putting through the necessary legislation.

By the time of British entry the official Labour position was to oppose the terms negotiated and the tactics employed by the Government—the traditional means of forcing legislation through parliament. Consistent with this, Labour boycotted the Communities, sending no MPs to the European Parliament—an action paralleled by the TUC in respect of the Economic and Social Council. Labour's manifesto for the February 1974 election called for a full-scale renegotiation of the Treaty of Accession with the results to be put to the British people in the form of a further election or a referendum. A Labour Government, facing enormous economic problems and needing to keep on reasonable terms with the other members, could not be quite so blunt. The solution was to work from within the Community to seek improvement in the terms of entry rather than adopt a position of partial withdrawal pending renegotiation of the actual treaty. Effectively this decision determined that Britain would remain inside the Community, but left open the means of reconciling the party. The latter was to be the function of a referendum, given that a third general election in eighteen months was unacceptable, When Wedgwood Benn had first proposed a referendum, he had been laughed to scorn by every other leading politician. However, early advocates of the referendum had seen it as a means of *determining* an issue cutting across normal party lines: now it was to be used by a majority in the Labour Cabinet as a kind of plebiscite against entrenched opposition from a large part of the Labour Party.

Formally the referendum was on the renegotiated terms, but most of the changes were totally incomprehensible to the average voter who could only express views on the principle of entry. Given that the Labour Party at a special conference determined by a large majority to campaign for a 'no' vote, the referendum result—67 per cent 'yes' on a 65 per cent turnout—demonstrates the unrepresentativeness of the rank and file. However, the course of the campaign showed the strength of Labour opposition. On the Labour side the most enthusiastic meetings were those listening to leading 'antis' such as Benn and Shore. Although most established leaders urged a 'yes' vote and were backed in this by almost every national newspaper, nearly 50 per cent of Labour supporters who voted must have been in the 'no' camp. The referendum neutralised and circumvented the Labour opposition and extricated a Labour Government from part of its own ideological legacy, but the price has been to make it virtually impossible for the party as such to work out any further European programme. Since the referendum Britain has been a fairly normal member of the Community, if occasionally a little reluctant or recalcitrant, but the Labour Party has been schizophrenically trapped between its old gut-reactions and unwillingness to flout a popular verdict. Thus the party has unwillingly and half-heartedly sent a delegation to the European Parliament, but Conference has turned down the idea of direct elections to which the Government is formally committed.

The preceding analysis of party attitudes towards the European question has also suggested ways in which Europe and the Communities have influenced the parties, but it is not easy to give any overall assessment. Because arguments about British membership usually cut across parties, leaderships have often sought to keep the issue under wraps. Macmillan's hoped-for tactical advantage in using the issue to rejuvenate the Conservatives was thwarted by de Gaulle, while Heath's later dedication was in large part personal. Once Margaret Thatcher became leader, the Conservatives tended to show less interest. After 1970 Labour might have launched a major anti-European crusade, but were held back, partly through fear of driving out some of the most respected parliamentary figures and partly through realisation by Wilson, Callaghan and others that in office there might be little alternative to continued membership as Britain's economic weakness became ever more evident. At one time the Liberals hoped that their early espousal of the European cause might give them some reward, but this is rarely the lot of prophets: their revival in the late 1960s and early 1970s owed little to this issue.

Finally, a word on contacts between British and other European political parties, although these have produced little feedback to date. Labour has adopted a rather off-hand approach towards other Social Democratic parties, initially boycotting the European Parliament and eschewing all links, later even implying that they might not join the official group, and finally refusing to participate in any preparatory work for a common programme for the direct elections. Although Conservatives have played a significant role in the Parliament, they had no obvious group to join, not wanting any organic links with the formally Christian parties. In turn the latter considered the Conservatives too right-wing. Equally unable to link with either of the major right-wing groups in France, the Conservatives have been limited to alliance with the small Danish party. There have even been problems for the Liberals. In terms of popular votes the largest such party in the Community, their influence is inevitably limited by the impact of Britain's electoral system. Unless some form of proportional representation is adopted for filling Britain's seats the Liberals are likely to be excluded from the Parliament after direct elections. Now that the French Independent Republicans have joined the Federation of Liberal Parties the latter has swung well to the right, to the increasing discomfort of the British party. All in all it seems likely that when direct elections are held the various British parties will campaign individually on a national basis rather than as part of Community-wide coalitions. Assuming that we use the normal British electoral system – first past the post in 81 huge constituencies – the result is also likely to be extremely unrepresentative.

4 Conclusion—the impact of Europe on British politics

Europe may have occasioned the most important structural change this century in British political processes by introducing the referendum. This is not the place to join speculations about the alleged 'ungovernability of Britain'. They are not, in any case, borne out by the results of the referendum and it is by no means clear that contemporary problems—balance of payments, prices and incomes, Northern Ireland and devolution—are politically more intractable than those of the past. However, the Community controversy did spotlight one weakness in political practice. Although many issues cut across parties, governments can normally enforce their view through our 'majoritaire' system. In the case of the Community the government formulated a view based on 'objective' factors which its own party would not accept. Given that governments do not in such circumstances simply resign, a new constitutional means is needed for resolving the issue. The referendum offers a means of settling issues which cut across parties and may also give governments a method by which they can appeal directly to the people over the heads of parties and interest groups alike. Devolution as an issue is having a far greater impact on British politics than the European Community, but the controversy over the latter may have provided the constitutional weapon which will settle the former.

Entry into Europe has far-reaching theoretical constitutional implications, affecting and limiting the powers of Britain's legally sovereign institutions – Cabinet, Parliament and the Courts. It is certainly true that for a range of questions formal decision-making powers are moved away from Westminster. Certain pieces of legislation can now be passed through the Community machinery which take direct effect inside the United Kingdom, and our own government can be directed to legislate in particular ways on some subjects. On the other hand the Community's own decision-making machinery is certainly not autonomous from national institutions—government is directly represented in the Council of Ministers, which works by consensus rather than votes, and also helps determine the composition of the Commission and the European Court of Justice. It is also important to recognise that Britain's theoretically independent decision-making power was being eroded in all spheres by extraneous factors outside our control long before we joined the Communities. Entry formalises a major part of that network of links which surrounds our own decision-making institutions and gives us some influence over the external environment. However, it also raises in a particularly acute form a general problem concerned with relations between executive and legislature and government and governed. As Western society becomes more complex the role of government increases, and as states become more integrated with one another it may be increasingly difficult for parliamentarians or people to influence national decisions. In many spheres decisions are now made in Brussels but implemented by national civil servants, directed in our case from London. The general public are in contact with the national administrators but not with those who make the decisions. At the present state of Community development, mechanisms for feedback and control through Parliament or the Economic and Social Committee are quite inadequate. Nor can the problem be adequately tackled on a national scale by the nine individual national parliaments establishing mechanisms for 'vetting' decisions from Brussels. In the long term, solutions to these problems of alienation might be found in development of the Community's own political institutions. Squaring the circle so that political integration accompanies the economic integration—which partly caused the Community and is partly caused by it—was implied in the thinking of those who produced the original treaties. Community institutions, never intended to be more than temporary, show a certain danger of acquiring permanence because they suit the convenience of Europe's executives. Political parties clearly have a major role in determining patterns of institutional evolution which will bring about effective Community-wide political institutions for decision-making and representation. In their reaction to both the contemporary problems of our own national institutions and the European challenge of the last thirty years, the British parties hardly inspire much confidence that they will be in the vanguard of this thinking.

Postscript

During the early part of 1977, it continued to seem possible that Labour would be split by a major effort through Conference and the NEC to commit the Party and, therefore, the government to ultimate withdrawal from the Communities after a general election fought specifically on the issue. The vote against withdrawal at the 1977 Annual Conference of the TUC was a decisive defeat for this strategy, and it was subsequently confirmed at Labour's own Conference. Europe will continue to affect British politics and parties, but it seems certain that it will not cause any organic split in Labour and it will not – at least in the issue's past and present form – be the chief subject of any general election.

Index